Perspectives on the State Borders in Globalized Africa

Assessing the different kinds of borders between African nations, the contributors present a borderland and trans-region approach to understanding the challenges and opportunities facing the peoples of the African continent.

Africa faces rampant violence, terrorism, deterioration of water-energy-food provision, influxes of refugees and immigrants, and religious hatred under the trends of globalization. Solutions for these issues require new perspectives that are not attempted by conventional state-building approaches. Statehood is limited in many places on the African continent because many states are combined by loose political ties. African states' borders tend to be regarded as porous and fragile. However, as the contributors to this volume argue, those porous borders can contribute to cultural and socio-economic network construction beyond states and the creation of active borderlands by increasing people's mobility, contact, and trade.

A must read for scholars of African studies that will also be of great value to academics and students with a broader interest in nationhood, globalization, and borders.

Yuichi Sasaoka is a professor in the Graduate School of Governance Studies at Meiji University, Japan.

Aimé Raoul Sumo Tayo is a senior researcher at the Center for Strategic Studies and Innovations, Yaoundé, Cameroon.

Sayoko Uesu is a research associate at National Graduate Institute for Policy Research (GRIPS), Japan.

Routledge Advances in International Relations and Global Politics

The Frontiers of Public Diplomacy
Hegemony, Morality and Power in the International Sphere
Colin R. Alexander

Security and Safety in the Era of Global Risks
Edited by Radomir Compel and Rosalie Arcala Hall

Laws of Politics
Their Operations in Democracies and Dictatorships
Alfred G. Cuzán

Climate Change and Biodiversity Governance in the Amazon
At the Edge of Ecological Collapse?
Joana Castro Pereira and Eduardo Viola

Mega-regionalism and Great Power Geo-economic Competition
Xianbai Ji

De Facto State Identity and International Legitimation
Sebastian Klich

Perspectives on the State Borders in Globalized Africa
Edited by Yuichi Sasaoka, Aimé Raoul Sumo Tayo and Sayoko Uesu

Making Sense of Cyber Capabilities for Small States
Case Studies from the Asia-Pacific
Francis C. Domingo

The Uneven Offshore World
Mauritius, India, and Africa in the Global Economy
Justin Robertson and Michael Tyrala

For information about the series: https://www.routledge.com/Routledge-Advances-in-International-Relations-and-Global-Politics/book-series/IRGP

Perspectives on the State Borders in Globalized Africa

Edited by Yuichi Sasaoka, Aimé Raoul Sumo Tayo and Sayoko Uesu

LONDON AND NEW YORK

First published 2022
by Routledge
2 Park Square, Milton Park, Abingdon, Oxon OX14 4RN

and by Routledge
605 Third Avenue, New York, NY 10158

Routledge is an imprint of the Taylor & Francis Group, an informa business

© 2022 selection and editorial matter, Yuichi Sasaoka, Aimé Raoul Sumo Tayo and Sayoko Uesu; individual chapters, the contributors

The right of Yuichi Sasaoka, Aimé Raoul Sumo Tayo and Sayoko Uesu to be identified as the authors of the editorial material, and of the authors for their individual chapters, has been asserted in accordance with sections 77 and 78 of the Copyright, Designs and Patents Act 1988.

All rights reserved. No part of this book may be reprinted or reproduced or utilised in any form or by any electronic, mechanical, or other means, now known or hereafter invented, including photocopying and recording, or in any information storage or retrieval system, without permission in writing from the publishers.

Trademark notice: Product or corporate names may be trademarks or registered trademarks and are used only for identification and explanation without intent to infringe.

British Library Cataloguing-in-Publication Data
A catalogue record for this book is available from the British Library

Library of Congress Cataloguing-in-Publication Data
A catalog record for this book has been requested

ISBN: 978-1-032-06433-8 (hbk)
ISBN: 978-1-032-06434-5 (pbk)
ISBN: 978-1-003-20231-8 (ebk)

DOI: 10.4324/9781003202318

Contents

List of figures	vii
List of tables	viii
Name of the box	ix
List of contributors	x
Introduction	xi

1 New perspectives on the African state borders   1
   YUICHI SASAOKA

2 From contested borders to cross-border cooperation in the Lake Chad Basin: Stakes and challenges   17
   AIMÉ RAOUL SUMO TAYO

3 A porous border and economic activity in the Kampala – Kinshasa market, West Nile, North-western Uganda   34
   NOBUKO YAMAZAKI

4 Cross-border refugee crisis and local governments in the West Nile Region, Uganda   54
   SATOMI KAMEI

5 Mobility as a culture in rural Africa   71
   YUICHI SEKIYA

6 Micro-regionalism in Southern Africa   86
   YUICHI SASAOKA

7 Transnational violent actors in the borderlands of the Sahel and challenges for stabilization: Any role for Japan?   102
   SAYOKO UESU

8 Insecurity in the Horn of Africa and the role of IGAD   122
   RIE TAKEZAWA

9 The hardening of African borders in the Era of growing
   security threats and the global War on Terror   138
   AIMÉ RAOUL SUMO TAYO

10 Porous boundaries and anisotropic mobility: Migration
   and cross-border trade between Nigeria and Japan   155
   HISASHI MATSUMOTO

11 Decentralization and conflict prevention in East Africa   170
   YUICHI SASAOKA

   Conclusion   187
   Index   202

Figures

Photo 3.1   Arua main market   46
Map 4.1   The West Nile Region and Districts (prior to 2019)   55

Figures

10.1   Population trends of Japanese living in Nigeria (1972–2017)   157
10.2   Population trends of Nigerians living in Japan (1984–2018)   160
10.3   Change of legal status among Nigerians in Japan (1984–2010)   161

Tables

3.1	Number of pedestrians arriving at the Kampala market	39
3.2	Number of bicycles arriving at Kampala market	40
3.3	Products brought to Kampala market on foot (21 October 2018)	41
3.4	Products brought to Kampala market by bicycle (21 October 2018)	41
3.5	Sale price at markets in 2018 (Uganda shilling: UGX)	43
4.1	Top 3 country of origin and number of refugees in Uganda	61
7.1	Security-related assistance to Northwest Africa since 2013	113
10.1	Population of Japanese Nationals Overseas according to region (October 2017)	157

Box

7.1　Japan's contributions for Africa – peace and stability　　　114

Contributors

Satomi Kamei is a local government planning expert in Uganda (June 2020).

Hisashi Matsumoto is a professor at the Infrastructure and Urban Society (Global Studies), Graduate School of Urban Innovation, Yokohama National University.

Yuichi Sasaoka is a professor in the Graduate School of Governance Studies at Meiji University, Japan.

Yuichi Sekiya is a professor at the Department of Cultural Anthropology, Interdisciplinary Cultural Studies, Graduate School of Arts and Science, University of Tokyo.

Aimé Raoul Sumo Tayo is a senior researcher at the Center for Strategic Studies and Innovations, Yaoundé, Cameroon.

Rie Takezawa is a Ph.D. candidate at Hitotsubashi University and previously a political advisor at the Embassy of Japan in Ethiopia (March 2020).

Sayoko Uesu is a research associate at National Graduate Institute for Policy Research (GRIPS), Japan, and previously worked as a terrorism analyst for the Japan International Cooperation Agency and the Japanese Ministry of Foreign Affairs.

Nobuko Yamazaki is a postdoctoral researcher at the Ryukoku University and Research Fellow, Kyoto University.

Introduction

Yuichi Sasaoka, Aimé Raoul Sumo Tayo, and Sayoko Uesu

Africa faces rampant violence, terrorism, deterioration of water-energy-food provision, an influx of refugees and immigrants, corruption, vote-buying, ethnic manipulation, and religious hatred. Solutions for these issues require new ideas that are not attempted by the conventional *state-building approach*. We know that limited statehood can be found in many places in African Continent (Risse, 2013) because the state was formerly combined by loose political ties (Herbst, 2014). African state borders tend to be regarded as porous and fragile, and therefore, ordinary state border arguments tend to stress the danger of fragile states and the necessity of strengthening border controls.[1] However, another view is also possible that porous borders can contribute to cultural and socio-economic network maintenance beyond states and create active borderlands by increasing people's mobility, contact, and trade (Alemu, 2019). The existence of cross-border ethnic and cultural groups could allow regional cooperation if such groups' activities are given freedom and facilitated. That approach can be called the *borderland and trans-region approach*.[2]

The *borderland and trans-region approach* helps consider future possibilities of designing and constructing a wider region or zone, including the present state border areas, as well as providing new understandings on the stability, welfare, and identity of the borderland. Establishing strong border controls may be necessary for a weak state, but it would also perish a bright future as a side effect and delay the schedule for future transnational and subregional governance. The post-modern, interdependent, and transnational state relations were partly realized in the European Union (EU). The EU does not necessarily exemplify the post-modern region, but it shows the advanced pattern of state-building. However, present African state relations are not so heavily backward as suggested by the *state-building approach*.[3] They may have dual-negative and dual-positive characters that must be modernized to be equipped with stable and strong borders and need to retain a pre-modern loose and free boundary simultaneously. Post-modern sub-regional integration could be realized earlier and safer by activating African societies and states' *borderland and trans-region approach*. Africa's pre-modern state vacuum could be utilized for gaining the base for post-modern sub-regional and transnational society.

We need to consider the border issues from global perspectives. The contemporary globalized world can be analysed from three levels of governance structure: (i) globalization, (ii) interstate system, and (iii) culture (Sasaoka, 2011, 2016). The interpenetration of these three levels shapes today's global governance. Globalization is the latest modernization segment that started around the end of the Cold War (Rosenau and Czempiel, 1992). To differentiate globalization from modernization, some researchers call it "IT globalization." The interstate system was originated in Europe and has been accompanied by modernization and industrialization processes. The modern era was created when advances in science and technology, such as the inventions of the telephone (1876) and the airplane (1903), brought changes to people's lives. Buzan and Lawson (2015) eloquently state that the 19th century's unique characteristics are industrialization processes, rational state-building, and technological development of transportation modes and military weapons. Mainly agreeing with this argument, the authors would like to suggest that the changes and multiplication of transportation routes may be more important than transportation modes such as engines of steam trains and jets, mainly focusing on developing countries because transportation routes are linked with regional cultures, histories, state construction, and globalization in the developing countries.

State-building approach emphasizes modern states' significance and tends to disregard two other levels: globalization and culture. The author worried about such a narrow stance and found that three levels of governance correspond to German anthropologist Dobler's (2016) border classification.[4] Firstly, the globalized border shares Dobler's "blue border – from the colour of the ocean on which container ships and oil tankers operate, and the sky across which freight planes fly (p. 160)," used for "commodity trade" facilitated by actors who work in the Capitals. "Blue" border has ameliorated the quality of infrastructure that reflects the globalization process. Secondly, modern state borders share Dobler's "grey border – a border the colour of tarmac (p. 156)," of roads, railways, and border towns used for "locally embedded trade" on grey tarmac roads or railway lines "passing through official border posts (p. 157)" and dependent on dense local networks. They have been developed from the 19th century to the present, accompanied by modern state functions. However, in Africa, this level of infrastructure is so weak and poorly maintained in rural areas. It is equivalent to the underdeveloped landline telephone system while mobile phone usage is much progressed under globalization (leapfrog technology). Thirdly, African small and de facto borders share Dobler's "green border: bush, savannah or desert and myriad paths across it (p. 155)." They are used for "local trades" of everyday goods carried across boundaries and "daily traffic" in and across local cultures. At this level, the border has retained the cross-border-patterned behaviors of people since pre-modern times.

The authors' message is to remind the importance of the combined effects of three types of borders and the significance of *borderland and trans-region approach* in Africa. There are also regional variances and mixed types of approaches with modern state-building. To understand African border problems accurately and provide countermeasures to them precisely, we need to consider the complex dynamics of three levels of governance structures in Africa. The authors hope this book will give some important clues to fundamental questions of state borders and initiate a long-overdue debate about state consolidation and transnational development in Africa.

Regional differences

We would like to see the regional differences of state borders in Africa from the security point of view. The security issue is just one of the issues but tends to be linked with the volatility of state borders. West Africa demands the highest level of care for volatility which is not limited to a few countries. In East Africa, insecurity is somewhat limited to countries such as Somalia, Sudan, South Sudan, and Ethiopia at present. However, East Africa was not free from terrorist fear in the past. There were Al-Qaeda terrorist bombings on the embassies, buses, and restaurants. Lord Resistance Army (LRA) often assaulted northern Uganda and killed and abducted local people, causing nearly a million internally displaced persons. We had better note that the scale of violence by LRA was more significant than today's Boko Haram violence in West Africa (Shirato, 2017). Since Sudan and South Sudan made a peace pact, LRA lost the stable home ground and assistance from Sudan and escaped to other neighbouring countries. Southern Africa provides relatively stable state borders and borderlands except for northern Mozambique, but the region is characterized by smuggling, crime, human trafficking, and corruption. While intensified conflicts existed, they were mainly internal conflicts in Zimbabwe, South Africa, Angola, and Mozambique. The interstate conflict between Namibia and South Africa and interstate debate was harsh at the apartheid time, but they do not exist.

There are sharp increases of insurgency or self-proclaimed Jihad in state border areas in West and Central Africa. Therefore, various solutions have been attempted by research institutions and international organizations (IOs) to incorporate transnational aspects. The International Crisis Group (ICG) focuses on the neglected causes of violence in the border areas, trying to demystify the increase of "international Jihad" in Sahel or Lake Chad and propose recommendations for various actors. Similar views are expressed by Pérouse de Montclos (2018), Mohammed (2018), Saïbou Issa (2018), and Chétima (2020). As Africa has been the theatre of numerous external military operations by the United States, France, the United Kingdom, and others, they try to encourage subregional security cooperation by supporting a rise of the African Peace and Security Architecture and its appropriation by Africans. France strongly assisted the sectors of communication and transmissions, equipment maintenance, and auditing to the new architecture of peace and security (Koungou, 2010). The dynamics have accelerated with the rise of Jihadism and have led to the creation of ad hoc regional coalitions such as G5 Sahel and the Multinational Joint Task Force of the Lake Chad Basin Commission. African strategic partners have also warned the risks derived from only focusing on the hardline policies and the cooperation of states, mainly led by the security apparatus. In contrast, L'Alliance Sahel aims to promote education, livelihood and food security, energy and climate, governance and decentralization, and local service delivery. The tasks are much broader than ordinary military and strategic operations.

Contrary to Europe, where borders were drawn from interstate conflicts (Tilly, 1990), those of Africa were artificially drawn by European powers. In Africa, rich land tends to be concentrated in the central and coastal parts of a country. In peripheral areas, the land quality is usually poor; much of it is arid and semi-arid. Therefore, there is little regard for the capture of the land in border areas. In such a circumstance, people do not need to define the borderline clearly. Africa did not experience a modern state formation war (Herbst, 2000). One of the exceptions might be the Ugandan dictator's, General Amin. He unilaterally specified the Kagera River as the state border between Uganda and Tanzania and sent a unit to control exceptionally fertile land. This behaviour was very much close to the modern European War. However, African conflict used to be intrastate, and political actors struggled over power in a modern state formation and did not pay much attention to the state border. Finally, a new type of conflict has been emerging as a trans-state conflict. Ugandan LRA conflict was one of the initial cases of this type. Nowadays, major ongoing conflicts in Africa can be classified into trans-state conflict, and West Africa and Sahel are now the focus of this type.

With these backgrounds, there are three research questions. Firstly, what kind of state borders exists in Africa? It is estimated that there are three types of state borders from transportation aspects, as mentioned previously. The border with small paths dated back to precolonial time and was linked with local people's business and culture. Still, people walk across the border on foot and ride on bicycles and animals. The modern state border began to be built for the benefit of Colonizers, and trunk roads and railways have been maintained and expanded after the independence. The third dimension is the globalized border, developing in many parts of Africa. They have a link with the globalized world utilizing super-modern facilities, IT, and automation networks. Three levels of state border can be seen in any part of the world, but African uniqueness is an almost equal combination of three types.

Secondly, the authors need to check the validity of the *state-building approach* for the policy prescriptions. The lack of effective border controls allows defeated armed groups to find safe heavens in neighbouring countries easily. The weak state border is a fact of life. Moreover, border control can hardly be attained when the government capacity is inadequate, where the central and peripheral ethnic groups confront each other, and the latter often connect with other neighbour groups. Kanuri, the bulk of Boko Haram's insurgents, live in Nigeria, Cameroon, Niger, and Chad. This group has taken advantage of prevailing situations of borders to extend its activities from Nigeria to other countries. In the Lake Chad Basin, the configuration of borderland areas has always been a factor of insecurity (Issa, 2000). Terrorist groups take advantage of the state's absence in the margin and the weaknesses of cross-border security cooperation. Considering the present situation, it is beyond the imagination that each state can maintain strong and durable borders. Furthermore, the concept of a strong border is a European concept that may not be suitable for Africa. African states had better not follow the European state formation process with many accounts.

Thirdly, the root causes of African Jihadism and terrorist attack may be found in the social structures and governance of the state and region rather than their radical and alleged ideologies and the lack of border controls. The critical point is the border society's structure where security is not tight, welfare is not provided, identity is fluid, and all these issues are entangled. If you agree to think that way, what kind of policy and strategies should we embark on? In Western Sahel, how can people balance the growing security concerns with the need to keep "the sheer adaptability of pastoralists, who favor flexible and opportunistic responses to climate and political uncertainties as well as smuggling and semi-official trade networks" (Walther et al., 2017)? Instead of confining people's mobility, we need to observe violent non-state actor (VNSA)'s social support base and links in the stateless area (Varin & Abubakar, 2017).

Global governance

Global governance seems to be located between rule-oriented societies (Rosenau and Czempiel, 1992) and rule-disregarded societies (Bremmer, 2013). European nation state power and authority are declining, and the United States and China, two superpowers, recently started a heavy confrontation. The new sets of rules and identities are emerging in a globalizing world, but they are still in an infant stage. Therefore, two contrasting phenomena are taking place at the same time. The process of globalization of trade, investment, and travel is paradoxically accompanied by the partitioning of spaces and the hardening of borders.

Regarding complex dynamics, Debray (2010) argues that the notion of borderlessness is wishful thinking in *global governance* arguments: The illusion of deterritorialization contrasts with the reality of multiplication of new states, walls, barriers, and fences. The nationalistic moves to strengthen borders and border controls have been quite evident in Israel, United States, China, and even Europe in recent years, and they may be a repercussion of the swift globalization trends. This book will tackle these dynamics of "partitioning of space" from the administrative registration with visa, military registration with mining, physical registration with checkpoints with or without strong symbolic dimensions (Damiani, 2013).

Thus, global governance is in the middle of a passage from the interstate system to a global society; it is also primarily affected by regional cultures. While state powers and the authority of interstate systems have been eroded, global rules, ethics, and identities are not yet established agreeably. But widespread popular disillusion with the abilities of secular state leaders can feed into perceptions that they hold power illegitimately and that image constructs a global religious revitalization (Haynes, 1999). François Burgat (2003), for example, considers that political Islam is both "a result of globalization and a reaction to its hold." Many researchers point out that global religious revitalization and terrorism can appear as a violent response of groups to the uniformly globalized cultures and lifestyles (Baudrillard and Derrida, 2015) and "the daily crushing of so-called marginal or minority cultures by the industrial cultures of the center." Therefore, techno-economic globalization can lead to politico-cultural Balkanization (Debray, 2007). The rise of a puritanical form of religiosities, such as Salafism and Pentecostal movement in Africa, can paradoxically be seen as a product of globalization and the result of the imperfection of a global form of governance. As a result, culturally based people's identities tend to clash everywhere in a different modality that Samuel Huntington predicted in the Clash of Civilization (2011 [1996]): globalization trends tend to stimulate social groups, and they can interact with negatively each other and with the government by using religious, cultural, and political symbols.

The international economy is still vulnerable due to a lack of rules and norms, which allows speculation of hot money and tax havens. G7 economies stagnate and cannot take the lead in creating a new world economy and recent pandemic controls (Stewart, 2020). While BRICS and G20 have become powerful, their positions are diverse and tend to make tentative slogans for their partial gains. G20 members are so various, and making a unified opinion is so difficult (Bremmer, 2013). The harmful effects of globalization occurred as coronavirus pandemic in 2020, although pandemic is not a new thing. It was caused by people's higher level of mobility and furthered by weak national health and hygiene systems and a lack of government transparency and accountability. Regionalism can be seen as another pillar of globalization, but many major formal moves are now paralysed. The cultural repercussions caused by globalization tend to crystalize into the minority and peripheral group's antipathy against the center and nationalistic arrogance and dominance in the game of the superpowers and regional rivalry politics.

The contemporary globalized world can be analysed from three levels of governance: (i) globalization, (ii) interstate system, and (iii) culture. The three levels of the idea are influenced by *The Mediterranean* by Fernand Braudel. Braudel (1982) explains history from three structural levels: (i) geographical time with a slow change (long wave); (ii) long-term social, economic, and cultural history (medium wave); and (iii) events caused by individuals and heroes (short wave). In the author's classification, IT (Information Technology) and related socio-economic globalization can be categorized as a short wave (the phenomena occurring especially after the 1980s and 1990s). The bulk of modernization processes correspond to a medium wave (the 17th century to the present). Culture and religion formation processes can be a long wave, as it has been chronologically continued from ancient, precolonial, and pre-modern times, but its mission has been suddenly transformed under globalization (Sasaoka, 2011).

As a globalization trend, globalized transportation modes can be seen in many parts of Africa. Durban, Mombasa, Dar es Salaam, Abidjan, and Lagos can be assigned as a pillar of a globalized transport network. They carry cargos in massive scale, high speed, and superior quality to all over the world. In Africa, 90% of the trade cargos are unloaded in the ports. Kenyan and Ethiopian farmers send cut flowers, especially rose, by air freight to all the cities, including Amsterdam, by using a cold chain to keep their products fresh. Another pillar is One-Stop Border Post (OSBP), a bonded transfer area for moving cargos to inland countries. They aim at simplifying the custom procedure and enhancing efficiency. After Chilund OSBP was built in 2009, transit time was successfully halved (Watanuki, 2019). A few dozen OSBP is operated at the state border between countries and between Regional Economic Communities (RECs).

Introduction xvii

This book attempts to synthesize the approaches of political science, geopolitics, and social anthropology, blending macro-, meso-, and micro-views on state borders. It sorts out the characteristics of border porosity yet negates the stereotypical perception of African borders and tries to rediscover *borderland and transregion approach*. The related attempt is to deal with the relationship between the physical character of the borders and security issues. This needs to be captured in a multidisciplinary way. In this regard, we can provide views about the livelihood of borderland people. The sociopolitical formation processes across state borders have been described by culture (long), economy (short), and political security (medium wave). There are contrasting cases regarding whether the culture goes beyond the border or remains inside the border. The potentiality of the regional formation process is contingent on the cultural homogeneity of adjacent regions (long wave, culture) and economic complementarity connecting adjacent societies across borders (short wave, globalization).

The general capacity of a state and the interstate system is a precondition of modernity (medium wave). Richer countries, having a high economic capacity, tended to restrict the inflow of workers from neighbouring more impoverished countries. South Africa had an electronic wire fence at the border with Zimbabwe, whereas Zimbabwe had no specific barriers except the Limpopo River. However, South Africa decided to accept immigrant workers without passports to obtain a cheap labor workforce. Hence, there is evidence that border policies are closely linked with labor and immigration policy.

Moreover, the central and local relations in a country are crystalized into a decentralization policy to mitigate internal group conflicts and frustrations. Decentralization can provide internal stability if resource allocation to a rural area is conducted fairly by the center, although it can risk segregating the region from the state (Sasaoka, 2008). Furthermore, the roles of civil society and outsiders to engage in trans-border activities need to be verified. The National Redemption Front, a rebel group in Darfur and eastern Chad, collected financial support from Zaghawa people's overseas network. Local people and outsiders carry out informal trade. The nomads or pastoralists in the Sahel, often associated with Jihadists or smugglers, are also holding onto a regional network (McDonnell, 2016). Based on these points of view, border porosity can be viewed differently from state-centric perspectives, leading to a new recognition, perception, and policy direction.

The fragility of a border is a concern to all the people. However, only emphasizing the *state-building approach* would prevent further development of transnational and regional policy under a unique and valuable institutional setting in Africa because the African state was constructed by external forces and did not follow the path of European state-building. Africa can unite without emphasizing state sovereignty and nationalism fanatically and respecting the culture and accepting globalization. This "the last shall be the first" approach may contradict modern state-building and interstate system formation. However, it can be called *a dialectic development approach*. The three different and opposite epochal disjuncture is required and can take place simultaneously. African state centralization is necessary for modern state-building. However, as a relic of colonization and a character of state artificiality, it is linked with the *predatory state* and *neo-patrimonial state* arguments, favouring limited power groups residing in the capital and/or political center. Therefore, the *borderland and trans-region approach* can give the African community authenticity and natural flexibility and create a more useful regional framework for rural people.

Structure of the book

Sasaoka, Sumo Tayo, Uesu, and other writers share the fundamental standpoint of arguments even though they have different foresight on the concrete issues. Editors provide a macro-side of interpretation on porous borders instead and capture complex prospects of the whole African borders in a longer perspective by looking at the merits of different borders. But they also provide relatively cautious views on the borders, mainly from a security point of view. Moreover, they share an opinion that only coercive and militaristic means cannot be the only desirable options to solve security problems. They also think *borderland and trans-region approaches* and *rebordering* are not antithetic since the process of *rebordering* can be seen as the rehabilitation of classical border functions of protection and control in a context of transnational threat. We share recommendations of summarizing the arguments and the aspirations that African societies can and should solve the issue by themselves through cooperation.

In Chapter 1, Sasaoka provides a basic conceptual framework of three layers of governance, regional variance, and the borders linked with globalization and culture. He recommends a *borderland and trans-region approach*, which does not consider porous borders so problematic, and this approach can provide an effective way to stabilize borderlands by confirming the historical and cultural connections of communities and new frontiers of emerging transnational society across state borders. At the same time, Tayo explains in Chapter 2 that since the beginning of the 2010s, there is a paradigm shift in national borders governance and cross-border relations in the Lake Chad Basin. Until the early 2000s, states of the Lake Chad Basin had an exclusive conception of their borders. The settlement of multiple territorial disputes, considering the sociopolitical configuration of border areas, and above all, shared security threats have forced the four Chad, Cameroon, Niger, and Nigeria to enshrine their border governances in a cooperative approach.

In Chapter 3, Yamazaki focuses on economic activities of residents at local markets on the border with the DRC in the West Nile, north-western Uganda, where people cross the border through *panya* road daily. By examining this case, she will discuss how rapid urbanization and improvement of the road infrastructure connecting various parts of the West Nile both with the capital area and with portal cities in neighbouring countries has increased logistics and characterizes the current trans-border trade in the region.

In Chapter 4, Kamei focuses on the cross-border refugees and Uganda's West Nile region to examine how the recent refugee influxes from South Sudan have impacted on the local governments (LGs) in the region. She illustrates prominent issues and challenges faced by the refugee-hosting LGs and communities and concludes that locally generated commitments and capacity for refugee responses must be further reinforced by the international donor community in light of tackling the globalized refugee crisis in peripheral West Nile region.

In Chapter 5, Sekiya will discuss the current situation where mobility as a culture has been accepted. Next, he will discuss the current condition of many migrant workers from rural Africa. This will be followed by a discussion of how rural communities maintain their functions. For example, he will take up relevant phenomena in Niger, Malawi, and Kenya. Then, he will point out again the mobility as a culture in Africa. Finally, he will argue the effectiveness of viewing the relevant events as an interplay of issues at three levels: micro, meso, and macro, as a way of analysing the sedentariness and mobility that exist in rural Africa.

In Chapter 6, Sasaoka looks back on micro-regionalism in Southern Africa, a show case of spatial planning and advanced type of transportation system, where top-down development approaches are usually preferred but tend to neglect ordinary, informal sector, and poor people's life and peace. Top-down nature development planning is also found in the recent economic corridor-related approach and finally failed. Super-modern transport can decrease corruption levels by automation technology and assure the benefits to some segments of people but does not guarantee an equitable distribution to all. Redistribution and attention to local people were disregarded concerning the modern oil pipelines such as Niger Delta: local share of oil revenue allocation finally reached 13% since 2000.

In Chapter 7, Uesu mainly deal with modern states but essentially fragile borders at the time of crisis. Uesu describes the different narratives surrounding a transnational pastoral community caught in a vicious circle of violence in the borderlands. The latter part reviews how the borderland has been governed and assisted with hardening the borders. The chapter concludes with a set of conclusions for Japan's new approach for peace and stability, which needs to incorporate some emerging trends on assisting the borderlands and its actors.

In Chapter 8, Takezawa talks about IGAD, the post–Cold War unique regional organization. As the Horn of Africa's regional body, IGAD has faced a wide range of tasks addressing transboundary threats from desert locusts to violent extremism. This chapter examines the evolution of IGAD's role over the years given the changing security environment and political landscape in the region including the conflict in Somalia and South Sudan.

Chapter 9 concentrates on the post-modern border issues closely linked with globalization. In a complementary investigation to his study on cross-border cooperation to fight against contemporary security threats (Chapter 2), Sumo emphasizes the paradoxical dynamics of hardening state borders in Africa with a focus on these mechanisms of partitioning space on the continent, the forms they take, as well as the securitization processes that led to their implementation.

In Chapter 10, Matsumoto will examine the transnational migration between Nigeria and Japan, triggered by cross-border trade. Instead of focusing on a single direction flow, he will consider the bilateral migration of Japanese and

xx *Introduction*

Nigerians and analyse interrelationships of the multiple actors involved. By examining the bilateral migration between two countries, Matsumoto will show inequalities among the actors, which is generated by the anisotropic nature of border-crossing activities.

Chapter 11 deals with thematic issues. Decentralization processes in East Africa are investigated. Sasaoka is convinced that these are essential elements and policy options to activate trans-border activities. In three countries, such policies have been successful, except for some uncertainty. He compared Uganda, Tanzania, and Kenya and extracted clear similarities and differences in their politics and policies. Decentralization can be a successful case when resource transfer is substantially conducted from the center to the periphery. Due to the open character of state borders, African societies have a transnational substructure, which can always facilitate local and trans-border trade and mobility. Also, a true sense of micro-regionalism cannot be constructed without a good stretch of decentralization policy.

In conclusion, we can highlight and categorize all the issues of state borders and consider the role of micro-regionalism and transnationalism. Since the conflict type is changing from intrastate conflict in the 1990s and the 2000s to trans-sate conflict from the 2010s, militia and violent non-state actor run across several countries easily. Conversely, economic integration can be made not bilaterally, usually more actor's multilateral framework. To cope with these issues, we need to have perspectives about micro-and/or sub-regionalism, and these supranational and/or trans-national perspectives can be matched with decentralized, bottom-up, and grassroots approaches. Finally, future perspectives on the state borders are provided.

Strengthening the state border is necessary for various reasons for modern state management. However, this measure tends to empower the central power groups controlling state apparatus and weaken the peripheral and borderland people and group, thereby deteriorating internal group relations and facilitating trans-state violence. The reverse trend is necessary: while modern state-building is still required for Africa, a new way of thinking is essential for combining the adjacent societies across state borders. The European nation state borders were formulated in the process of state competition and interstate wars, which is a history of modern state-building. On the other hand, recent African conflicts are not interstate conflicts, and intrastate conflicts are also limited in several countries such as Somalia, Cameroon, and Chad. African conflicts are trans-border and local conflicts at present. Therefore, applying *the state-building approach* to these conflicts does not fit well with the African historical state-building processes in scope, actors, time frame, and modality. With a long-term state-building strategy in mind, Africa needs to adopt the best combination of state border policies and the best sequence to their development prospects.

Notes

1 The World bank has categorized the countries of LICUS since 2002 and set the assessment criteria of CPIA. USAID focused on the crisis analyses and set the

Fragile States Indicators. Fund for Peace announces Fragile State Index in Foreign Policy and Brookings Institution announces Index of State Weakness.
2 Here, the trans-region means a region across a country, not like a continental scale such as trans-regional approach between Africa and Middle East.
3 State-building concept and jargon were noticed and emphasized when peacebuilding approach was considered necessary and important in the countries of the former-Yugoslavia, Afghanistan, and Iraq in the post–Cold War era. Therefore, this kind of concept tends to stress that without national and state security, state mechanism cannot be constructed firmly.
4 Gregor Dobler is a scholar and member of African Boderlands Research Network (ABORNE).

References

Alemu, M.G. (2019). "Trans-border trajectories of violence capabilities for peace and cooperative engagement in the Afar Horn", in Moyo, I., et al. (eds.), *African Borders, Conflict, Regional and Continental Integration*. London: Routledge.

Baudrillard, J. and Derrida, J. (2015). *Pourquoi la Guerre Aujourd'hui?* Paris: Ligne.

Braudel, F. (1982). *Civilization and Capitalism 15th–18th Century, Vol. I, II, III*. New York: Harper & Row Publishers.

Bremmer, I. (2013). *Every Nation for Itself: What Happens When No One Leads the World*. New York: Portfolio.

Burgat, F. (2003). *Face to Face with Political Islam*. London: I. B. Tauris.

Buzan, B. and Lawson, G. (2015). *The Global Transformation: History, Modernity and the Making of International Relations*. Cambridge: Cambridge University Press.

Chétima, M. (2020). "Comprendre Boko Haram à partir d'une perspective historique, locale et régionale", *Canadian Journal of African Studies/Revue Canadienne Des Études Africaines* 54(2): 215–227. https://doi.org/10.1080/00083968.2019.1700814

Damiani, I. (2013). "Ferghana: Les étapes d'une matérialisation frontalière entre intention et réalité", *L'espace Politique* 20. https://doi.org/10.4000/espacepolitique.2651

Debray, R. (2007). *Un mythe contemporain: le dialogue des civilisations*. Paris: CNRS Editions.

Debray, R. (2010). *Eloge des frontières*. Paris: Gallimard.

Dobler, G. (2016). "The green, the grey and the blue: a typology of cross-border trade in Africa", *Modern African Studies* 54(1): 145–169.

Haynes, J. (ed.) (1999). *Religion, Globalization and Political Culture in the Third World*. London: Palgrave Macmillan.

Herbst, J. (2000, 2014). *States and Power in Africa – Comparative Lessons in Authority and Control*. Princeton, NJ: Princeton University Press.

Huntington, S. (2011 [1996]). *The Clash of Civilizations and the Remaking of World Order*. London: Simon & Schuster.

Issa, S. (2018). *Attaques et attentats de Boko Haram dans l'Extrême-Nord du Cameroun*. Paris: L'Harmattan.

Koungou, L. (2010). *Défense et sécurité nationale en mouvement. Dynamiques des reformes, mutations institutionnelles en Afrique subsaharienne*. Paris: L'Harmattan.

McDonnell, N. (2016). *The Civilization of Perpetual Movement: Nomads in the Modern World*. London: Hurst & Co. (Publishers) Ltd.

Mohammed, K. (2018). "The origins of Boko Haram", in Levan, C. and Ukata, P. (eds.), *The Oxford Handbook of Nigerian Politics* (pp. 582–604). Oxford: Oxford University Press. https://doi.org/10.1093/oxfordhb/9780198804307.013.42

Pérouse de Montclos, M.-A. (2018). L'Afrique, nouvelle frontière du djihad ? *La Découverte*. www.documentation.ird.fr/hor/fdi:010072883

Risse, T. (ed.) (2013). *Governance without a State?: Policies and Politics in Areas of Limited Statehood*. New York: Columbia University Press.

Rosenau, J., & Czempiel, E.-O. (1992). *Governance without Government: Systems of Rule in World Politics*, Cambridge: Cambridge University Press.

Sasaoka, Y. (2008). "The effects of decentralization on conflict prevention in sub-Sahara Africa", *Journal of International Cooperation Studies* 16(1): 45–69.

Sasaoka, Y. (2011, 2016). *Development and Politics in Global Governance*. Akashi Shoten (written in Japanese).

Shirato, K. (2017). *Boko Haram – The World's Most Dangerous Organization beyond ISIS*. Tokyo: Shincho-sha (written in Japanese).

Stewart, P. (2020). Expanding the G7 makes sense, including Russia does not. *The Internationalist, Council on Foreign Relations*, 8 June.

Tilly, C. (1990). *Coercion, Capital, and European States, AD 990–1990*. Oxford: Basil Blackwell.

Trémolières, M. and Walther, O. (eds.) (2017). *Cross-border Co-operation and Policy Networks in West Africa*. Paris: SWAC/OECD.

Varin, C. and Abubakar, D. (2017). *Violent Non-State Actors in Africa – Terrorists, Rebels and Warlords*. Cham Switzerland: Palgrave Macmillan.

Watanuki, M. (2019). *Logistics in Africa and Its Private Business Chance, March 12, 19*. Tokyo: Nittsu Research Institute and Consulting (written in Japanese).

1 New perspectives on the African state borders

Yuichi Sasaoka

The borders are considered troublesome for people, local community, and sovereign states. As a recipe, there has been a *state-building approach* to strengthen state capacity and border controls by upgrading state functions to a higher level. However, authors consider that another approach may be more meaningful; a *borderland and trans-region approach*, which does not consider porous borders so problematic. This approach can provide an effective way to stabilize borderlands by confirming the historical and cultural connections of communities and new frontiers of emerging transnational society across state borders. Therefore, we had better turn to a page from a *state-building approach* to a *borderland and a trans-region approach* to connect communities or space that were forcibly separated by artificial state borders during colonial times. A strong connection could be realized by facilitating human mobility, cultural penetration, and sharing social and economic benefits with neighbouring societies.

Another motivation we recommend a new approach is that if African state follows the similar patterns of European state formation, the government needs to spend a lot of money for hardening the border and strengthening military and police capacity. That can be anticipated huge opportunity costs, and the government could utilize the same amount of money for other purposes such as health and education. The government should utilize more meaningful public investments for the bright future. Moreover, if African states follow European state formation process, and they have cumbersome confrontations with neighbours, they might result in an unnecessary trap – interstate conflict. That is the inevitable process that European states repeatedly experienced, even though the war modality would be different in a globalized environment. Modern time is the age when state border is fixed half-violently throughout all the regions (Iyotani, 2002). However, European-type state formation process, still ongoing, may not be mandatory for the African states' future.

Fragile and porous borders are not the main reasons of the conflict in Africa. The possible reasons may be the fundamental state issues such as the lack of good governance and the limited political legitimacy of the governments. Ero (2014) mentions that groups located in the center and groups located in the border tend to confront each other, whereas the former tends to obtain political power. In Kenya and Uganda, centrally located ethnic groups took power after

DOI: 10.4324/9781003202318-1

independence in the 1960s. The central region is land rich, and the battle for capturing the rich land makes an intrastate conflict. After the capital city was set up in the central region, intrastate struggle has been accelerated. To draw a line of the border was never considered as an important work, even though it was a rational work in the colonial regime and modern state-building in the 19th and 20th centuries.

The intrastate conflict was still important after the end of the Cold War. Due to the trends of democratization, political party made a struggle for a power, linking with the support base of ethnic groups. For political elites, the threat exists within the border, not outside the border (Takeuchi, 2003). After 2000, African governance is becoming mostly a hybrid regime, which is the mixture of formal democratic institutions and informal authority. Thereafter, the intrastate conflict has been reduced, as the struggle for power tends to be confined in the hybrid regime. While the influence of modern state-building lingered on, globalization started to influence larger and abrupt moves of the person, goods, and money beyond the border, causing a new type of conflict: trans-state conflict. Therefore, the border line is not without problems. Its funny shape in Hala'ib Triangle, Ilemi Triangle, and Ogaden has the potential risk. Newly discovered natural resources near the border could be the source of conflicts. Confirming the sizable share of interests from oil exports, Sudan and South Sudan agreed to sign the Comprehensive Peace Agreement, while the territorial jurisdiction of Abyei, the oil-producing area, was left behind. The activity of violent non-state actor has been conspicuous these days, linking with traditional migration patterns, culture, contraband, resource capture, and the religious fundamentalism.

A *borderland and trans-region approach* is useful for considering future possibilities of designing and constructing a wider region including the present states' borderland, as well as providing new understandings on the stability, welfare, and identity of the borderland. Establishing strong border controls is necessary for a modern state, but it would also perish a bright future as a side effect and delay the schedule for active transnational and sub-regional relationships. The post-modern, interdependent, and transnational state relations were partly realized in the EU. The EU does not necessarily exemplify the post-modern region, but it shows the advanced pattern of state-building. Present African state relations are actually not so heavily backward as suggested by *state-building approach* arguments. They may have dual-negative and dual-positive characters that must be modernized to be equipped with stable and strong borders and need to retain pre-modern loose boundary at the same time. Post-modern sub-regional integration could be realized earlier by activating African societies and states' *borderland and trans-region approach*. Africa's pre-modern state vacuum could be utilized for gaining the base for post-modern sub-regional society.

Academic background of the research and its core questions

The solutions for African problems require new perspectives that are not attempted by conventional *state-building approaches* (Olowu and Chanie, 2015).

Various research approaches have been attempted by Western research institutes and aid organizations. Institut Français des Relations Internationals has been engaged in the projects of Sahel G5 (Mali, Mauritania, Niger, Burkina Faso, and Chad) and Nigeria entrusted by the French Ministère de la Défense to set up military and humanitarian operations. The research outputs are utilized in French defense and development policies, but they tend to converge on the military and hardline policy areas and the related cooperation among states. Contrastingly, International Crisis Group investigates terrorism as a part of their regional focus and is good at analysing social backgrounds, politics, and geopolitical situations about terrorism – what kind of social factors harbour armed groups and their support bases. In a long term, a desirable strategy seems to be not just containing armed groups by force but making steps for inclusive development based on the understanding of social structures in armed groups' homeland.

There are two views on the understanding of static African state borders: the revisionists and the anti-revisionists (Nguendi, 2012). AU and OAU clearly endorsed anti-revisionists' position and argued strongly for the maintenance of status quo. Recently, AU has started the African Union Border Governance Strategy (AUBGS) aligned with the AU's Agenda 2063, which provides fairly progressive and balanced views on the state border (AUC, 2020). Starting from the adoption of the Strategy, the first implementation period was scheduled to be 2017–2022 (AUC, 2017). While the Niamey Convention on Cross Border Cooperation (CBC) still awaits its entry into force, the African Union Border Programme is now widely adopted by three levels of actors: AU, Regional Economic Communities (REC), and member countries (AUC, 2020). AUC (2017) explains that the function of borders shall be understood as an instrument to promote peace, security, and stability and as zones of facilitation of regional integration and sustainable development. AUBGS is good at providing multi-level governance scopes, but the strategy does not impose any enforcement mechanism upon member states yet.

Considering the theoretical analyses on the border, firstly, we need to know the changing type of the conflicts. African conflict used to be an interstate conflict in the Cold War period. In the late 1950s to the 1990s, more or less Cold War period, major sources of conflicts were trans-boundary minorities, trans-boundary resources, and frontier/decolonization (Nguendi, 2012). The typical conflicts were Chad/Libya, Ethiopia/Somalia, Ethiopia/Kenya, Cameroon/Nigeria, and Mali/Burkina Faso. This type has been dramatically decreased since the 1980s. Secondly, the major source of conflict has shifted to the intrastate conflict. "Who captures the state" became the main topic in the post–Cold War period. The political legitimacy was not seriously questioned in the Cold War time, if authoritarian rulers were committed to either the Western or Eastern bloc. When the Cold War was ended, the support from the East was vanished and the support from the West was conditioned: economic and political liberalization. Under the external pressure, the old neo-patrimonial regime weakened, and intrastate conflict occurred seeking for the new power. Democratization tended to spur inter-group conflicts because multi-party politics was introduced and political party was linked with the support base of specific ethnic groups. This political confrontation often turned into violent conflict. This type has been decreased since the 2000s. By that time, hybrid regime was established and neo-patrimonial rule was reconstructed in many states, reducing the cases of the intra-state conflict. Hybrid regime was a mixture of formal democratic institutions and informal authority. The third type is trans-state conflict, having transnational nature and at least one party is VNSA. It has been growing with the eye-opening event of 11 September 2001, by Al Qaeda and is linked with the dark side of globalization (Khan and Estrada, 2017).

The precolonial and colonial governance inconsistency is basically the cause of the first type conflict: interstate conflict. The modern state formation process through the struggles over power and democratization is the cause of the second type: intrastate conflict. At present, we are witnessing the third type: trans-state conflict. Al Qaeda terrorist's motivation is linked with anti-Americanism, and the resurrection of Islam and their activity is facilitated by IT globalization. In Africa, three types of conflict coexist and interact each other. They are connected with each layer of the governance: culture, state system, and globalization. The first type was negative heritage of colonialism. OAU confirmed "the principle of the respect of borders existing" in the Charter, by Cairo Resolution AHG/Res. 16(I) in 1964, and the principle was reconfirmed in article 4(b) of the Constitutive Act of the AU (AUC, 2000). To be sure, this principle has had some deterrence effects on the border conflict. The second type was not involved with state border and border retrieved the recognition in the third type. In the second type, defeated group can run away from the country to other adjacent countries easily and thereby intrastate conflict never ends. The similar element can be found in the third type that militia can go beyond the border easily but that does not entail the battles for winning the political legitimacy, just capturing home base and resource advantage.[1]

The research in global contexts

This book needs to focus security issues as well as other issues, with the inability of states to control their margins. The authors therefore observe a process of questioning the principle of the impenetrability of states and its corollary territorial exclusivity (Kelsen, 1952). The concept of state border inviolability was established in the European history, and it was aiming at the fixation of state borders because frequent border changes had taken place due to chronic interstate conflicts in the modern state-building process (Tilly, 1990). The African territorial integrity principle has been applied to postcolonial state borders (Cammack, 1988). While political rulers have not controlled sovereign territory in an effective way, actual border changes have rarely taken place. Capacity building is aimed at avoiding any kind of fragility by a *state-building approach* (Olowu and Chanie, 2015). But the greater capacity of a state may not lead to the openness of state border. Some say that African states are basically equipped with state capacity and functions. Some researchers have praised the African state and people's efforts to manage the imposed borders after the independence (Zartman, 2010, 2019) and appreciated that they have created stable nationalism within a given state framework (Young, 2012).

Security situations in Africa have deteriorated in the 2010s–2020s compared with those around the 2000s, due to resource capture, climate change, and terrorism. However, the current advantage for rural people is that people can easily communicate using mobile phones around borders, where regional integration proceeds to open a mobile phone market. In East Africa, a country code is not necessary when dialling other countries, although terrorism warnings tend to restrict foreigners' phone usage. Transport network between the center and periphery is not so closely linked. Contrastingly, close communication across state borders can be seen as neighbours, mobile phone networks, and informal trade networks. Informal cross-border trade is carried out by local civil societies, and outsiders are engaged in the trade using various networks (Moyo, 2017). Fulani in Burkina Faso is said to be linked with Jihadists, but it does not mean that all the Fulani are violence seekers – they are marginalized in a society under the globalization and holding onto an existing regional network. Border porosity can be seen differently and can be considered the future opportunity to substantiate regional formation, leading to new policy direction.

Transborder cooperation is especially important for inland states because they can be isolated without links with coastal countries. In the same vein, regional cooperation is also important for inland states to facilitate economic relations. Shifting authority to regional or sub-regional organization from the central government can be considered as upward decentralization, while shifting authority to the local government is downward decentralization. In the double directions, the validity of a decentralization policy for stabilizing the regions and mitigating ethnic group conflicts is crucial. Regarding regionalism, it is considered that African states can expect European level potential to facilitate regional interpenetration for the future. Therefore, a similar regional integration approach can be employed by the AU (Adam and Peter, 2016). From that view, the neo-functionalism may be the main principle to promote regional economic integration by activating Free Trade Agreements (FTAs) to remove tariffs, constructing economic corridors across borders, and facilitating people's mobility. Similar ideas were expressed by EU's CBC strategy and its subsidy programme of INTERREG (EC, 2007). Many African leaders have expressed the view that EU type integration will be possible for Africa. Therefore, there is an argument that African borders are functioning, and their barriers should be lowered to facilitate market integration.

Moreover, state issues are not only capacity issues. Citizens' agreement on *stateness* usually predated the formation of democratic institutions in a modern state history, but the concept of democracy includes territorial citizens' consent on the procedures to make a government (Linz and Stepan, 1996). In a transition period to state democracy, deciding who are the citizens in a country is inescapable. In Africa, many of the political regimes were democratized immediately after independence and turned into authoritarian thereafter. Who are the citizens is a puzzle in the borderland. Many communities divided by Colonizers still connect with each other through historical, cultural, and economic networks, thereby providing the perspectives of sub-regional, micro-regional, and transnational linkages. Somali and Afar people went through regional or interstate conflicts but also retain the latent connectivity of the community, which has been restrained in the modern state-building processes.

Although there are a variety of views, the average *Fragile States* arguments point out that border porosity tends to cause state vulnerability in Africa. They undoubtedly stress the negative side of porosity and emphasize the importance of strengthening state functions and upgrading border controls. There are border posts that are in charge of immigration and customs, and many of them are open, but they are not immune from corruption and negligence. That view accepts the fact that African states have constructed roads and railways that are operational, but their functions are affected by colonial legacy, nepotism, and corruption, neither linking major parts of nation state nor advancing the welfare of the people. Weak border control and porous border are utilized by the dark business to their advantage and recently by the terrorist groups to their move. However, we need to be aware of who gets the benefit of the *Fragile States* arguments, which is focusing on not the states so labelled but the international donor's strategy to build their own operational capacity for intervention into developing countries (Kaplan, 2014; Woodward, 2017).

The related issue of porous border is corruption. In borderland, vendors can approach an inspector working in a transition. Smuggling means not only corruption in customs clearance but also the complicity of not paying attention to stolen articles. It is often protected by administrative and political powers because it is an assured way for local boss to make a profit under incomplete regulations and a lack of control. Smuggling can be regarded as strong interest-sharing on both sides across the border. However, the arguments on the borders are not always pessimistic; rather, they can be positive if we can change the standpoint. Due to porosity, people can enjoy higher levels of mobility across the border with lower costs without strict controls. Loose border can facilitate higher levels of mobility for people, goods, and money, which can create active transnational and sub-regional networks. It is true that loose border is not checking smuggling and corruption and not gaining proper revenues from tariffs. It is also damaging to the dignity of sovereign states, which should protect the border for the safety of people and the symbol of national pride. Loose border may not be good for modern state-building, but it may be good for a wider political and economic region in line with the globalization. It can advance the transnational relations in Africa, similarly to the EU region that realized such schemes three-and-a-half centuries after the Westphalian Treaty. Transnational relations can revive the pre-modern community relations, linking the past and future in the Continent.

Additionally, the borderland becomes an interpenetrative place when local products are different and local cultures are similar or accommodative on both sides. The combination of economy and culture across the border can be classified into four types, and it may be useful to add a political variable – the degree of autonomy or decentralization from the center – on both sides. The proximity of the markets to the borderline (Dobler, 2016) and FTAs are also important elements. If some markets are located far from the center and they are close to the borderland economy, local products can be sold to the outside market. Crop markets in Tanzanian border were linked with other countries, by the historical trade routes, whereas main trunk roads between the center and periphery were not well connected. In the Maputo Development Corridor, informal sector vendors in Mozambique tried to go beyond the fence to reach the South African market, while no such vendors existed in South African side (Söderbaum and Taylor, 2001; Taylor, 2002). People's perception was asymmetrical between South African business people and Mozambican informal vendors because the latter wanted to keep their informal business routes.

The context of international relations theory

Since James Rosenau (1995; Rosenau and Czempiel, 1992), an original thinker on global governance, there have been many debates that an interstate system consisting of nation states cannot properly manage rapid changes of global society in the post–Cold War period. The tradition of liberalist scholars had been critical of the overemphasized role of the state, the central government, and the interstate system. However, there are plentiful other views about the post–Cold War world. Keohane and Nye (2000) have cautiously interpreted the effects of globalization as relatively minor issue, and they considered global governance to be a supplementary mechanism to the interstate system. Krasner (1999) was sceptical about the relativized positions of sovereign states caused by globalization but admitted the erosion of states' sovereignty. In the 1990s, scepticism was mounting on the role of the central governments from the views of New Public Management, while negative views on the interstate system became prominent through global governance theory. Global governance theory and globalization affected governance arguments in Western Europe and Japan and the role of nation states and central governments.

While global governance theory tends to stress the transition process from modernity (interstate system) to post-modernity (global governance), it rarely touches on the issues of pre-modern society (pre-existing governance and culture). Therefore, the third layer of governance, culture, needs to be added in the overall governance framework (Robertson, 1992; Tomlinson, 1999; Sasaoka, 2011, 2016). Moreover, owing to IT, today's world becomes smaller when communication is viable to any part of the world. People can visit distant foreign countries by air and can ask the family which souvenir is better by mobile phone. However, the contraction process of the globe brings about unexpected cross-cultural friction: hatred, fear, and misunderstanding. Huntington's (1996) "Clash of Civilization" argument might be positioned in such a spectrum. At the time of the birth of globalization theory, the interstate system was considered to be unipolar system dominated by the United States in the 1990s. Through the events of Iraq War and Leeman's collapse, unipolar system seemed to be ended: the alternative system arguments can be bipolar system (Friedberg, 2005; Ikenberry, 2006, 2008), multipolar system (Birdsall and Fukuyama, 2011), and non-polar system (Bremmer, 2012; Haass, 2017).

There are various views of globalization, based on the start period. If we consider globalization is the distribution of goods, people, and money beyond a state, it can be captured by many ways. Giddens (1990) considers that the globalization process is started from Modern times, and Sen (2002) captures Ancient times as the start period because he considers the propagation of civilizations throughout the Continent can be the process of globalization. Another definition is asserted by Rosenau and Fukuyama's (1992) post–Cold War period: global scale political and economic expansion and transformation promoted by democracy and IT revolutions. The three layers of governance view: culture, interstate system, and globalization more or less correspond to three types of interpretations of globalization here. After Rosenau and Fukuyama predicted the flourishing of liberal world, that followed the end of the Communism, the world was shaken by unexpected events, the revival of identity groups, resource battles, and obstinate authoritarianism. The bright future images seem to be declining, but positive elements are found in the emergent countries' economic growth and prosperity. Recently, another trend of global governance theory has been stressed by Global South scholars, Acharya and Buzan (2019). Their criticism on the dominant position of Eurocentric IR theory could have provided alternative IRs based on pre-existing governance structures and cultures and recent socio-economic development in non-European regions. Global South IR theory and Western traditional IR theory can have equal weight in theoretical underpinning. Acharya (2014) considers that US-led world order is deteriorating due to the loss of authority and trust especially after the Iraq War, and the future world is going to be a multiplex world that is consisted of the fluid combination of US-oriented order, the rise of emerging powers, and open regionalism.

With using three layers logic: culture, interstate system, and globalization, the author would like to explain the generating mechanism of Arab Spring in 2011. Firstly, the globalization element was evident through IT by which young protesters expressed opinions and exchanged information using social networking. Another element was a trigger factor brought about by Lehman's collapse, which was the result of the unregulated global economy and undisciplined excessive investment to induce a heavy credit crunch in the United States; the subsequent depression gravely affected the European and the Middle East economy. Food prices were hiked suddenly due to the investment of a commodity futures trading market. After many migrant workers arrived back home from Europe and the European tourists visiting Middle East sharply decreased, frustration in the youth accumulated. IT and the global economy were the main forces of globalization, and both of them are not yet tame. The reason behind the scenes is that global politics cannot sustain global economic order in a stable way.

Secondly, the state system in Middle East was advancing a slow pace of democratization in the 2010s, without strong external pressures, thereby its political regimes had been firmly characterized as an authoritarian. People were accustomed to be silent, not criticizing political rulers in the public, but that does not mean they are supportive. Since youth bulge brought about demographic changes to increase young population, young unemployment was increased. The interstate systems between Middle East and Europe have historical relationships and influence each other, especially through social media free from the government control and immigrant networks, while Arab regional identity augmented the political adventure. Middle East is rather wealthy region in a developing world, but the epicenter of Arab Spring has been concentrated in the Mediterranean sub-region rather than the wealthy Gulf sub-region.

Thirdly, cultural aspects binding people here are strong beliefs in Islam and arid region culture. At the time of crisis, secular leaders in Middle East did not behave well to people. People put up with despotic rule; however, once they conceive the serious injustice in long-time dictators, they are ready to start the collective action to change the old regime (nizam). Their human networking is surprisingly robust, formulated in Al-Jumua and communities. There are various debates whether Muslim's culture is adaptable to the Western-type democracy or not, but anti-government groups did not share a clear and unified political vision before collapsing the old regime, and civil society is not so much Westernized as Indonesia which experienced democratization process in 1998–1999.

There are three major debates about the relationship of global governance and globalization in Africa. The debates concern the three layers of governance and corresponding border types: (A) the advantages of globalization, (B) the modern state system, especially its vulnerable side, and (C) cultural elements interacting with globalization. At each level, we can identify the general traits of African society and the related issues of state borders.

Firstly, (A) type represents advanced global infrastructure and management systems that are found in the Programme for Infrastructure Development in Africa (PIDA) initiated in 2010 (AfDB, 2014). Regarding African infrastructure, Continental level organizations are African Union Commission (AUC) and NEPAD (The New Partnership for Africa's Development) Planning and Coordinating Agency (NPCA), and Regional level organizations are RECs and their related bodies. PIDA includes infrastructure and energy sectors; economic corridors, OSBP, oil and gas deposits, Export Processing Zones (EPZ), port facilities, and airports. They include not only new projects such as ICT but also old ones which have been pipelined; 25% of Trans-African Highway project has not been completed yet (NEPAD, AU, AfDB, 2011). ICT develops remarkably advanced marital and terrestrial fibre optic cables used for extending the connectivity to landlocked countries. Over half a billion Africans could access the internet (CFR, 2019). The related post-modern technology is found in Drone Delivery, Logistic Management Systems, and Internet of Things. They are high-tech transportation systems, and their system is so automatic that it can cut personnel's arbitrary discretion including bribery. (A) type is developed in Southern and Eastern Africa, Nigeria, and EPZ, especially. These modern facilities are used for the urban dwellers, foreign enterprises, and foreign consumers and rather unfamiliar to borderland people, while these modern technologies are leapfrog nature, and also familiar to borderland people.

(A)'s claim is that globalization has been pushed by technological breakthrough and has made significant impacts on the interstate system to reshape new types of cooperation (Lund and Tyson, 2018; Derian, 2013; Friedman, 2007). FTA, economic corridors, and IT management have progressed in the post–Cold War era. With these renovations, globalization has been promoted by market competition among firms and strategic competition among states. However, these renovations are double-edged sword. FTA and economic corridor have facilitated economic growth, but the acquired wealth is not necessarily shared by all. Political and economic elites gain a lot, while many people and the poor are unaffected from the market expansion and profit shares. Informal traders who used to cross the borders easily tend to be shut out from the modern transportation and custom system. While the business and government cooperation develop through the diffusion of the Internet and mobile phones, IT fraud, hacking, and cyberwars also arise. Sharing IT operation norms and disciplining mutual member activities have not been established in the cyber area.

IT globalization can bring benefits to local businesses by enabling farmers to know the world price of goods, thereby activating trade beyond the border and upgrading their living conditions. Rural people receive small remittances at the cell phone shop from family members working abroad. The relative income disparity between neighbouring countries tends to make rural people in poorer countries become migrant workers. Immigrants and refugees from poor countries tend to increase by the trend of globalization, state failure, and lack of promising industries. Simultaneously, there is a cost side to globalization. Cheap labor from neighbouring countries affects the employment rate and salary scale of workers in a recipient country, thereby creating political turmoil and even violence against foreigners. The overall trend is that very efficient transportation system, making large profits, tends to expand the income inequality in African countries because super-efficient and safe transportation system is suitable for sending goods long distances and not benefiting the local markets and informal sectors.

Major trunk road networks have been promoted by donor assistance under the multi-year framework with the OECD countries, and China has started to provide the enormous projects of the main roads and bridges. African government was rarely in the driver's seat for selecting a large development project. In this sense, PIDA is very much symbolical for Africans' leadership. From the 2000s, Africa has started to take off economically, after the highly indebted poor country relief programs cut off their heavy debt and foreign investment was restarted. Simultaneously, emerging economies like China have started to import massive scale natural resources from Africa. The World Bank, African Development Bank (AfDB), and Japan have followed the Chinese development strategy, infrastructure project came back to the centre stage. Since China was reluctant to join OECD/DAC (Development Assistance Committee) policy dialogue and local donor meetings, there was no dialogue. However, after aid convergence takes place, donor competition is activated. The potential problem is that if donor promised to cover the major part of project construction costs (development budget), the recipient government needs to cover the recurrent budget for the project maintenance and also repay the principal and interest rates of said construction costs. They are charge in after years. Since the competition is harsh among donors and Chinese loan requires the higher interest rates, several countries have already faced the debt sustainability problems.

Contrastingly, (B) is main rural roads and local railway system which represent African modern state and transportation systems. Especially, in Africa, state weakness was emphasized in the *fragile state* arguments (Sandbrook, 1985; Jackson, 1993; Collier, 2009; World Bank, 2011). The national transportation systems are not well developed and maintained in many countries. Road access rate by local people is 34% in Africa, compared with 50% in other regions (AfDB, 2014). Actually, demand for national transportation is growing due to the expansion of domestic markets in recent economic growth. Road access rate can be the blockade which reduces regional trade ratio in Africa. The border town is often used for smuggling, corruption, and human trafficking across state borders. As the globalization facilitates the flow of goods, money, and people, inefficient, low quality, and immoral national transportation systems produce serious problems at the border. While globalization has heightened people's expectation of efficient transportation systems, national transportation systems tend to delay the procedures and paralyse the circulation of goods.

Modern type facility was poorly built and not maintained well in Africa. The disfunction of state system can be observed in not only African states but also the interstate system in general. The present globalization challenges have not been dealt with adequately by the interstate system: global issues seem to be greater than the management capacity of a state and its interstate system (Piketty, 2013; Rodrik, 2011). At the time of the extreme crises, public opinion is frustrated with African countries' low capacity and unwillingness. Held and McGrew (2002) consider that regionalism can be the springboard for transforming society from national to transnational and from transnational to global. Any alternative body other than state and the central government can be considered as important counterweights. Africa is busy in making a lot of FTAs and continental FTA; the speed of regional integration seems to be much quicker than Latin America and South Asia. With the help of regional organization (ROs), the state weakness and division can be fixed.

African border control is considered horrible, but recent coronavirus spread issues tell us that African people and government are rather doing well. One of the factors is the governments' quick response to the border and airport quarantine controls from the experiences of Ebola disease. The East African Community (EAC) leaders held the online meeting and agreed on the facilitation of logistics and safety check on the drivers circulating in the region. However, border security and the management of borders in ways that promotes national security have generally been given low priority in Africa compared to security provided for political elites in the capital city and other urban areas far-removed from the borders (Okumu, 2011). While national security strategies of some countries mention the importance of secure and peaceful borders, few governments have concrete border security strategies. The negligence of border security and poor management of the borders have largely contributed to a prevalence of threats such as cross-border crimes and severe social problems such as the prevalence of HIV/AIDS and STDs at border crossing points.

Multi-level governance approach may be an important framework for the regionalism (Marks, 1993) but tends to focus only on the formal institutions. Here, we had better emphasize informal regionalism and the role of non-state actors (NSAs) to deal with the grassroots' social dynamics (Söderbaum and Shaw, 2003). Regional, sub-regional, state, and non-territorial actors can provide accurate prospects of today's regionalization along with globalization. The Western donors are glad to stress the study of sub-regionalism and micro-regionalism in non-European region and also to focus on decentralization and local governance as not only institutional aspects but also social dynamics in Africa. However, we disagree with ordinary *fragile state* arguments. We need to clarify this book's distinctive features on the state border with micro-region and grassroots perspectives because political science has mainly focused on the actors, formal institutions, and governance (the partnership of actors) and paid a tiny attention to informal institutions, grassroots, and actual territoriality (Chilla et al., 2012).

Finally, (C) implies that the smooth and instant connections of distinct communities and cultures are facilitated by globalization. In the borderlands, many cultures interpenetrate each other, while the communities are divided by politics. Cultural homogenization has been promoted in a modern African state since independence, but cultural and religious groups were deeply divided inside the border (Appadurai, 2006). The borderlands are usually marginalized in a nation state context, but they can be linked closely with adjacent communities. Due to their geographic positions, many borderlands have obtained multiple inter-cultural conditions, which are common in a global milieu. Since state borders were imperialist's artificial construction, borderland people have tended to resist and ignore imposed boundaries (Alemu, 2019). As economic interpenetration with neighbours is actively facilitated under globalization, new perspectives need to be provided to consider sub-regional and transnational interpenetration.

However, cultures make frictions through globalization, when people see the other culture's pictures and hear the messages in the internet or television. The Christianity and Islam religion penetrate through the borders and sometimes create friction with local religions and between them. Those who ignite religious clashes are leaders of religious sects who are skilful at sensitizing people. Also, fundamental Islamists and Jihadists can go across the border and start violent activities and manipulate local people by using shock and terror. Identity beliefs and actions can often, albeit not always, strengthen the perception of friend and enemy in the conceived *zero-sum* situations. How to dissolve antagonism by identity groups is the cultural challenge in global governance.

IT and religion surely reflect globalized social changes – all are not confined by modern state boundary, while state leaders can utilize them to control people's mindsets. Porosity can be flexibility which is good at facilitating transnational activities and can restore cultural solidarity across the border. Porosity can also be a symbol of state weakness, and nationalistic leaders can utilize weak borders to sensitize people's emotions. After confirming merits and demerits of porous borders, the authors can recommend a *borderland and trans-region approach:* borderland can be designated as free zone and allow state engagement and facilitate interpenetration. How to promote this agenda? A recommendation may be an autonomous policy to the borderland areas in a country to facilitate flexibility, sovereignty, and interpenetration in a balanced way.

Note

1 The third type tends to occur in the borderland or "fragile" states where modern state capacity and control (the second layer of governance) are very weak, and culture (or religion; the first layer of governance) and IT globalization (the third layer of governance) can interact and interpenetrate easily.

References

Acharya, A. (2014). *The End of American World Order*, Cambridge: Polity Press.
Acharya, A., & Buzan, B. (2019). *The Making of Global International Relations: Origins and Evolution of IR at Its Centenary*, Cambridge: Cambridge University Press.
Adam, A., & Peter, A. (2016). Comparative analysis of AU and EU: Challenges and prospects. *International Journal of Peace and Conflict Studies*, 13(1).
African Development Bank (AfDB) (2014). *Programme for Infrastructure Development in Africa*, Abidjan: Côte d'Ivoire.
African Union Commission (2000). *Constitutive Act Draft*, Addis Ababa: African Union Commission.
African Union Commission (2017). *Draft African Union Border Governance Strategy*, Addis Ababa: African Union Commission.
African Union Commission (2020). *African Union Strategy for a Better Integrated Border Governance*, Addis Ababa: African Union Commission.
Alemu, M.G. (2019). Trans-border trajectories of violence capabilities for peace and cooperative engagement in the Afar Horn. In Moyo, I. et al. (eds), *African Borders, Conflict, Region and Continental Integration*, London: Routledge.
Appadurai, A. (2006). *Fear of Small Numbers: An Essay on the Geography of Anger*, Durham, NC: Duke University Press.
Birdsall, N., & Fukuyama, F. (2011). The post-Washington consensus: Development after the crisis, Working Paper 244, Washington, DC: Center for Global Development.
Braudel, F. (1982). *Civilization & Capitalism 15th–18th Century*, Vol. I, II, III, New York: Harper & Row Publishers.
Bremmer, I. (2012). *Every Nation for Itself: Winners and Losers in a G-Zero World*, New York: Portfolio.
Cammack, P., Pool, D., & Tordoff, W. (1988). *Third World Politics: A Comparative Introduction*, London: Macmillan Education Ltd.
Chilla, T., Evrard, E., & Schultz, C. (2012). On the territoriality of cross-border cooperation: "Institutional mapping" in a multi-level context. *European Planning Studies*, 20(6).

Collier, P. (2009). *Wars, Guns, and Votes: Democracy in Dangerous Places*, New York: Harper Collins Publishers.
Council on Foreign Relations (2019). Last month, over half-a-billion Africans Accessed the Internet, Blog poat John Campbell, July 25, 2019.
Denoon, D.J.N. (2009). The Transvaal Labour Crisis, 1901–6. *The Journal of African History*, 8(3): 481–494.
Derian, D. (2013). From war 2.0 to quantum war: Superpositionality of global violence. *Australian Journal of International Affairs*, 67(5): 570–585.
Dobler, G. (2016). The green, the grey and the blue: A typology of cross-border trade in Africa. *The Journal of Modern African Studies*, 54: 145–169.
Ero, C. (2014). Competing solutions to keeping peace in Africa, conversation at United Nations University. September 5 (https://unu.edu/events/archive/conversation-series/competing-solutions-to-keeping-peace-in-africa-a-conversation-with-dr-comfort-ero.html#overview).
European Commission (EC) (2007). Interregional co-operation programme: 'INTERREG IVC' (https://ec.europa.eu/regional_policy/index.cfm/en/atlas/programmes/2007–2013/crossborder/interregional-co-operation-programme-interreg-ivc).
Friedberg, A. (2005). The future of U.S.-China relations: Is conflict inevitable? *International Security* 30(2): 7–45.
Friedman, T. (2007). *The World Is Flat: Further Updated and Expanded (Release 3.0)* (2nd revised and expanded ed.), New York: Farrar, Straus and Giroux.
Fukuyama, F. (1992). *The End of History and the Last Man*, New York: International Creative Management.
Giddens, A. (1990). *The Consequences of Modernity*, Stanford, CA: Stanford University Press.
Haass, R. (2017). *A World in Disarray: American Foreign Policy and the Crisis of the Old Order*, New York: Penguin Press.
Held, D., & McGrew, A. (2002). *Globalization/Anti-Globalization*, Cambridge: Polity Press.
Huntington, S. (1996). *The Clash of Civilizations and the Remaking of World Order*, New York: Simon & Schuster.
Ikenberry, J. (2006). *Liberal Order and Imperial Ambition: Essays on American Power and World Politics*, Cambridge: Polity Press.
Ikenberry, J. (2008). The rise of China and the future of the west: Can the liberal system survive? *Foreign Affairs*, 87(1): 23–37.
Iyotani, T. (2002). *What Is Globalization?* Tokyo: Heibonsha.
Jackson, R. (1993). *Quasi-States: Sovereignty, International Relations and the Third World*, Cambridge: Cambridge University Press.
Kaplan, S. (2014). Identifying truly fragile states. *The Washington Quarterly*, 37(1): 49–63.
Kelsen, H. (1952). *Principles of International Law*, New Jersey: The Lawbook Exchange, Ltd.
Keohane., R., & Nye, J. (2000). Introduction. In Nye, S. & Donahue, J.D. (eds), *Governance in a Globalizing World*, Washington, DC: Brookings Institution Press.
Khan, A., & Estrada, A. (2017). Globalization and terrorism: An overview. *Quality and Quantity*, 51(4): 1811–1819.
Krasner, S. (1999). *Sovereignty: Organized Hypocrisy*, Princeton, NJ: Princeton University Press.

Linz., J., & Stepan, A. (1996). *Problems of Democratic Transitions and Consolidation*, Baltimore, MD: Johns Hopkins University Press.
Lund., S., & Tyson, L. (2018). Globalization is not in retreat: Digital Technology and the future of trade. *Foreign Affairs*, 97(3).
Marks, G. (1993). Structural Policy and Multilevel Governance in the EC. In Cafruny, A. & Rosenthal, G. (eds), *The State of the European Community*, New York: Lynne Rienner.
Moyo (2017). Zimbabwean cross-border traders in Botswana and South Africa: Perspectives on SADC Regional Integration. In Nshimbi, C., & Moyo, I. (eds), *Migration, Cross-Border Trade and Development in Africa*, London: Palgrave Macmillan.
NEPAD, AU, AfDB. (2011). Study on Programme for Infrastructure Development in Africa (PIDA), Phase III, PIDA Study Synthesis, Clichy-Cedex, France: SOFRECO.
Nguendi, F. (2012). Africa's international borders as potential sources of conflict and future threats to peace and security, Paper no. 233. Institute for Security Studies.
Okumu, W. (2011). Border management and Security in Africa, Working Paper, Addis Ababa: African Union.
Olowu, D., & Chanie, P. (2015). State Fragility and State Building in Africa, Cases from Eastern and Southern Africa (UNU Series), New York: Springer.
Piketty, T. (2013). *Capital in the 21st Century*, Éditions du Seuil, Paris and Harvard University Press (2014, English), Cambridge, Massachusetts.
Robertson, R. (1992). *Globalization: Social Theory and Global Culture*, London: SAGE.
Rodrik, D. (2011). *The Globalization Paradox*, New York: Norton & Company, Inc.
Rosenau, J. (1995). *Governance in the Twenty-First Century*, Brill, Leiden, The Netherlands: Global Governance 1.
Rosenau, J., & Czempiel, E.-O. (1992). *Governance without Government: Systems of Rule in World Politics*, Cambridge: Cambridge University Press.
Sandbrook, R. (1985). *The Politics of Africa's Economics Stagnation*, Cambridge: Cambridge University Press.
Sasaoka, Y. (2011). Decentralization and conflict prevention. *International Politics*, 165, Yuhikaku, Tokyo: The Japan Association of International Relations.
Sasaoka, Y. (2011, 2016). *Development and Politics in Global Governance*, Tokyo: Akashi Shoten (written in Japanese).
Sasaoka, Y. (2016). Governance revisited: Its multiplicity in a globalized era. *Meiji Journal of Governance Studies*, 3, Tokyo: Meiji University.
Sen, A. (2002). Globalization, inequality and global protest. *Development*, 45(2): 11–16, London, New York and Shanghai: Palgrave Macmillan.
Söderbaum, F., & Shaw, T. (eds) (2003). *Theories of New Regionalism: A Palgrave Reader*, Hampshire: Palgrave Macmillan.
Söderbaum, F., & Taylor, I. (2001). Transmission belt for transnational capital or facilitator for development? Problematising the role of the state in the Maputo development corridor. *Journal of Modern African Studies*, 39(4): 675–695.
Takeuchi, S. (2003). How to capture Asian and African conflict. In *State, Violence, and Politics: Over Asian and African Conflict*, Chiba: Institute of Developing Economies.
Taylor, I. (2002). The Maputo development corridor: Whose corridor? Whose development? In Breslin, S., & Hook, G.D. (eds), *Microregionalism and World Order*, Basingstoke: Palgrave Macmillan.

Tilly, C. (1990). *Coercion, Capital, and European States, AD 990–1990*, Cambridge, Massachusetts: Basil Blackwell.

Tomlinson, J. (1999). *Globalization and Culture*, Chicago, IL: University of Chicago Press.

Uesu (2020). New Partnership between Business and Development: A case study of Ethiopia's Industrial Development (co-authored, one chapter in *Designing Integrated Industrial Policies: For Inclusive Development in Asia and Africa*), Abingdon, Oxon, and New York: Routledge.

Woodward, S. (2017). *The Ideology of Failed States – Why Intervention Fails*, Cambridge: Cambridge University Press.

World Bank (2011). *World Development Report: Conflict, Security, and Development*, Washington, DC: World Bank Publications.

Young, C. (2012). *Post Colonial States in Africa*, Madison, WI: University of Wisconsin Press.

Zartman, W. (ed.) (2010). *Understanding Life in the Borderlands: Boundaries in Depth and in Motion*, Athens, GA: University of Georgia Press.

Zartman, W. (2019). I William Zartman: A Pioneer in Conflict Management and Area Studies, New York: Springer.

2 From contested borders to cross-border cooperation in the Lake Chad Basin

Stakes and challenges

Aimé Raoul Sumo Tayo

The African States have made the respect of the borders inherited from colonization the pledge of their stability, security, and sovereignty. These borders have a bad reputation, however. They are said to be "arbitrary and absurd, porous and subverted, indefensible and undefended" (Foucher, 2020). They are also known to be conflictual due to irredentism and rivalries for exploiting border resources. In the Lake Chad Basin, conflict and lack of cooperation between Chad, Cameroon, Niger, and Nigeria have long characterized border dynamics. Borders' inviolability and territorial exclusivity were the cornerstones of their respective border governance. The various countries had a strict conception of their sovereignty as it reaffirms the principle of impenetrability of their respective territories. However, since the beginning of the 2010s, there is a paradigm shift in national borders governance and cross-border relations.

This contribution focuses on the issues and challenges of this dynamic in which contested borders tend to become a symbol of cooperation in the Lake Chad Basin. It is about the reasons and the modalities of this paradigm shift. This chapter also addresses the conflictual aspect of local border relations, the transnationality of security threats, and bilateral and multilateral initiatives for cross-border cooperation. The work is based on administrative, diplomatic, and security archival documents, existing literature, and direct observations at the borders between Chad, Cameroon, Niger, and Nigeria between 2014 and 2020.

The geopolitics of borders in the Lake Chad Basin show that until the early 2000s, states had an exclusive conception of their borders. The settlement of multiple territorial disputes, the consideration of the sociopolitical configuration of border areas, and above all, the community of threats have forced the four founding states of the Lake Chad Basin Commission (LCBC) to enshrine their border governances in a cooperative approach. From this perspective, this work differs from pessimistic methods of the border-constraint paradigm and the victim-based and militant practice of the Africanist border studies. It is part of critical border studies that go beyond the fixed nature of the border and considers borders as a process and performance.

DOI: 10.4324/9781003202318-2

Background of the study

Understanding the new collaborative approach to border management in the Lake Chad Basin is influenced by the theoretical framework of this study and the geopolitics of the considered space.

Theoretical framework

The perception of the dynamics studied in this paper is influenced by theoretical assumptions. Understanding the conflicting dynamics that have long affected interstate relations between the countries of the Lake Chad Basin, for example, is influenced by realist approaches that postulate that the interests of states are more often in conflict than in harmony. Conflicts are thus the result of the selfish and aggressive nature of the actors of the international system. Scarcity (Homer-Dixon & Blitt, 1998), competition for access to resources (Hobbes, 2020), and territorial contiguity (Buzan, 1991; Vasquez, 2009) can explain conflicts. This approach also explains why security is the primary objective of states (Waltz, 2010), which agree to make sacrifices to strengthen it (Wolfers, 1952).

This work goes beyond realist theories to analyse cooperative state behaviour (Keohane, 1984; Wendt, 1992). It is inspired by transnational paradigms (Pries, 2008) as complementary models of state-centrism (Rosenau, 1990), despite the importance of the state over other actors (Keohane & Nye, 1977), especially in a context of interconnection of the world. This perspective explains the relationships between social actors belonging to different nationalities in a context marked by informal dynamics and multiple affiliations of individuals due to individuals' territorial and social situations. Game theory (Osborne, 2004), which studies the behaviour of decision-makers in positions of strategic interdependence, considers the inclusion in a cooperative approach as rational and optimal (Rusko, 2011). It stems from the discussion of game theory and social network theory (Corbetta, 2013). The last one explains the relationships between interdependent actors.

Despite anarchy and the desire to maximize their power, rational states will nevertheless choose cooperation. Thus, this work appropriates the concept of coopetition (Brandenburger & Nalebuff, 1996), which comes from strategic management. In the security field, this concept refers to the pooling of efforts to avoid the crystallization of criminal activities. This concept arises from the cooperation paradigm and the competitive paradigm. Each state engages in a coopetitive approach when it does not have sufficient internal resources to obtain a competitive advantage on its own, especially when the competitor has the additional resources (Fernandez & Roy, 2010). Such dynamics are generally cyclical, unstable, and scalable. It can have external determinants as the intervention of third-party actors (Chiambaretto et al., 2019). Above all, it questions the victim-based approach that has long characterized the Africanist current of borders studies.

In effect, the dominant approach to the study of African borders is the border-constraint paradigm. This paradigm is marked by historicism that, like the economism of liberal studies, does not account for the reality of African borders (Bach, 1995).

Geopolitics of the Lake Chad Basin

The "Lake Chad Basin" refers to both a geographical entity, the watershed, and a political entity, the conventional basin. The geographical entity is estimated to be 2,382,000 km² and includes the Sahelian shores of Algeria, Libya, Chad, Niger, Nigeria, Cameroon, and CAR (Njeuma & Malaquais, 2004). On the other hand, the conventional Basin of Lake Chad covers 967,000 km² and refers to the political and institutional dimensions. Institutionally, the LCBC was created on 24 May 1964 in Fort Lamy (Ndjamena) and included Cameroon, Niger, Nigeria, and Chad. The Central African Republic, although not directly bordering the Lake, became the fifth member state in 1994 (Roitman, 2004).

Despite the absence of the States at their margins, the Lake Chad Basin is an integrated area between at least four states due to the presence of regional and global financial and commercial networks, the contiguity of two economic zones, and the existence of Muslim religious networks (Roitman, 2004). The differentials in agro-ecological, demographic, monetary, regulatory, and customs orders have enabled a real integration "from the bottom up" (Chauvin et al., 2018), with emitting poles of agricultural or manufactured products such as the Diamaré plain or Maiduguri.

Lake Chad itself is divided between Cameroon (1/12), Niger (1/6), Nigeria (1/6), and Chad (1/2). This configuration makes it difficult for interstate cooperation, as recently seen against Boko Haram jihadists. The situation is complexified because Nigeria has difficulties when interacting with francophone countries. As a regional power, its goal is to be the hegemon of the system (Mearsheimer, 2014). The presence of France challenges this ambition. Ate & Akinterinwa (1992) have emphasized the "French Factor" as a source of Nigeria's conflictual relations with its francophone neighbours. The authorities perceive France as a threat and an obstacle to Nigeria's foreign policy and leadership aspirations because of the agreements, colonial ties, and cultural affinity with all francophones Nigeria's neighbours (Omede, 2006).

Cameroon, mainly, is considered a security challenge for Nigeria. Recently, the country was considered Nigeria's most vulnerable neighbour because the country served as a recruiting ground for Boko Haram (Guitta & Simcox, 2014). On the contrary, Niger and Nigeria's bilateral relations have always been cordial, even more so since the demarcation of their common boundary under the African Union Border Programme (Okumu, 2011). Nevertheless, globally, the perception of Nigeria by its francophones neighbours is tinged with mistrust. Nigeria is perceived as arrogant and violent as its diplomacy often consists of demonstrations of power (Pérouse de Montclos, 1994).

This mutual distrust has permitted the jihadist of Boko Haram, for example, to use the lake Chad Basin as space for recruitment and safe heaven because of its strategic position, at the junction between four states and by its difficult access, especially for the armies of the sub-region (Lavergne, 2017). They also took advantage of historical disputes and the lack of security cooperation between Chad, Cameroon, and Nigeria. This situation has made the Lake Chad Basin a highly conflicted space.

Globally, conflicts over access to resources, which are becoming scarcer because of climate change and strong population growth, characterize the security situation. Those local interpersonal disputes have sometimes evolved into international disputes. Beyond the international dimension of land conflicts between populations, climate change is having an impact on borders. Indeed, the floating islands of Lake Chad change their position and can be a source of border conflicts. Recently, Boko Haram has crystallized many conflicts among local communities on the shores of Lake Chad, which must then declare themselves for or against Salafism (Seignobos, 2014).

Disputed borders in the Lake Chad Basin

Borders' problems have long been an issue in the relations between Nigeria and its francophones neighbours of the Lake Chad Basin Commission. Frequent border clashes have long characterized the relations between Nigeria and Chad. It was the case when, from the Nigerian perspective, Chadian troops attacked the Army Rifle Company at Kainasara and other islands in Lake Chad between 18 April and 25 May 1983. Also, Chadian security forces are frequently accused of harassing Nigerian fishers in the Lake (Omede, 2006). These incidents led to the demarcation of the border under the auspices of the LCBC.

The Lake Chad has long been the scene of political, ecological, economic, and security issues. In recent years, in the face of demographic pressure, climate change, and desertification, populations have fled to lake areas where they found refuge. The resulting demographic concentration has further degraded the environment and the available natural resources. This situation has precipitated the fate of the region while fuelling community tensions. This high level of immigration is at the root of many land disputes (Bagadoma, 2007). Many agro-pastoral conflicts and community tensions also arise from this scarcity of resources. The arable land of the Lake has been a source of disputes between the local populations of Boumgour Makary (Cameroon) and those of Ngala (Nigeria). The gradual withdrawal of the Lake waters during the dry season led Nigerian herders to transhumance to these spaces, which Cameroonian fishers occupied in the same period.

The Lake Chad became more conflictual with discovering mineral resources such as chromium, cobalt, titanium, uranium, platinum, and with the potential in terms of industrial fishing and tourism (Ibrahim, 1989). The first incursions by Nigerian soldiers into the Cameroonian islands of Lake Chad dated back to the beginning of 1983. Following these initial incursions, Governor Ousmane Mey met with the Nigerian authorities in Gambaru. The latter had then ordered the chief officer of the Nigerian army detachment not to allow his elements to enter Cameroonian territory. The military momentarily respected this directive from the Nigerian authorities.[1] However, in 1987, Nigeria seized the Cameroonian islands of Karakaya, Nimeri, Kassoua Maria, Aïssakoura, Bazaka, Kinzimawadji, and Naïra and the towns of Darak, Katekimé I, Katekimé II, Gore Tchendji, Tchika, and Naga'a (Sumo, 2017). The International Court of Justice resolved this issue in The Hague through its judgement of 10 October 2002.

Environmental issues have also undermined relations between Cameroon and Nigeria. The Lagdo Dam on the Benue regularly causes deadly floods in Nigeria. In September 2012, for example, the accidental opening of the dam gates caused deadly floods within the Nigerian states of Borno, Taraba, Benue, Kogi, and some south-eastern states, killing 137 people and displacing 121,000 (Unknown, 2013).

During the 1980s, efforts to pool efforts to fight insecurity in Lake Chad had not been successful. Indeed, as part of the demarcation of the common border in Lake Chad, Niger, Nigeria, Cameroon, and Chad had decided to set up a joint international patrol (PAMINT). Very quickly, incidents occurred between soldiers of Nigeria and Cameroon.[2] The situation could partly explain why Cameroon has been reluctant to organize joint military patrols and give Nigeria a right to pursue.

In the same vein, Chad's former consul in Garoua, Mbodu Said, accused Cameroon of being reluctant to create a joint brigade to fight cross-border banditry. A Cameroonian officer explains his country's posture by the fact that the Chadian army was operational according to alliances and defections. Some Chadian officers are former rebels, and quite often, soldiers defect to join rebellions to power in place. Therefore, a joint brigade would allow former Chadian soldiers, who had become rebels, to access sensitive or secret-defence information (Koungou, 2010). This situation has long confirmed the idea of "the illusion of solidarity" in the sub-region. However, since the year 2000, there is a paradigm shift in national borders governance and cross-border relations in the Lake Chad Basin for various reasons.

Reasons for cooperation

Many factors such as the settlement of border disputes, cross-border communities, informal integration from below, and common security problems can explain the current dynamics of cross-border cooperation.

The settlement of border disputes

The final settlement of border disputes and the demarcation of the borders can explain the new dynamic of cross-border cooperation in the Lake Chad Basin. As a result of armed clashes between Chad and Nigeria over their boundary in 1983, the member states of the LCBC had demarcated their common international borders in Lake Chad between 1988 and 1990.[3] The process led to the precision of the Chad–Nigeria border and the normalization of bilateral relations between the two countries. The ICJ confirmed the process in a judgement of 10 October 2002. This decision led to the withdrawal of the Nigerian administration, military, and police in and transfer of authority in 28 Cameroonian villages. It also led to returning some villages to Nigeria (Sumo Tayo, 2017).

After settling their border disputes and normalizing their bilateral relations, Cameroon and Nigeria signed a cross-border security agreement on 28 February 2012, in Abuja.[4] Experts from the two countries meet regularly to discuss securing their joint borderlands. For example, they agreed to organize synchronized security operations and intelligence sharing and create a criminal activity database.[5] At the military level, the normalization that followed the final settlement of border disputes has led to active cooperation between the armies of both countries. Every year, Cameroonian officers are trained at the National Defense College (NDC) in Abuja or the Armed Forces Command and Staff College in Jaji. In return, Nigerian officers are trained at the Yaoundé International War College. This situation confirms that setting and demarcating borders are the prerequisite for genuine cross-border cooperation, the geopolitical stability of African states, and the progress of legitimate ambitions for regional integration (Foucher, 2020). Concerning border governance, there is a changing paradigm from barrier to bridge (Asiwaju, 2012).

The presence of cross-border communities

The design of African borders by the colonial powers has led to the partition of many ethnic groups (Asiwaju, 1984). In the Lake Chad Basin, colonial borders have divided some ethnic groups belonging to the "Chadic" group, with Paleo-Sudanese peoples such as the Mafa, Mafou, Daba, Kapsiki, Guidar, Guiziga, and Mandara, and many other micro-ethnic groups living on the massifs and foothills of the Mandara Mountains. The Mandaras, for example, are found in Cameroon in the sultanates of Kousseri and Logone Birni. Their former capital was Kerawa in Nigeria. Today, it is in Mora, Cameroon (Brann, 1989). In the same vein, the Kanuris live in north-eastern Nigeria, Cameroon, and Chad. There are also peoples belonging to the neo-Sudanese complex, including the Kotoko, the Musgoum, and the Massa. Some communities practise pastoral nomadism, such as the Shuwa Arabs (Roupsard, 1987). These *Sudanese Arabs* live in the areas of Dikwa (Nigeria), N'Djamena (Chad), and Kousseri (Cameroon) (Brann, 1989).

In the Lake Chad Basin, as elsewhere in Africa, border peoples participate in activities on both sides of the border and engage in similar agricultural activities. These groups often have common deities, ancestral shrines, and some of them "share annual festivals and rituals which all members of the ethnic group must attend irrespective of location vis-à-vis an international boundary" (Okon Ekpenyong, 1989). This presence of transborder communities has long been seen as a sign of the arbitrary borders division by colonial masters (Asiwaju, 2012). Despite the colonial separation, they have preserved a sense of shared belonging. People in borderlands recognize the existence of the border but do not suffer from it. During the colonial period, border peoples used boundaries for fiscal, political, and economic purposes. Despite international borders, these cross-border peoples continue to maintain relations to the extent that the slightest intercommunal conflict in a country has repercussions in a neighbouring state. During the Arab insurgency of 1919, the Shuwa had received reinforcements from their brothers from Chad and Nigeria. Similarly, between 1927 and 1931, the Manguilva Toumba Sedka mobilized the Moundang of Cameroon and Central-West Chad as part of an anti-colonial insurgency (Saïbou, 2001). Recently, during the January 1992 clashes between the Kotoko and the Shuwa Arabs, cross-border solidarity was mobilized (Saïbou, 2012).

It appears that, while states and researchers hold forth over the artificiality of borders and brandishing the existence of cross-border peoples as a stigma of Berlin butchery, on the ground, for local populations, the limit has not disturbed their everyday border crossing, notably those living near the border (Newman, 2011). Fractions of the various cross-border ethnic groups relate to each other across the borders. The possession of multiple national identity cards and international participation in votes following a subversion of elections manifests populations buoyancy, among other things (Roitman, 2004).

Cross-border populations do not see their situation as dramatic. Instead, they consider it as an advantage: "their mastery of one or more local languages, dress codes and networks offers them greater opportunities to swap national and ethnic identities, as required, allowing them to cross borders and negotiate with officials" (Foucher, 2020). Apart from cross-borders ethnic languages in the Lake Chad Basin, the Hausa serves as lingua *franca*. On the borders of Chad, this language is strongly competing with Arabic. The existence of these cross-borders vehicular languages creates a blur in the spatial structure of border, as well as a kind of border continuum because, for the local population, their natural border is the linguistic border, thus creating discontinuities in the space of social relations (Claval, 1974). Also, in the Lake Chad basin, border populations usually gravitate in the orbit of the neighbouring territory. Sometimes, they lose national sentiment, and their ethnic solidarity prevails over national solidarity (Saïbou, 2001).

Territorial space versus social space: integration from below in the Lake Chad Basin

Michel Foucher (2020) noted the weakness of intracommunity exchanges and the introversion of the African continent. A vernacular approach to the border (Perkins & Rumford, 2013), which analyses borders through the prism of people's daily lives (Amilhat Szary, 2015), tends to question this thesis. A study of borderities in the Lake Chad Basin shows that border relations have never been an obstacle for people. The colonial border has failed to impose "territorial space" in the face of "social space," and local populations have modes of belonging that goes beyond the framework of the state" (Egg & Herrera, 1998).

Like elsewhere in Africa, border areas in the Lake Chad Basin have specific characteristics. Territorially, culturally, and economically, they are transitional areas. There is a significant interaction between them. The border is not always materialized, and the same peoples live on both sides. The exchange is effective because the local population interacts like any two neighbours (Adejuyigbe, 1989). Globally, borders are transparent because of the absence of any traffic barriers and the lightness of controls. This situation creates a sort of regional integration "from below." These dynamics create alternative spaces that do not necessarily challenge the existence of borders but instead use it as an opportunity (Brunet-Jailly, 2019). Despite the relative failure of institutional sub-regional integration, the lake Chad Basin is an informal cross-border trading region based on ethnic, family, or religious networks (Bennafla, 2012). This informal regionalization exploits dysfunction and disparity, which derives from existing boundaries.

Economic disparities between Nigeria and the countries of the CFA zone are at the origin of the border dynamics. The continued depreciation of the Naira has made the CFA a guarantee of financial security for economic operators on the outskirts of Lake Chad. The differentials created by the border make them multidisciplinary resources. This situation is at the root of what Bennafla (2012) calls "commercial fermentation."

In the Lake Chad Basin, there is a polarization towards Nigeria, in particular, because of ecological differentials and the resulting trading systems (Chauvin & Magrin, 2020). Niger and Nigeria's bilateral relations have always been cordial, even though in the 1980s, the Nigerian authorities had closed their land borders to deal with smuggling (Grégoire, 1992). The two countries are members of the Ecowas, which established, in 1979, a protocol on the free movement of persons, goods, and services. Structural factors such as the landlocked situation of Niger, agro-pastoral complementarity, monetary differentials, and size and economic weight can also explain the dynamism of these bilateral relations. In addition, cyclical factors are arising from disparities in economic policies (Grégoire, 1992). In the Konni area on the border with Nigeria, kinship, religious considerations, ethnicity, and commercial communities influence cross-border relationships (Bibata, 2000). The mobility of Koranic masters and Nigerian students to the Koranic centres renowned for perfecting their education, creating a certain homogeneity of Islam and its currents of thought in the region (Ibrahim, 2019).

A pre-existing regional system has favoured the regionalization of insecurity in the Lake Chad Basin. It has also prompted neighbouring countries to cooperate, collaborate, and co-produce security policies (Brunet-Jailly & Dupeyron, 2007).

Security interdependence, common enmity, and sub-regional security cooperation

The regionalization of insecurity in the Lake Chad Basin has prompted the various affected states to reconsider their strict conception of territorial exclusivity, which they considered the first manifestation of their sovereignty. The regionalization threats such as Jihadism, rural and cross-border banditry, and Public Health Emergency of International Concern had forced Cameroon and its neighbours to rethink their security and conflict resolution approaches. The trend was towards pooling security efforts through collective security initiatives to a pluralistic security community (Buzan, 2000).

Common security problems

Rarely, ecological region coincides with international boundaries (Cunningham, 2012). There is a paradigm shift in border management related to biodiversity globally. In the past, nature was the ultimate justification for dividing the territories. Today, nature becomes a possible place of cooperation. Moreover, border resources, which were the alibi of wars, support cross-border cooperation (Amilhat Szary, 2015). The LCBC, created to ensure the sustainable and equitable management of Lake Chad and the other shared water resources of the eponymous Basin, is animating a Bioregionalism. It has also been mandated to preserve the Lake Chad Conventional Basin ecosystems and promote the integration and preservation of cross-border peace and security in the Lake Chad Basin. So, there is a long tradition of cooperation on combating the effects of climate change, desertification, and food security (Kerins & Mouaha-Bell, 2018).

On the other hand, there is informal cross-border cooperation in biosecurity with a logic of co-building networked borders against global or regional pandemics. It is because automobility and self-replication challenge the functions of borders, creating danger for agriculture, the environment, and public health (Smart & Smart, 2012), in the Lake Chad Basin.

Rural and cross-border banditry is also a common security problem for the Lake Chad Basin states. In effect, the crisis of pastoral societies, since the 1990s, has led to the rise of militarized rural and cross-border crime, which emblematic manifestations are ambushes on the roads and kidnappings (Seignobos, 2011). They were true multinationals of crime whose members were citizens of all the countries of the region and Sudan. These groups took advantage of the configuration of border areas and the difficulties of cooperation between the States concerned to act. To do this, they set up their bases either at short distances from one of the international borders and in very difficult-to-reach areas.[6] Those groups are not subject to the same constraints as the States, the same as Boko Haram.

In effect, since 2009, the Nigerian jihadi group, Boko Haram, has taken advantage of the geopolitical, anthropological-sociological, and socio-economic configuration of borderlands to expand its activities to neighbouring countries. Very early, the United Nations Department of Safety and Security (UNDSS) revealed Boko Haram sleeper cells at the Niger border area adjacent to Nigeria (UNDP, n.d.). At the same time, despite the denials of officials, Cameroon has long served as a rear base from which the insurgents prepared their offensives in Nigerian territory. The country also served as *Safe Heaven* when it came to escaping pressure from the Nigerian army. Similarly, Cameroon is a primary and essential logistical base for the sect. In 2013, unable to take refuge in the deep bushes of Bornou State, Boko Haram fighters took shelter on the western side of the Mandara Mountains, thus wanting to take advantage of the Gwoza Hills' defensive domain. In addition, this strategic area offers opportunities for control of the Yola, Maiduguri, Damaturu, and Cameroon axes (Seignobos, 2014).

From 2014, the movement has thus moved from isolated assaults to the actual occupation of localities and military installations. After occupying, apparently without much resistance, Gambarou, Kalagubdou, Kirawa, Pulka, Gwoza, Madagali, and, later, Banki, the sect gradually expanded its operational area to Cameroun, for example. As soon as the international coalition against Boko Haram was set up, many jihadists migrated into Lake Chad (Seignobos, 2018). They played ethnic rivalries and forged alliances that had allowed them to get their hands on the local informal economy (Lavergne, 2017).

As a result, since 2003, Boko Haram's operational area has expanded to neighbouring countries, including northern Cameroon, Niger, and Chad. The jihadist has taken advantage of the ignition delays observed in the start of a concerted response between the states bordering Lake Chad. However, finally, the regional dimension of the problem has led to the establishment of the multinational joint task force, an international antiterrorist coalition comprising the states of the sub-region.

Bilateral and multilateral cooperation mechanisms

Cross-border cooperation refers to collaborating across borders to achieve a common goal. It consists of three stages: convergence, collaboration, and co-management (Pavlakovich-Kochi, 2011). In the Lake Chad Basin, the cooperative approach to border management consists of bilateral and multilateral initiatives. Common security problems have led to intense diplomatic activity at the bilateral level. The regular sessions of the Cameroon–Chad mixed commission on security are an opportunity to discuss these problems of cross-border crime. Cameroon and Chad had committed to joint action to defeat the armed robbers, locally known as Zaraguina (Seignobos, 2011). They had even developed a chronogram of activities with well-identified actions. The two countries had agreed to exchange information and telephone contact information between the two countries' security forces.[7]

Since the colonial period, local authorities have cross-border cooperation in the same vein. This form of territorial diplomacy is carried out parallel with that of the central state (Wassenberg, 2019). This "territorial diplomacy" or "secondary foreign policy" (Klatt & Wassenberg, 2017) aims to end tensions between border populations and fight against cross-border insecurity. The process has resulted in a *multi-level-governance* system and decentralization processes (Catala & Wassenberg, 2019). The economic tours of the Cameroonian administrative authorities were usually an opportunity to meet their Nigerian counterparts in the adjoining constituency. Good-neighbourly relations need to regulate transhumance in Cameroon and combat cattle theft.[8]

The cooperative approach to border management is made through Regional Integration Arrangements with a disappointing performance (Asiwaju, 2012). Nevertheless, some multilateral initiatives have been successful in tackling some security problems. Since 1998, for example, Ecowas has created a mechanism to regulate the cross-border movement of herders and livestock.

This pooling of efforts against various insecurities is encouraged and supervised by economic and military partners of the countries concerned. These countries regularly organize international military exercises to enhance the interoperability of the armed forces of the sub-region.[9] International partners, including Japan, support this cross-border/multi-country approach. The latest country, for example, is sponsoring a project to "Strengthen Community and Regional Capacity for Security Improvement in Niger" that provides vehicles and communications equipment for the security forces (UNDP, n.d.).

Military and security cooperation

Cameroon and Chad have built a coalition to fight against Boko Haram on the Cameroon–Nigeria border at the bilateral level. On 17 January 2015, Chadian troops entered Cameroon via Kousseri, and later, on January 30, the Chadians launched their offensive against Boko Haram from Fotokol. In the framework of "Operation Logone 2015," Chad had sent a contingent of 2,500 men with armoured vehicles, pickup trucks, and helicopters.

At the multilateral level, the four founding states of the Lake Chad Basin Commission have convened a military coalition against Boko Haram: the Multinational Joint Task Force, a concerted and temporary structure of regional state actors, with troops from Cameroon, Chad, Niger, and Nigeria (International Crisis Group, 2020). The MJTF was created in 1994 as a purely Nigerian force fighting insecurity at the Far North–East border. In 1998, it included troops from Niger and Chad, with headquarters in Baga. Cameroon was not part of the initiative since the country has a long territorial dispute with Nigeria on the Bakassi peninsula and more than 18 islands in Lake Chad. However, the MJTF was reformed in 2015 as a coordinated response to Boko Haram's insurgency (Comolli, 2015). The transnationality of the threat has led to operational concepts and standard rules of engagement. The MJTF serves as an international framework, but each country operates with its troops and other means on its territory or, exceptionally, in the adjacent border.

The pooling of efforts to convene this coalition was complex. Until January 2014, the response to Boko Haram's insurgency was primarily domestic. Cameroun, for example, did not want to buy a problem perceived as purely Nigerian. Also, before 2014, the Nigerian president had tried unsuccessfully to meet his Cameroonian counterpart. Similarly, during the high-level meetings between Cameroonians and Nigerians, following the example of the one held on 27 January 2014, the Cameroonian authorities had expressed their "extreme reservation" about the Nigerian request for the right to pursue the insurgents.[10]

France had to intervene for the French-speaking neighbours of Nigeria to agree to pool their efforts. In effect, the Paris summit on 17 May 2014, marked the beginning of the mutualization of actions against Boko Haram's fight. It has helped overcome some historical disputes and stereotypes and fears that have long prevented the pooling of efforts. It has also helped define and conduct a coordinated response to the insurgency.

Before the Paris summit, field unit leaders had developed informal mechanisms for intelligence sharing. For example, the retreats of the Nigerian military garrison of Kirawa, Banki, and Gambaru through Cameroon have been the occasion for soldiers of the two countries to mingle and establish contact based on trust with neighbouring counterparts. It permitted informal intelligence sharing between militaries of the two countries. In the same vein, as early as 2012, the State Security Service (SSS), Nigeria's domestic intelligence service, reportedly given the Cameroonian authorities an updated list of Boko Haram members or their accomplices living in Cameroon. This dynamic led to the arrest of some 50 suspected Boko Haram members in Amchidé on 19 December 2012.[11]

Conclusions and proposals

This contribution dealt with the issues and modalities of the paradigm shift in border management in the Lake Chad Basin, where contested borders become a symbol of cooperation. It shows that until the early 2000s, margins were conflictual. The various states had a strict conception of their sovereignty as they reaffirm the principle of impenetrability of their respective territories. Distrust then marked their bilateral relations. However, because of the settlement of border disputes, the consideration of the political and social configuration of border areas, and, above all, the existence of common threats, since the beginning of the 2010s, there is a paradigm shift in national borders governance and cross-border relations in the Lake Chad Basin, with more cooperative approaches.

However, the current dynamics are perfectible. Thus, several prerequisites must be settled: firstly, build trust and destroy stereotypes. Misperception has been the leading cause of conflict between Cameroon and Nigeria. Indeed, the first will always fear the second's domination because of its size, population, and resources. The presence of a critical Nigerian community in Cameroon, a quarter of the total population, is seen as a threat by the authority (Ngubane, 2003). In return, Cameroon is considered Nigeria's main defence issue (Ate & Akinterinwa, 1992).

Secondly, it is imperative to clarify some border sections in the Lake Chad Basin to avoid future litigation. For example, there are many contentious points on the border between Cameroon and Chad. For instance, at the Department of Logone-and-Chari, Chadians had set up houses and plantations on the Cameroonian bank of the Chari River between Blangoua and Saban-Dabang, as well as on the Cameroonian islands of Kofia, Bini-Goni, and Kofia II. Also, Chadian forces had even occupied the islands of Nimeri, Karakaya, in the Darak district. Similarly, the Chadian government had built a full-cycle school in Ngargousso, near Kousseri.

Thirdly, for optimal cooperative border management in the Lake Chad Basin, multi-level diplomacy needs to be institutionalized. African Union has adopted a convention on cross-border cooperation on 14 June 2014, to promote cross-border cooperation at local, sub-regional, and regional levels. However, it has not yet entered into force. The countries of Lake Chad could sign bilateral agreements on cross-border cooperation that exist informally.

In the meantime, in a context of a legal vacuum, "cross-border engineering" (Wassenberg, 2019) should be developed. In any case, local communities must be involved in managing the border, and there should be a synergy among border management stakeholders.

From a military and security point of view, the international community must accompany the cooperative dynamics of border governance. The challenge here is that of a genuine pooling of efforts. The primary constraint is linked with structural weakness of the MJTF since every force is fighting with proper resources, on its territory mainly. There is also a problem of national fierce by Nigeria when Cameroon and Chad conduct operations on its soil (International Crisis Group, 2020). Also, differentiated perception of the threat depending on the proximity to the epicentre of the insurgency and a lack of political will undermine this ad hoc military coalition (Alio, 2017).

On the other hand, the difficulties of mutualization lie mainly in the command, funding, and capacity gaps of the national armies (Susnjara, 2016). In the long term, because insecurity and various crises often occur at the border areas, it is necessary to work on interoperability of the armies of the sub-region, create the tactical link, and address the diversity of the units that could be involved.

Notes

1 Border Issues Unit (BIU), Letter from the Governor of the North to the Minister of Territorial Administration, 23 February 1983.
2 BIU, Minutes of the joint meeting held on 20 July 1988 in Kousseri between the border authorities of Gambaru Ngala (Nigeria) and those of the department of Logone-et-Chari, Far North Province (Cameroon).
3 BIU, LTBC, Report of the extraordinary session, Lagos, 21–23 July 1983, Lagos, 27 July 1983.
4 *Cameroon-Tribune*, n° 10893/7092, Wednesday, 29 July 2015.
5 *Cameroon-Tribune*, n° 10463/6664, Monday, 11 November 2013.
6 *Cameroon-Tribune*, n° 9515/5716, Tuesday, 12 January 2010.
7 *Cameroon-Tribune*, 9515/5716 of Tuesday, 12 January 2010.
8 National Archives Buea (NAB), 5th Military Sector Monthly Intelligence Summary, January 1983.
9 *Cameroon-Tribune*, n° 10117/6318 Tuesday, 19 June 2012.
10 *Mutations*, n°3577 Tuesday, 28 January 2014.
11 *L'œil du Sahel*, n° 513, 7 January 2013.

Bibliography

Adejuyigbe, O. (1989). Identification and characteristics of borderlands in Africa. In A. I. Asiwaju & P. O. Adeniny (Eds.), *Borderlands in Africa a multidisciplinary and Comparative Focus on Nigeria and West Africa*. Lagos: Lagos University Press.

Alio, M. (2017). *Les défis et enjeux sécuritaires dans l'espace sahelo-saharien. La perspective du Niger*. Dakar: Friedrich-Ebert-Stiftung.

Amilhat Szary, A. (2015). *Qu'est-ce qu'une frontière aujourd'hui?* Paris: Presses Universitaires de France. https://doi.org/10.3917/puf.amilh.2015.01

Asiwaju, A. I., (ed.). (1984). *Partitioned Africans: Ethnic Relations across Africa's International Boundaries 1884–1984*. London: C. Hurst & Co.; Lagos: University of Lagos Press.

Asiwaju, A. I. (2012). The African Union Border Programme in European comparative perspective. In T. M. Wilson & H. Donnan (Eds.), *A Companion to Border Studies*, Blackwell Companions to Anthropology 19. Chichester: Wiley-Blackwell. https://doi.org/10.1002/9781118255223.ch4

Ate, B. E., & Akinterinwa, B. A. (1992). *Nigeria and its immediate neighbors: Constraints and prospects of sub-regional security in the 1990s*. Lagos: Pumark Nigeria Limited.

Bach, D. (1995). Contrainte et ressource de la frontière en Afrique subsaharienne. *Revue Internationale de Politique Comparée*, 2(3).

Bagadoma, M. I. (2007). *La commission du Bassin du lac Tchad: structure probante ou coquille vide* [mémoire de Géopolitique]. Collège interarmées de Défense.

Bennafla, K. (2012). *Pour une géographie des bordures à l'heure globale: Frontières et espaces d'activités 'informelles'* [Thesis]. Université Paris Ouest Nanterre La Défense.

Bibata, D. (2000). *Frontières et développement régional. Impacts économique et social de la frontière Niger-Nigéria sur le développement de la Région de Konni* [Thèse de doctorat de Sciences économiques]. Université Lumière Lyon 2.

Brandenburger, A., & Nalebuff, B. (1996). *Coopetition*. New York: Doubleday.

Brann, C. M. D. (1989). A sociolinguistic profile of Nigeria's Northern and Eastern Borders. In A. I. Asiwaju & P. O. Adeniny (Eds.), *Borderlands in Africa a multidisciplinary and Comparative focus on Nigeria and West Africa*. Lagos: Lagos University Press.

Brunet-Jailly, E. (2019). Why read Michel Foucher's African borders: Putting paid to a myth? *Journal of Borderlands Studies*, 35: 1–2. https://doi.org/10.1080/08865655.2019.1671212

Brunet-Jailly, E., & Dupeyron, B. (2007). Introduction: Borders, borderlands, and porosity. In E. Brunet Jailly (Ed.), *Borderlands: Comparing Border Security in North America and Europe*. Ottawa: Les Presses de l'Université d'Ottawa | University of Ottawa Press. http://books.openedition.org/uop/159

Buzan, B. (1991). *People, states, and fear: An agenda for international security studies in the post-cold war era*. Boulder, CO: L. Rienner.

Buzan, B. (2000). The logic of regional security in the post-cold war world. In B. Hettne, A. Inotai, & O. Sunkel (Eds.), *The new regionalism and the future of security and development: Volume 4* (pp. 1–25). London: Palgrave Macmillan. https://doi.org/10.1007/978-1-137-11498-3_1

Catala, M., & Wassenberg, B. (2019). Introduction. *Relations Internationales*, 3(3), 3–7. https://doi.org/10.3917/ri.179.0003

Chauvin, E., & Magrin, G. (2020). Violence and regionalization in Central Africa. *Revue belge de géographie*, 4. https://doi.org/10.4000/belgeo.43632

Chauvin, E., Charline, R., Lemoalle, J., Magrin, G., Raimond, C., Sylvain, A. D., Fougou, H., Abdourahamani, M., Tafida, A., & Tukur, A. (2018). La région du lac Tchad avant Boko Haram. Le système régional: Environnement, populations et ressources. In Magrin, G., Pérouse de Montlos, M-A. (Dir.). *Crise et développement. La région du lac Tchad à l'épreuve de Boko Haram*. Paris: AFD.

Chiambaretto, P., Fernandez, A., & Le Roy, F. (2019). 10. La coopétition ou l'art de coopérer avec ses concurrents. In D. Sébastien Liarte (Ed.), *Les grands courants en management stratégique* (pp. 281–312). Caen: EMS Editions. https://doi.org/10.3917/ems.liar.2019.01.0281

Claval, P. (1974). L'étude des frontières et la géographie politique. *Cahiers de géographie du Québec, 18*(43), 7–22. https://doi.org/10.7202/021173ar

Comolli, V. (2015). The regional problem of Boko Haram. *Survival, 57*(4), 109–117.

Corbetta, R. (2013). Cooperative and Antagonistic networks: Multidimensional affinity and intervention in ongoing conflicts, 1946–2001. *International Studies Quarterly, 57*(2), 370–384. https://doi.org/10.1111/isqu.12020

Cunningham, H. (2012). Permeabilities, ecology and geopolitical boundaries. In T. M. Wilson & H. Donnan (Eds.), *A Companion to Border Studies*, Blackwell Companions to Anthropology 19. Chichester: Wiley-Blackwell.

Egg, J., & Herrera, J. (Eds.). (1998). Echanges transfrontaliers et intégration régionale en Afrique subsaharienne. *Autrepart, 6*.

Fernandez, A., & Le Roy, F. (2010). Pourquoi coopérer avec un concurrent: Une approche par la RBV. *Revue française de gestion, 5*(5), 155–169.

Foucher, M. (2020). African borders: Putting paid to a myth. *Journal of Borderlands Studies, 35*(2), 287–306. https://doi.org/10.1080/08865655.2019.1671213

Grégoire, E. (1992). Quelques aspects des échanges entre le Niger et le Nigeria. In C. Robineau (Ed.), *Les terrains du développement: Approche pluridisciplinaire des économies du Sud*. Paris: ORSTOM.

Guitta, O., & Simcox, R. (2014). *Terrorism in Nigeria: The Threat from Boko Haram and Ansaru*. London: Henry Jackson Briefing.

Hobbes, T. (2020). *Leviathan by Thomas Hobbes*. Independently published.

Homer-Dixon, T. F. & Blitt, J. (Eds.). (1998). *Ecoviolence: Links among Environment, Population and Security*. Lanham, MD: Rowman & Littlefield.

Ibrahim, A. M. (2019). *L'insécurité transfrontalière en Afrique de l'Ouest: Le cas de la frontière entre le Niger et le Nigeria* [PhD thesis]. Université Côte d'Azur (2015–2019).

Ibrahim, J. (1989). Lake Chad as an instrument of international cooperation. In A. I. Asiwaju & P. O. Adeniny (Eds.), *Borderlands in Africa: A multidisciplinary and comparative focus on Nigeria and West Africa*. Lagos: University of Lagos Press.

International Crisis Group (2020). *What role for the Multinational Joint Task Force in Fighting Boko Haram?* Report 291/Africa. ICG: Nairobi/Brussels.

Keohane, R.O. (1984). *After Hegemony: Cooperation and Discord in the World Political Economy*. Princeton: Princeton University Press.

Keohane, R. O., & Nye, J. S. (1977). *Power and interdependence: World politics in transition*. Boston: Little, Brown.

Kerins, P. M., & Mouaha-Bell, S. V. (2018). *Boko Haram's Rise and the multinational response*. [Thesis] Monterey, CA: Naval Postgraduate School.

Klatt, M., & Wassenberg, B. (2017). Secondary foreign policy: Can local and regional cross-border cooperation function as a tool for peace-building and reconciliation? *Regional & Federal Studies, 27*(3), 205–218.

Koungou, L. (2010). *Défense et sécurité nationale en mouvement. Dynamiques des réformes, mutations institutionnelles en Afrique subsaharienne*. Paris: l'Harmattan.

Lavergne, M. (2017). *Le lac Tchad, entre l'assèchement et l'intrusion de Boko Haram: La faute au changement climatique, ou à l'immobilité politique?* [Research Report]. Tours: Sawa Consulting. https://halshs.archives-ouvertes.fr/halshs-01494017

Mearsheimer, J. (2014). *The tragedy of great power politics – Updated edition*. New York: W. W. Norton & Company.

Newman, D. (2011). Contemporary research agendas in border studies: An overview. In Wastl-Walter, D. (Ed.), *The Ashgate Research Companion to Border Studies*, Ashgate Research Companion. (pp. 33–47). Farnham: Ashgate.

Ngubane, L. P. (2003). *Nigeria-Cameroon military relations, issues, and prospects*. Lagos: National War College.

Njeuma, M., & Malaquais, D. (2004). Coopération internationale et transformation du Bassin du Lac Tchad: Le cas de la Commission du bassin du lac Tchad. *Politique africaine*, 2(2): 23–41. https://doi.org/10.3917/polaf.094.0023

Okon Ekpenyong, J. L. (1989). Potentials of Nigerian boundary corridors as sources of international economic conflict. In A. I. Asiwaju & P. O. Adeniny (Eds.), *Borderlands in Africa a multidisciplinary and comparative focus on Nigeria and West Africa*. Lagos: Lagos University Press.

Okumu, W. (2011). Border management and security in Africa. *Concordis Briefing*, 4(4), 1–18.

Omede, A. J. (2006) Nigeria's relations with her neighbours. *Studies of Tribes and Tribals*, 4(1), 7–17. https://doi.org/10.1080/0972639X.2006.11886532

Osborne, M. J. (2004). *An introduction to game theory*. New York: Oxford University Press.

Pavlakovich-Kochi, V. (2011). Cross-border cooperation and regional responses to NAFTA and globalization. In Wastl-Walter, D. (Ed.), *The Routledge research companion to border studies*. Farnham: Ashgate.

Perkins, C., & Rumford, C. (2013). The politics of (un)fixity and the vernacularisation of borders. *Global Society*, 27(3), 267–282. https://doi.org/10.1080/13600 826.2013.790784

Pérouse de Montclos, M.-A. (1994). *Le Nigéria*. Paris: Karthala.

Pries, L. (2008). *Rethinking transnationalism: The meso-link of organisations*. Abingdon: Routledge. https://doi.org/10.4324/9780203893692

Rosenau, J. N. (1990). *Turbulence in world politics: A theory of change and continuity*. Princeton, NJ: Princeton University Press.

Roitman, J. (2004). Les recompositions du bassin du lac Tchad [1]. *Politique africaine*, 2(2), 7–22. https://doi.org/10.3917/polaf.094.0007.

Roupsard, M. (1987). *Nord-Cameroun ouverture et développement*. Coutance: Roupsard.

Rusko, R. (2011). Exploring the concept of coopetition: A typology for the strategic moves of the Finnish forest industry. *Industrial Marketing Management*, 40(2), 311–320. https://doi.org/10.1016/j.indmarman.2010.10.002

Saïbou, I. (2001). Cameroun-Tchad: image de l'autre et attitude. In D. Essomba, J.-M. Njeuma, & M.-Z. de la Ronciere (Eds.), *Dynamique d'intégration régionale en Afrique Centrale* (tomes 1 et 2). Yaoundé: PUY.

Saïbou, I. (2012). *Ethnicité, frontières et stabilité aux confins du Cameroun, du Nigeria et du Tchad*. Paris: L'Harmattan.

Seignobos, C. (2011). The phenomenon of the *Zaraguina* in Northern Cameroon: A crisis of Mbororo Pastoral Society. *Afrique contemporaine*, 3(3), 35–59. https://doi.org/10.3917/afco.239.0035

Seignobos, C. (2014). Boko Haram: Innovations guerrières depuis les monts Mandara: Cosaquerie motorisée et islamisation forcée. *Afrique contemporaine*, 4(4), 149–169. https://doi.org/10.3917/afco.252.0149

Seignobos, C. (2018). Chronique d'un siège (2): Boko Haram dans ses sanctuaires des monts Mandara et du lac Tchad (2017). *Afrique contemporaine, 1*(1), 99–115. https://doi.org/10.3917/afco.265.0099

Smart, A., & Smart, J. (2012). Biosecurity, quarantine, and life across the border. In T. M. Wilson & H. Donnan (Eds.), *A Companion to Border Studies,* Blackwell Companions to Anthropology 19. Chichester: Wiley-Blackwell. https://doi.org/10.1002/9781118255223.ch

Sumo Tayo, A. R. (2017). *Héritage colonial et gestion des conflictualités des frontières internationales du Cameroun* [Thèse de doctorat en Histoire]. Université de Yaoundé 1.

Susnjara, P. (2016). Révolution dans les affaires militaires africaines. *Revue Défense Nationale, 7*(7), 38–42. https://doi.org/10.3917/rdna.792.0038

UNDP (n.d.). Countries: Burkina Faso, Chad, Mauritania, Mali, and Niger Border Management & Border Communities in the Sahel. Programme Document.

Unknown (2013). *Foreign policy and national interest: A case study of Nigeria-Cameroon relations.* Abuja: National Defense College.

Vasquez, J. A. (2009). *The war puzzle revisited.* Cambridge: Cambridge University Press.

Waltz, K. N. (2010). *Theory of international politics* (Reissue edition). Long Grove: Waveland Pr Inc.

Wassenberg, B. (2019). Diplomatie territoriale et coopération transfrontalière en Europe depuis 1945. *Relations internationales, 3*(3), 9–24. https://doi.org/10.3917/ri.179.0009

Wendt, A. (1992). Anarchy is what States Make of it: The Social Construction of Power Politics. *International Organization, 46*(2), 391–425. http://www.jstor.org/stable/2706858

Wolfers, A. (1952). "National security" as an ambiguous symbol. *Political Science Quarterly, 67*(4), 481–502. https://doi.org/10.2307/2145138

3 A porous border and economic activity in the Kampala – Kinshasa market, West Nile, North-western Uganda

Nobuko Yamazaki

General characteristics of the East African borderlands

The West Nile sub-region[1] (hereinafter, the West Nile) of north-western Uganda is geographically marginalized from the central government, but this does not necessarily mean that the borderlands are isolated. To investigate how the development of road infrastructure and the resulting expansion of logistics has impacted people's lives in the region, I analyse how residents use several markets throughout the West Nile, including local markets on the border of Uganda and the Democratic Republic of the Congo (DRC), as well as the impacts of the rapid urban development in the region.

The West Nile has long been socially, politically, and economically marginalized within Uganda. However, the lives of the people are not restricted, given that they can move freely across the borderline and take advantage of the linguistic and cultural proximity as well as the social ties that transcend national boundaries. Rather, it is by not restricting trans-regional mobility that the potential for flexible regional development is realized. In this book, I analyse the borderlands by using a trans-regional approach from a grassroots perspective, focusing on the porous nature of African borders.

Negative descriptions of the borders and borderlands in Africa often reference their artificial nature, which is due to the history of colonization. However, there have been studies that focused on the potential of borderlands, shedding light on their positive aspects, and it has been pointed out that they have complex dimensions. Also, it has been argued that the borderlands of East Africa are made vibrant by active socio-economic relations based on cultural and geographical proximity with neighbouring countries, even though these areas are often neglected by the central government (Khadiagala 2010). Such views are highly compatible with Feyissa and Hoehne's (2010: 8–12) arguments that borders and borderlands provide resources and opportunities for people, inspired by Asiwaju and Nugent's argument that "borders are opportunities" (1996: 1–14). Titeca and Herdt (2010), focusing on cross-border trade and smuggling in frontier areas, conclude that residents are more likely to negotiate with state agents such as customs officials, military personnel, and police officers in frontier areas, which are often considered to be beyond the reach of the rule of law due to their remoteness from the centre of the state.

This chapter focuses on the economic resources that the borderlands can give to its residents (Feyissa and Hoehne 2010) and refers to Dobler's (2016) typology of African borders with the aim of deepening our understanding of the situation in the West Nile. The porousness of the border in the region will be portrayed as relatively positive, but it will not be praised outright because new challenges are presented by rapid urbanization. This chapter is based mainly on empirical data collected during fieldwork conducted by the author in urban and rural areas of the West Nile. To protect the privacy of the people in the villages, pseudonyms are given instead of the actual names and locations of places the author visited.

Research site

The West Nile consists of 12 administrative districts (as of 2021), the boundaries of which were drawn based on ethnic settlements. However, it was only after the introduction of decentralization in the 1990s and afterwards that new districts were successively established. Multiple ethnicities with different language groups coexisted within administrative sites, including the Lugbara, Madi, Kakwa, Kebu, Alur, and Nubi. Most of the groups consist of segmentary societies, which do not have a centralized political structure, in contrast to the ethnic groups that form the southern kingdoms. The majority group in village Y is the Lugbara. The Lugbara people live mainly in north-western Uganda and the north-eastern DRC and also have communities in southern Uganda and South Sudan, with others living abroad for work or study. The Lugbara's main livelihood is agriculture, and they also engage in petty trading and seasonal work. Intermarriage with neighbouring ethnic groups is common.

The rainy season (*ayi*) is from March to early October, and the dry season (*eli*) is from October/November to the end of February, although it varies slightly from year to year. Even in the dry season, there is no month without rainfall, and the average annual temperature does not fall below 18°C, and so, farming is widely practised as a livelihood. The soil at the research site is classified as Ferralsol. Although it is not very fertile, it is more food-productive compared with other areas of the West Nile. In fact, the local name of the area comes from its abundant harvests, and the people there see the area as a "food basket."

The staple food of the West Nile is the cassava (*g'banda*) and the main dish is *enya*, which is made from dried cassava flour kneaded in hot water. *Enya* is often served with side dishes of leafy greens, small fish (*ngeje*), mushrooms (*'drika*), and meat (*za*) sauces, mainly for lunch or dinner. For breakfast, sweet potatoes (*maku*), cassava, and avocados (*'avoka*) are sometimes served with tea, but it is not uncommon to go without breakfast when there is no agricultural work to be done. Some people go to a restaurant in a small town nearby, whereas others return home for lunch and then go back to work. In addition to cassava, maize (*kaka*) and beans are also grown. Livestock and poultry raised in the area include cattle (*ti*), sheep (*kabilo*), goats (*ndri*), pigs (*ezoo*), chickens (*au*), and to a lesser extent, ducks (*bata*), turkeys (*kulukulu*), and rabbits (*etoo*). Even today, with the penetration of the market economy, cattle, sheep, goats, and chickens continue to play an important role in marriage ceremonies and as offerings to oracles and for other rituals. These livestock and poultry are also sold at the market.

The current boundaries of the West Nile date back to part of the former Equatoria province settled in 1870 in Sudan and later incorporated into Belgian Congo (the Congo Free State) as the Lado Enclave in 1900. Anglo-Egyptian Sudan acquired parts of the territory in 1910 after King Leopold II passed away (Leopold 2009: 468). At the end of 1912, a survey team departed from Khartoum to demarcate the border between Sudan and the Uganda Protectorate, and when they finished in 1913, the inevitable result was the division of the groups living in the area into different states (Blake 1997; McEwen 1971). In the following year, the administrative officer of the Uganda Protectorate arrived in the West Nile for the first time. The border between the West Nile and the DRC was defined in an agreement between the British and the DRC in 1894, which roughly overlaps with the present-day border (INR 1970).

As some researchers have already pointed out (Titeca 2009: 3; Dobler 2016), the north-eastern DRC and southern Sudan (before South Sudan became an independent state) are much closer geographically to the West Nile than to their respective capitals of Kinshasa and Khartoum, and the West Nile is much more economically interconnected with these neighbours than with the Kampala, distant capital of Uganda. In the West Nile, with its web of inter- and intra-ethnic social relations across the three countries, there are, as in many other border areas, numerous people who come to the West Nile to attend school, to visit the hospital, to gather for various kinship events, and to work as farmers. Ugandans do not carry passports, visas, or other forms of identification with them when they travel to the DRC, but they do bring their Ugandan ID cards (National ID Card) just in case they are stopped by local security forces, known as *askari*.

Around 2015, stone pillars were erected along the Uganda–DRC border, starting with one of the most important border checkpoints, the Vurra customs post in southern Arua, and construction finished in 2017/2018. Of the 79 pillars erected so far, some are located on the land of local residents, which means that sometimes a single household straddles both Uganda and the DRC. In addition, large trucks with license plates from the DRC, South Sudan, Kenya, Tanzania, and other countries pass through the Vurra customs checkpoint. Immigration officials,[2] soldiers from the Uganda People's Defence Forces (UPDF), Ugandan police, and Uganda Revenue Authority (URA)[3] officials are stationed on the Ugandan side of the checkpoint, whereas DRC police officers and immigration officials are stationed on the DRC side. A total of 79 stone pillars have been placed on the borderline, starting from this checkpoint and extending to the southern tip of Arua District, making it visible to the local residents as the border between Uganda and the DRC was redrawn.

A local market on the border between Uganda and the DRC

The transborder movement of populations following the outbreak and the end of conflicts creates new markets and diminishes the existing ones. For example, because of the intensification of armed conflicts in Uganda following the fall of the Amin regime in April 1979, the population flowed out from the West Nile to southern Sudan and the DRC, and new markets were formed in and around the refugee settlements in southern Sudan (Harrell-Bond 1986). It has also been noted that after conflict broke out in Uganda in 1979, the size of the Ariwara market, which was originally located in the DRC, expanded at the same time (Meagher 1990). The influx of Ugandans into the DRC was also relevant here.[4]

The local market on the Uganda–DRC border is another market that emerged during the 1990s, when people flowed into Uganda from the DRC (Zaire), where civil war was raging. This market, which straddles the border between Uganda and the DRC, is called the "Kampala – Kinshasa market" by local residents, with those residing on the Ugandan side in particular referring to it as the "Kampala market." As mentioned previously, there are several stone pillars in this market, which clearly shows that this market is located on the border.

The Kampala market was initially formed in the 1990s when women gathered from time to time on the DRC side of the border between Uganda and the DRC to barter for vegetables, grains, and bananas. In the 1990s, as the civil war in the DRC worsened, many Congolese began to flow into Uganda, and numerous markets were set up in the border areas on the Ugandan side where agricultural products were sold (Titeca 2009). In the early 2000s, the Ugandan local government became more involved in the management and operation of the Kampala market, which led to the collection of various taxes and the development of the market. During my visit, I used a GPS device (Garmin eTrex 20J) to measure the market area before and after its expansion, mainly on the Ugandan side. I was accompanied by a man who belonged to the association responsible for the management and operation of the market. I found that in the 1990s, the market covered an area of only 166 square metre, whereas in 2018, it had grown to 5,911 square metre, a 36-fold increase. As of 2020, the Kampala market is one of the largest regular markets in the West Nile in terms of area, compared with the permanent market in Arua.

The Kampala market was previously limited to Thursday evenings and sold mainly agricultural products, but as the number of customers increased in the 2000s when tax collection began systematically, the Local Council chairman (LCIII) decided to open the market two days a week starting in 2011 or 2012.[5] In addition to agricultural products, various goods are sold, including charcoal, sisal mattresses, clothing (new and used), furniture, pots and pans, farming tools, radios, and other daily necessities. There is also a livestock market, although it is much smaller than the ones in Arua and Terego. Industrial products such as plastic products, bottled beer, and boxed cigarettes flow mainly from the Ugandan side into the DRC, whereas cheaper agricultural products flow from the DRC side into Uganda. Most of the sellers are from the DRC and the West Nile in Uganda, although a small number of clothing sellers on the Ugandan side come from the capital city and do not speak the local language of the north.

The market accepts only the Uganda shilling as payment, and Ugandan traders pay with Uganda shillings when they buy large quantities of produce brought by DRC residents. The primary language spoken in the market is Lugbara, and there are many Lugbara speakers in the area. If the seller and buyer are from neighbouring villages, they communicate in their first language, whereas traders who come from more distant areas often speak Lugbara.

The market also has bars and restaurants, and, in the evening, DVD movies are shown, and people gather on the dance floor to dance. The open square is crowded with people drinking alcohol or chatting without drinking. Although most of the people who gather at the stalls selling agricultural products and clothing are middlemen and retail traders from the cities, most of the people who gather at the bars are residents of neighbouring villages. The mother of the LCI of village Y is from the DRC near the Kampala market and her son told me that they go to the market not only to buy foodstuffs and daily necessities but also to meet their relatives and acquaintances to talk and share recent news. In other words, the border markets serve as a place for socializing among the residents living on both sides of the border.

There are three entrances that are wide enough for large vehicles to pass through, located on the northern, southern, and western sides of the road. The road is wide enough to accommodate pedestrians, bicycles, trucks, and passenger buses (hereinafter, *matatu*). The northern and southern entrances are located inside Uganda, whereas the western entrance is located on the DRC side of the border. Vehicles with DRC license plates arrive in smaller numbers at the western entrance than at the northern and southern entrances on the Ugandan side. *Matatu* arrive at the southern entrance, bringing passengers from areas south of the market. The number of buses is limited, and the number of passengers is not large. Nearly, all the large vehicles and *matatu* from the city of Arua, the capital of Arua District, and other parts of the West Nile arrive at the northern entrance. All vehicles must pay a parking fee at the north entrance when they leave the market. Two UPDF soldiers are stationed at the northern entrance from around 8 a.m. to 9 p.m. on Thursdays and Sundays when the market is open. If any vehicle tries to leave without paying the parking fee, UPDF soldiers and market association officials confront them and instruct them to comply with the fee collection. All sellers are required to pay "market dues" according to the type and amount of goods they sell; market association clerks collect the dues.

From 30 August to 21 October 2018, I conducted a traffic survey each Thursday and Sunday from 7 a.m. to 3 p.m., when the regular Kampala market was held. This period is during the rainy season and corresponds to the peak agricultural season. Pedestrians, bicycles, motorcycles, and heavy vehicles were counted at the northern entrance for a total of 13 days during this period. Most foot and vehicle traffic passes through the northern entrance.[6] On most days, a few people arrived at the market before 7 a.m., shortly after sunrise. At around 7 a.m., some of the employees of the market association arrived, opened the association's office, and started preparing to collect the market dues. Around 8 a.m., the number of sellers and customers gradually began to increase. The market became crowded with people selling produce, merchants make purchases, retailers and vendors selling various goods, and shoppers. Around 4 p.m., the clerks tallied up the total amount of market dues collected and closed the office. To coincide with this time, I finished my traffic survey at 3 p.m. and made my way to the union office.

I counted the number of people walking or biking to the market and the number of vehicles arriving at the market. I found that 1,011–1,411 pedestrians, 249–309 bicycles, and 24–31 vehicles arrived at the northern entrance on Thursdays, whereas 2,098–2,602 pedestrians, 405–482 bicycles, and 20–44 automobiles arrived on Sundays (Tables 3.1 and 3.2). In terms of congestion, foot traffic peaked by 9 a.m. and bicycle traffic peaked by 8 a.m. on Thursdays. On Sunday, foot traffic peaked between 9 a.m. and 10 a.m., and bicycle traffic peaked by 8 a.m. (Tables 3.1 and 3.2). The slightly later peak time for foot traffic on Sundays compared with Thursdays was likely because many local residents go to the market after first attending church on Sunday mornings.[7]

For most hours of the traffic survey, the number of walk-in visitors was higher on Sunday than on Thursday (Table 3.1). The highest number of walk-in visitors was between 8 a.m. and 10 a.m. on both Thursday and Sunday (Table 3.1). For example, the highest number of walk-in visitors was 556 on Sunday, September 16 between 10 a.m. and 11 a.m., and the lowest was 388 on Sunday, October 14 between 9 a.m. and 10 a.m. In contrast, the peak for a Thursday was on August 30 between 9 a.m. and 10 a.m., and the low was 211 people on October 18 between 9 a.m. and 11 a.m. On Sundays, the number of visitors did not fall below 100, even during the lowest hours of

Table 3.1 Number of pedestrians arriving at the Kampala market

Date\Time	7–8am	8–9am	9–10am	10–11am	11am–12pm	12–1pm	1–2pm	2–3pm	Total/day
Thursday (2018)									
30-Aug	118	293	352*	272	104	64	46	20**	1,269
6-Sep	119	278	321*	230	107	149	97**	110	1,411
13-Sep	134	281	264*	183	84	57	64	45**	1,112
20-Sep	148	252	281*	158	86	64	51	43**	1,083
27-Sep	148	253	261*	131	97	62	49**	58	1,059
18-Oct	107	233	211*	202	110	36**	50	62	1,011
Total/hour	774	1,590	1,690*	1,176	588	432	357	338**	6,945
Sunday (2018)									
2-Sep	174	383	542*	542*	458	285	110	100**	2,594
9-Sep	219	376	504	523*	295	306	243	136**	2,602
16-Sep	224	367	489	556*	357	246	174	145**	2,558
23-Sep	148	310	386	504*	399	330	212	133**	2,422
30-Sep	277	251	431	470*	365	318	207	160**	2,479
14-Oct	140	346	388*	385	288	215	186	150**	2,098
21-Oct	111	297	387	478*	285	231	196	128**	2,113
Total/hour	1,293	2,330	3,127	3,458*	2,447	1,931	1,328	952**	16,866

Note: *Highest **Lowest
Source: compiled by author

Table 3.2 Number of bicycles arriving at Kampala market

Date\Time	7–8am	8–9am	9–10am	10–11am	11am–12pm	12–1pm	1–2pm	2–3pm	Total/day
Thursday (2018)									
30-Aug	29	64*	55	37	28	13	17	6**	249
6-Sep	43	69*	46	37	27	24**	29	34	309
13-Sep	59	72*	49	32	16	12**	26	20	286
20-Sep	59	68*	51	34	27	11**	11**	12	273
27-Sep	54	69*	48	29	19	14	10**	13	256
18-Oct	49	85*	50	31	24	9	6**	12	266
Total/hour	293	427*	299	200	141	83**	99	97	1,639
Sunday (2018)									
2-Sep	40	103*	96	74	40	44	30	16**	443
9-Sep	63	103*	82	75	56	56	29	17**	481
16-Sep	77	66	93*	67	48	42	34**	35	462
23-Sep	41	77	100*	83	48	51	50	32**	482
30-Sep	49	100*	68	73	53	48	40	36**	467
14-Oct	49	106*	81	62	30	36	22	19**	405
21-Oct	67	83*	83*	55	41	37	32	16**	424
Total/hour	386	638*	603	489	316	314	237	171**	3,154

Note: *Highest **Lowest
Source: compiled by author

the day. Both the highest and lowest number of bicycles during peak hours were larger on Sunday than on Thursday. The same was true for the number of motorcycles.

Looking at what people who walked or biked to the market brought to sell, agricultural products were the most common item on both days. For example, on Sunday, October 21, more than half of the people who came on foot brought produce and the peak time in the morning (Table 3.3). The same was true for bicycles, with more than half of the visitors bringing their produce in the morning (Table 3.4). Nearly all the people who walked to the market to sell produce were women, and most of the produce sellers who came by bicycle were men.[8] All these visitors brought produce from nearby rural villages. Livestock such as goats, sheep, and chickens were also traded, but cattle were far less common; the number of heads of cattle traded on Sundays was higher than that on Thursdays.

Regarding vehicles,[9] some arrived in the morning and some in the afternoon. The total number of vehicles arriving at the market was higher on Sundays than on Thursdays, and the time that vehicles left the market tended to be concentrated between 11 a.m. and 12 p.m. on Thursdays but was more varied on Sundays. There are two reasons for this. Firstly, the vehicles coming to the market on Thursdays often carried regular vendors and middlemen, who finished their business quickly and left the market in the early afternoon. On Thursdays, the vendors' vehicles also returned to town as soon as they had delivered their goods to the permanent stores in and around the market or had received their orders. This is because the arrival and departure times were roughly fixed. Secondly, there was a higher overall number of customers on Sundays, and thus, there were more vehicles that came only on Sundays. The vehicles that came to the market on both Thursdays and Sundays had a regular mix of passengers, whereas those that carried an unspecified number of passengers did not depart until a certain

Table 3.3 Products brought to Kampala market on foot (21 October 2018)

	7–8am	8–9am	9–10am	10–11am	11am–12pm	12–1pm	1–2pm	2–3pm	Total
Agricultural products*	47	158	218	269	158	80	87	29	1,046 (52%)
Matoke	0	34	23	31	16	4	1	0	109 (5%)
Livestock	0	11	12	0	0	2	0	0	25 (1%)
Charcoal	6	1	3	0	1	0	0	0	11 (1%)
Firewood	2	3	0	4	0	0	0	0	9 (0%)
Empty-handed	47	49	114	148	115	120	135	67	795 (40%)
Total	102 (5%)	256 (13%)	370 (19%)	452 (23%)	290 (15%)	206 (10%)	223 (11%)	96 (5%)	1,995 (100%)

Note: *Except matoke
Source: compiled by author

Table 3.4 Products brought to Kampala market by bicycle (21 October 2018)

	7–8am	8–9am	9–10am	10–11am	11am–12pm	12–1pm	1–2pm	2–3pm	Total
Agricultural products*	32	46	34	18	10	5	5	2	152 (42%)
Matoke	16	19	16	3	1	0	0	0	55 (15%)
Livestock	0	0	1	0	0	0	0	0	1 (0%)
Charcoal	0	0	0	0	0	0	0	0	0
Firewood	0	0	0	0	0	0	0	0	0
Empty-handed	11	19	28	27	16	23	21	7	152 (42%)
Total	59 (16%)	84 (23%)	78 (22%)	48 (13%)	27 (8%)	28 (8%)	26 (7%)	9 (3%)	360 (100%)

Note: *Except matoke
Source: compiled by author

number of passengers were ready to leave, resulting in greater variation in the time they left the market.

Daily-use markets and Kiosks in the rural trading centre

Village A is a 30- to 40-minute walk from village Y. As in many villages with large populations throughout the country, there is a trading centre in village A.[10] This trading centre is a market that is open every day from 5 p.m. to 7 p.m. According to a Lugbara gentleman in his 60s who was working as a market clerk, the market had already been established in 1977 when he was in his mid-teens, and traders from the DRC and Arua visited the market in those days.[11] Residents of neighbouring villages come to the market to buy and sell agricultural products, which are used for daily consumption. The residents of village Y produce cassava and sweet potatoes, which are consumed mainly for their own use as staple foodstuffs. Twenty-two per cent of all households in village Y had more than one female household member who sold their produce, either as is or processed, at the market in village A for cash. For example, women from village Y sell sweet potatoes and use their earnings to buy leafy greens for side dishes at the market in village A as well as other small markets in neighbouring villages. Other women sell a paste made from peanut (*funyo*)[12] harvested from the fields.

The number of sellers and customers at the market in village A fluctuates according to the day of the week because large regular markets are held in many neighbourhoods. This is due to the fact that some businesses buy produce at a lower price in smaller markets and then sell it for a profit at larger markets. The number of people who visit the market in village A increases on the day before a large regular market is held. For example, because the larger market in village F is open on Tuesdays and the Kampala market is open on Thursdays and Sundays, the market in village A tends to attract more customers on Mondays, Wednesdays, and Saturdays – the days before the larger markets are held.

In addition to agricultural products, smoked fish, salt, cooking oil, charcoal, peanut paste, and snacks are also sold at the market in village A. Some people carry portable flour mills to the market, and customers pay to have their cassava and maize ground. When people come to sell agricultural products, they must pay dues to the market keeper based on the type and quantity of the goods they sell. Nearly all the people I observed selling and buying goods at the market were women. The only male visitors were the two clerks who collected the dues, one fishmonger, the two men who operated the flour mill, and a few boys who came to the market because they were asked to run errands for their families.[13]

Other than foodstuffs such as sugar, salt, rice, pasta, and cooking oil, daily necessities could be obtained at retail stores in village A or at nearby kiosks. Here, kiosks refer to huts made of wooden boards and tin sheets that are small enough for only one shopkeeper to enter. The kiosks sell the plastic sandals that most villagers wear as well as razor blades for cutting nails and shaving hair, soap, cigarettes, matches, and plastic bags for storing goods when shopping. In village A, there is a pharmacy and a clinic that sells painkillers, intestinal medicine, antimalarial medicines, and so on. The residents of village Y get the medicines they need for daily life from the shops in village A and from other nearby retail stores.

Direct roadside sales and utilization of markets in rural areas

Residents of village Y not only sell their agricultural products at markets to earn a cash income but also sell their agricultural products from their own residences. The purchasers of this locally sold produce resell it at the main market in Arua or to middlemen who have travelled from urban areas to visit the Kampala market. In other cases, the produce is sold among villagers when they need a large amount of staple food ingredients for a wedding or funeral.

In February 2019, Lily, a trader, visited Anna's home in village Y. Lily often buys cassava from Anna and then sells it at the Arua main market for UGX 700/kg.[14] An amount of 147 kg of cassava was purchased at 500 UGX/kg and transported to the main market in Arua and sold at UGX 700/kg, netting a profit of UGX 29,600. According to Lily, the cost of transportation between village A and the city of Arua was UGX 4,000/passenger and UGX 6,000/unit luggage one way. Thus, although the residents of village Y rarely bring cassava to the main market in Arua, the presence of traders like Lily allows the rural residents to earn cash income indirectly through this access to the market.

On another occasion in the same month, Kayla, a resident of village M, came to visit Anna and bought a large quantity of dried cassava. Kayla needed to prepare a meal for her daughter's wedding. The cassava was sold at a lower price than what Lily paid, partly because Kayla is related to Anna.[15] On another day, Fatima,

Economic activity in the Kampala market 43

Table 3.5 Sale price at markets in 2018 (Uganda shilling: UGX)

	Market in village A	Kampala Market	Arua Main Market
Sweet potatoes (small basin)	1,000	1,000	2,000
Dried cassava (kg)	500	400–500	700–800
Matoke (share)	4,000–5,000	5,000–7,000	8,000–15,000
Avocado	200–500/7seeds	200–500/3–5seeds	200–500/seed
Cabbage (head)	500	500–1,000	2,000
Mushroom (stalk)	1,000–1,500	2,000–	8,000
Charcoal (basin)	2,000	2,000–3,000	5,000

Source: compiled by author

a long-distance trader who owns a large truck, was passing through village Y and stopped to buy dried cassava from Anna. She sold the cassava to Fatima at a slightly higher price than she did for Lily and Kayla.

I examined what these direct sales mean to Anna's household by referring to her income and expenditures. The following data were obtained over an 11-day period from 9 February to 19 February 2020, when Anna's household consisted of three adult women and one boy, namely Anna, her mother, her sister, and her sister's son. Anna's sister also has a daughter, who lives in a dormitory at a government secondary school and Anna pays her tuition. The breakdown of expenditures was 4% for food, 60% for the rent on the land they use for cultivation, 5% for gratuities to the locals who helped with the farm work, 30% for the children's school fees, and 1% for church maintenance.[16] It is difficult to pay the tuition in one lump sum, so it is usually paid in instalments over the semester. It is not uncommon for households to rent land outside the village or to cultivate land belonging to relatives in other villages, as in the case of Anna. At least 27% of all households rent land outside the village, where they grow cassava and other crops on a large scale, mainly to sell. In 2019, the rainy season lasted until late November, spoiling many of the leafy greens, especially in the dry season when market prices were higher than usual.

Based on the household data I collected in October 2018, I estimated that Anna earned UGX 41,000[17] cash income from the sale of sweet potatoes at a nearby market.[18] The sweet potatoes were sold in bulk at the Kampala market to traders from urban areas, which generated more revenue than when sold to neighbours at 1,000 UGX per serving. Price changes at the markets (Table 3.5), and this is how rural residents take advantage of using several markets to sell their produce.

Improvement of road access and innovations at the main market in Arua

With improvements to road infrastructure, it took about 8–9 hours to travel by long-distance bus from the West Nile to the capital city of Kampala in 2014. However, it took decades for the region to develop this infrastructure after independence. This section introduces the changes in transportation access from rural villages to towns within Arua District, between Arua and other parts of the West Nile, and between the West Nile and southern Uganda over the past 30 years.

The West Nile experienced intermittent armed conflicts from the late 1970s to the early 2000s. The main road between Kampala and the West Nile was built in the 1970s during the Amin regime, but even in the 1980s, it took several days for a large truck to travel between Kampala and the West Nile, or possibly a week during heavy rains (Meagher 1990).

The security situation stabilized after Museveni took power in 1986, but the rise of the anti-Museveni forces such as the Lord's Resistance Army (LRA) in Gulu and other parts of the Acholi sub-region in the 1990s brought chaos back to northern Uganda. Although the damage caused by the LRA in the West Nile was not as severe as that in the Acholi sub-region, long-distance buses running on the main highway between the West Nile and Kampala were often attacked, residents were shot or kidnapped, and transports were cut off.[19] During this period, people had to take another route via Mukono to avoid the LRA, meaning it took at least three days to reach their final destination.

This lack of security delayed the progress of development in northern Uganda. It was not until 2002 – when the current Museveni administration signed a peace agreement with the Uganda National Rescue Front II (UNRF II), an armed group based in the West Nile – that stability was brought to the area (RLP 2004). Even with the signing of the peace agreement in 2002, development did not proceed immediately, and the main roads were not paved until the 2010s. Since the end of 2013, the West Nile has seen an influx of refugees fleeing the conflict in South Sudan. Many Ugandans who were doing business (e.g. selling vegetables, shoes, and commodities) in South Sudan lost their jobs and returned to the West Nile at that time. Aid sent to support the livelihoods of the refugees has in turn led to improvements in local infrastructure.[20] In 2010, the first phase of Uganda's domestic development policy, which I discuss later, was launched. When I first visited Arua in 2014, the main street was under construction and the project was completed only within the last few years. Northward from Arua, a paved road was completed, linking Koboko District in the border region with South Sudan. But heading eastward from Koboko to Yumbe and on to Moyo, the road still consists only of murram and is quite dusty. It has been decided that this road will be paved by 2025, with financing from the World Bank.[21]

For example, in the case of village Y, there were only two cars to carry people from the village to Arua until the 1990s, so most people had to walk or ride bicycles to get around. As of 2020, three *matatu* were operating between the villages and Arua six days a week except on Sundays, making it easier to access urban areas and markets from rural areas.

There is a *matatu* stop at a bus terminal called the taxi park in the centre of Arua where passengers get off the bus and head to their respective destinations. In addition to the people who have come to Arua from all over West Nile to visit the Arua main market, many residents return home from jobs or schools outside the West Nile. The *matatu* picks up passengers who have gathered at the trading centre early in the morning and departs Arua in the afternoon. When weddings and funerals are held in town, the *matatu* returns several times to collect the people from the village to bring them into town. The taxi park in Arua was renovated to coincide with the construction of new roads and the renovation of the market. The tenants of the taxi park include not only locals but also Asians and Ugandans from the southern and eastern parts of the country who run tea stores, clothing stores, and wholesale egg stores.[22] There is a *matatu* service that runs between Aru in the DRC and Arua on the street to the right (north) of the new taxi park. People also travel between the DRC and Uganda by bicycle, motorcycle, or on foot. Vendors from the DRC were also seen in Arua. They crossed the border on foot, by bicycle, and by *matatu* to sell products such as *kitenge* fabric and palm oil.

Retail traders from all over the country sell mainly agricultural products at the main market in Arua and at markets along the main roads in the more populated rural areas nearby. Agricultural products purchased at markets throughout the West Nile tend to accumulate at the Arua main market. Middlemen transport these products to the Arua market in the early morning hours and sell them to retail traders. At least, this was the situation after the main market was demolished and replaced by a temporary market, where early in the morning (from 6 a.m. to 7 a.m.), vehicles carrying goods gather all over the country gathered and retail merchants bought vegetables and other items from the middlemen. The market's "sales floor" was neatly divided into sections according to the product. There were four entrances to the temporary market, and dues were collected at two of them. People who came to sell their goods paid the prescribed amount at the entrance to the market and were given a receipt.

Commodities are brought to the main market from markets all over the West Nile. According to Middleton (1962), who lived in the West Nile from 1949 to the early 1950s, more than 500 traders a day used the main market in 1950. He describes in detail the market and commerce in Arua in the 1950s: "These merchants paid dues for the use of the market, while street vendors selling their goods outside the market operated their businesses without paying dues" (Middleton 1962: 569, 571–573).

Considering Middleton's (1962: 572) account, it seems that some of the goods sold at the market and the people selling them have not changed much since the early 1950s, whereas others have changed substantially. In the temporary market in Arua, men sell knives and razor blades in retail stores or peddle them outside. Salt, sugar, tea, soap, and other consumables are sold by both men and women but more often by men. Men are responsible for selling all meat products, whereas women often sell grains, legumes, and other foodstuffs. New products that were not seen in the 1950s include ceramic dishes, stainless steel and plastic kettles, thermos bottles, cups, dining plates, and cutlery made in China. Although the unit price of these products is not cheap, they have become daily necessities and nearly every household now has at least one set.

I met a man in his 60s from village Y who had gone to the Arua main market in 1980 to help his parents sell the maize and other agricultural products they had harvested. He described his visit to the town of Arua as follows:

My parents used to go to Arua to sell maize. In the 1970s and 1980s, Arua did not have any tall buildings like today, and the only thing that stood out was the local government office and the market. The wide open landscape stretched far into the distance, and you could see the roofs of the huts in the distant villages. The roads were not paved, so the dust from the heavy vehicles would rise up and block our view, especially in the dry season.[23]

The landscape of Arua, as described by this man, was very different from the way it looks today, with paved roads and buildings all over the town. To get to Arua from the surrounding villages, people had to ride a bicycle or walk in those days. A man in his 50s also recalled that Arua had only government offices and the market at that time.

As of this writing, the main market is being renovated (Photo 3.1) under the supervision of a consulting company run by a resident of Arua District. When the renovations are completed, some 9,000 retail traders will be able to do business in the all-weather market. The market will be divided into sections for fresh vegetables, grains, fish, and meat. It was expected that more than 4,000 retail traders would be able to start operating by May 2021.[24]

However, when the old market was dismantled in 2017, many of the retailers who had been operating there were evicted by the city government and lost their

Photo 3.1 Arua main market

Source: [A] The old market (30 August 2017). [B] After demolition (2 December 2017). [C] Foundation of the new market (20 July 2018). [D] Nearly complete (4 November 2019). All photos taken by the author.

livelihoods. Many of these traders had no choice but to sell their produce on the streets. However, following a series of problems, including vehicle accidents and an increase in garbage on the streets, residents and customers began to complain. In response, the city government cracked down on street vendors, but the traders were increasingly critical of the government for simply chasing away street vendors and not providing any compensation.[25]

Temporary markets were set up in various parts of the city. Some of the merchants who had tried to sell their goods on the streets moved their businesses to these temporary markets. The old market was located in the heart of the city and was therefore easy for most people to access. However, the temporary markets that were set up in 2017 were located in different places across the city, with one food market and one second-hand clothing market in the north and another of each in the south. The food and clothing markets in the south were located relatively close to the Arua Municipal office and were larger than the markets in the north.

Arua expanded: invented marginalization and magnification of investing in the borderlands

Along with the aforementioned reconstruction of the main market, renovation of the taxi park and construction of a new hospital ward and a sports stadium with commercial facilities are underway in Arua. By the end of 2019, most of the retail space in the stadium had already been rented to the residents of the West Nile or businesspeople from Kampala in the south who were looking for opportunities in the West Nile. This rapid pace of urbanization is due largely to the first National Development Plan (NDP), which was formulated and implemented in FY2010/11, followed by the second NDP in 2015 and the third NDP in 2021 (NPA 2015, 2020). The Ugandan government has been working to transform the major markets throughout the country into large, all-weather markets under its Markets and Agricultural Trade Improvement Programme (MATIP), with funding from the African Development Bank (AfDB). The reconstruction of the Arua main market is part of MATIP II.[26]

Along with these rapid developments, it was decided that two divisions of Arua Municipality[27] would form the new administrative city of Arua in July 2020.[28] Arua Municipality is the fourth most densely populated city in Uganda as of 2014 (UBOS 2014), with a population of more than 800,000 people in 2016. Due to improved road access and job creation in the construction industry, not only is there a flow of people from rural to urban areas but also an influx of workers and traders from southern Uganda. To meet the food needs of this growing urban population, agricultural products are being brought in from all over the West Nile.

In 2016, there were three "Asian-owned" supermarkets, at least five electrical appliance stores, and four pharmacies, all of which had been in operation for the last 30 years. There were about 40 stores in the town of Arua in the early 1950s (Middleton 1962),[29] and it was clear that Arua had grown substantially when

I conducted a fact-finding survey in Arua within a 1-km radius of the district government in early February 2018. This area included pharmacies and kiosks, stationery stores, tea stores, restaurants and bars, electronics stores, mobile phone stores, barber shops, supermarkets (six), bank branches and ATMs (seven), foreign currency exchanges (two), and newsstands. In total, there were more than 200 stores.

The East African Community (EAC), which had been founded in 1967 and dissolved in 1977, was re-established in 2001. The EAC initiated free trade with the Common Market for Eastern and Southern Africa (COMESA) and the Southern African Development Community (SADC) in 2008. Although the DRC is not a member of the EAC, it has been a member of COMESA since the 1980s and has a long history of bilateral trade with Uganda. Partly thanks to these alliances, local residents who regularly visit the Kampala market are not required to pay extra fees at the border market, and it can be said that the local government benefits from so-called informal cross-border trade given that the market dues collected at the Kampala market are one of its most important sources of revenue. Similar phenomena might be seen at markets in many other African borderlands.

In 2013, plans to build a railroad connecting (i) Kenya to Uganda and (ii) South Sudan to the DRC began to take shape.[30] Cargo arriving in Mombasa will be transported to Kampala via Malaba, or from Tororo to Gulu. As part of efforts to encourage such cross-border economic activities, One-Stop Border Posts (OSBPs) administering simplified concessions at border points are being promoted (Nugent and Soi 2020). OSBPs have been established mainly between Kenya and Uganda, Rwanda and Uganda, and the southern DRC and western Uganda. They aim to reduce the need to re-enter a neighbouring country by checking visas once and to simplify the inspection of the goods being transported.[31]

As I have shown, the construction of roads into the West Nile and the capital region has led to the emergence of retail traders and middlemen who travel to several regular markets weekly and make a profit by reselling agricultural products and commodities. This route overlaps with the commercial zone historically used by long-distance traders between the north-eastern DRC and southern Sudan and northern Uganda: the markets in Yei, Yambio, Maridi, and Juba in South Sudan, Kaya and Oraba on the border between South Sudan and Uganda, Ariwara and Aru in the DRC, the main market in Arua, and the large regular markets throughout the West Nile. The road infrastructure on the Ugandan side is far better than that in the DRC, and access to the wider economic zone including Mombasa is secure (Mukohya 1991: 63–65), allowing the West Nile to serve as a key transit point for economic activities such as cross-border trade.

When it comes to long-distance trade, residents of the West Nile use mobile phones to communicate with their customers. For example, a woman in her mid-20s, one of the author's informants since 2014, started a small business to sell used clothes at local markets. She contacts her customer in the capital to check whether good items are available and then travels by night bus and to get there early the next morning. After purchasing the clothes, she returns home and sells the items at a market in Adjumani District, which shares a border with South Sudan. She plans to start selling at the Kampala market in the near future.[32]

Mobile phones play an important role in cross-border trade, and people sometimes use several lines to facilitate their business. In many cases, services provided by mobile carriers such as MTN Uganda and Airtel do not work deep inside the DRC but do work in border towns such as Aru and Ariwara. Vodacom DRC users can communicate with people in the West Nile, even from far away. In South Sudan, Ugandan services also work in the border areas, and people can use South Sudanese services such as Vivacell in Uganda. According to local residents, MTN is superior to Airtel in neighbouring countries, but Airtel is improving its network and provides better service in some border areas. In Juba, as the author has seen in the field, it was Ugandans that who normally sold fresh vegetables in the markets, but many retail traders and peddlers left Juba and returned to the West Nile after conflict broke out in December 2013. More of them returned to Uganda in July 2016 when the situation worsened but have continued to monitor the situation by texting or calling their contracts in Juba, hoping to resume business as soon as.

Connecting to wider economic opportunities

Drawing on Dobler's (2016) typology of "green," "grey," and "blue" borders, the case of the West Nile in this chapter focuses mainly on how local population use green and grey borders. Borderland residents cross green borders each day on foot or by bicycle, using small paths (*panya* roads) to transport contraband and retail goods. Goods, both smuggled and legally recognized, are transported via the grey border, which consists of tarmac roads and railroads large enough to accommodate heavy vehicles. Meanwhile, on the blue border, goods are imported and exported by ships and planes at seaports and airports respectively.

This chapter did not focus on what Dobler mentions the collusion between grey border actors and residents, or the competition between grey and blue border actors. The West Nile was marginalized for a long time during the colonial period and after independence, and its economic activity was based mainly on cross-border trade with the DRC and South Sudan (the green and grey borders). Since the 2000s, when the security situation stabilized after the turmoil of the post-independence period, roads have been built and the role of the grey border line has become increasingly important. In addition, the improved roads lead from the West Nile to Uganda's central (southern) region and to port cities such as Mombasa in Kenya and Dar es Salaam in Tanzania (the blue border).

This chapter shows that the geographical distance of the West Nile from the central government does not necessarily mean isolation of the borderlands. The first and foremost factor in this situation is the improvement of road infrastructure. With the influx of refugees from neighbouring countries and the end of the conflicts within Uganda, the major highways connecting the area to the capital have been improved and means of transport between rural and urban areas have expanded logistics within the region. As a result of these changes, rural residents of the borderlands have gained access to economic opportunities in urban areas and increased their earnings potential from traders passing through rural areas.

The residents of village Y already have discerned some of these opportunities, including selling surplus produce at the small markets near their homes, reselling produce at higher prices at the larger markets along the main road, and selling produce to middlemen and retail traders who buy in bulk at borderline markets. The latter two are expected to accelerate, especially when considering that the villagers themselves will use multiple markets for resale. In villages located along the main road, the increased traffic of trucks carrying middlemen and retail traders to the various markets might enable them to sell their goods in large quantities to passing merchants. Thus, it may be possible to earn a large cash income in a single transaction by selling a large amount of agricultural products, rather than the conventional method of selling small amounts at nearby markets or through direct sales to local residents. However, the availability of arable land in village Y is limited, so more and more households are renting land to cultivate produce for sale.

In the case of agricultural products sold at regular markets on the border, there is no outstanding difference in price between one side of the border and the other. However, the price difference increases as the products move towards urban areas where the population has been growing within Uganda, and a reasonable profit can be expected after deducting transportation costs. This can be explained by the fact that many traders travel to several regular markets on different days of the week, taking advantage of the improved road infrastructure that connects the markets and facilitates access.

It can be said that the population growth of nearby cities due to rapid development and the rising prices of agricultural products are attracting local merchants. It is also worth noting that in the north-eastern DRC, which continues to face logistical challenges, the connection to the larger market on the border with Uganda has created relatively stable cash earnings opportunities for the residents on the DRC side. Securing a supply of cheaper agricultural products from the DRC is important for residents on the Ugandan side of the border because the urbanization of Arua is expected to further increase food supplies as the number of people moving from rural to urban areas increases in the future.

Acknowledgements

I would like to express my sincere gratitude to everyone who encouraged me in various ways during my fieldwork. Without the help of the people of the West Nile, this research would not have been possible. This work was supported by a Research Grant for Graduate Studies (Shibusawa Fund for Ethnological Studies) and a grant from the Field Survey Support Program for Next-generation Researchers (JSPS Project No. 16H06318).

Notes

1 Uganda's administrative divisions, in descending order of size, are region, sub-region, district, county, sub-county, parish, and village.
2 It is under the jurisdiction of the Ministry of the Interior. In principle, visas are issued upon payment of a fee based on the length of stay and the purpose of the visit.
3 An agency under the jurisdiction of the Ministry of Finance, it inspects goods imported and exported from Uganda and the DRC and collects taxes according to the contents.
4 By the end of 1979, some 30,000 people had taken refuge in southern Sudan and another 50,000 refugees had gone to the DRC. As a result of intensified looting and killings by Ugandan government forces still in the West Nile, the number of Ugandan refugees in southern Sudan swelled to 130,000 by 1982 (Crisp 1986: 164), and by 1984, between 240,000 and 260,000 people were living as refugees in southern Sudan and the DRC. Since the late 1990s, there has been a gradual repatriation to the West Nile (Crisp 1986; JRP 2014).
5 Interview with the former LC III in the very sub-county where the Kampala market is located. The heads of administrative units are as follows: district (LCV), county (LCIV), sub-county (LCIII), parish (LCII), and village (LCI). The Local Council system was introduced in the 1990s.
6 There are no walls or fences around the Kampala market, and pedestrians can enter and exit from practically anywhere.
7 Interview with users of Kampala market and residents nearby the market.
8 There was only one lady came to this market by bicycle during the whole survey period.
9 The author counted the number of arriving/departing vehicles by recording their make and model and license plate number at northern entrance. The total number of arriving vehicles varied from 18 to 44 a day during the survey period, averaging more than 30 on Sundays.
10 There is waiting area for motorcycle taxis called "boda boda" as well as a number of restaurants and kiosks.
11 Interviewed on 13 October 2018.
12 It is locally called "g-nut" which comes from the word "groundnut," particularly referring to the peanut here. This peanut paste is added to salted water and used to flavour side dishes.
13 Based on the author's observations on Saturday, 13 October 2018.
14 3,700 Uganda shillings (UGX) = 1 US dollar (October 2019). Interview was on 26 October 2019.
15 Kayla's father-in-law is Anna's paternal grandfather. Kayla's mother-in-law and Anna's paternal grandmother are different people.
16 It cost 267,600 UGX in total. The rent on the land was paid in instalments.
17 Calculated by adding UGX 11,000 from the sale of mushrooms and UGX 30,000 from sweet potatoes.
18 However, from the rainy season of 2019 to the dry season of February 2020, Anna's household was unable to sell sweet potatoes, so she had no way to earn this kind of cash income and was struggling to make ends meet.
19 From interviews with a number of local residents in Arua District. The attacks by the LRA have been reported in previous studies.
20 Uganda was hosting 1.4 million refugees as of the end of 2020, the third largest number of refugees in the world and the largest in Africa, with more than half residing in the West Nile. Of these, more than 880,000 are from South Sudan, 410,000 from the DRC, less than 50,000 from Burundi, and others from Somalia, Rwanda, Eritrea, Sudan, and Ethiopia (UNHCR 2021: 10).

21 World Bank. 10 September 10 2020 (www.worldbank.org/en/news/press-release/2020/09/10/world-bank-provides-1308-million-to-upgrade-road-infrastructure-in-areas-hosting-refugees-in-ugandas-west-nile-sub-region) last accessed on 25 June 2021. Apart from this, JICA's "National Road Rehabilitation Project in Refugee Hosting Areas in West Nile Region" has launched to provide support for the development of national roads from FY2020.
22 In October 2019.
23 Interview on 24 October 2019.
24 Daily Monitor. 2 April 2021. (www.monitor.co.ug/uganda/news/national/arua-main-market-nears-completion-3346616) last accessed on 25 June 2021.
25 A news program broadcast by an FM radio station in the West Nile featured the voices of residents and customers in the vicinity of the temporary markets (October 2018).
26 Interview with Arua local government officials and the general manager of the Arua Main Market Vendors' Association (27–28 November 2017).
27 Arua Hill division and River Oli division.
28 The Independent. 28 April 2020. (www.independent.co.ug/parliament-approves-15-new-cities-for-uganda/). 1 July 2020. (www.independent.co.ug/excitement-as-arua-mbarara-assume-city-status/) last accessed on 25 June 2021.
29 In the early 1950s, there were seven British officials, about a dozen Anglican and Catholic missionaries each, three British tobacco growers, and about a dozen Indian shops in the Arua at that time (Middleton 1992: 6–7). These Indians fled Uganda after a 1972 presidential decree during the Amin administration expelling them from the country, but some are now returning to Uganda and others are newly migrating to Uganda.
30 The East African. 15 May 2021. (www.theeastafrican.co.ke/tea/news/east-africa/uganda-kenya-team-up-on-old-metre-gauge-rail-project-eyeing-congo-s-sudan-340103) last accessed on 25 June 2021.
31 This helps logistics much, but it seems to bring other problems at the same time especially amid COVID-19. The number of patients increased gradually first with the long-distance drivers from neighbouring countries passing Arua without enough quarantine period. Hospitals are run out of space, and Uganda is now under second lockdown except heavy lorries as of 2021 June (West Nile Web. 24 April 2020. (www.westnileweb.com/news-a-analysis/pakwach/covid-19-four-positive-truck-drivers-to-be-managed-in-arua) last accessed on 25 June 2021; West Nile Web. 1 October 2020. (www.westnileweb.com/news-a-analysis/arua/arua-hospital-covid-19-center-runs-out-of-space) last accessed on 25 June 2021), and phone calls from people in Arua.
32 Interview in October 2018.

References

Asiwaju, A. I. and Nugent, P. (eds.) (1996). *African Boundaries: Barriers, Conduits and Opportunities*. London: A Cassell Imprint.

Blake, G. H. (1997). *Imperial Boundary Making the Diary of Captain Kelly and the Sudan-Uganda Boundary Commission of 1913*. Oxford: Oxford University Press.

Crisp, J. (1986). Ugandan Refugees in Sudan and Zaire: The Problem of Repatriation, *African Affairs* 85(1): 163–180.

Dobler, G. (2016). The Green, the Grey and the Blue: A Typology of Cross-Border Trade in Africa, *Journal of Modern African Studies* 54(1): 145–169.

Feyissa, D. and Hoehne, M. H. (eds.) (2010). *Borders and Borderlands as Resources in the Horn of Africa*. Oxford: James Currey.

Harrell-Bond, B. (1986). *Imposing Aid: Emergency Assistance to Refugees*. Oxford: Oxford University Press.

INR. (1970). *International Boundary Study No. 108- Democratic Republic of the Congo (Zaire) – Uganda Boundary*. Washington, DC: Office of the Geographer, Bureau of Intelligence and Research, Department of State, United States of America.

JRP. (2014). *It Was Only the Gun Speaking, with a Pool of Blood Flowing the Ombaci Massacre: June 24, 1981* (JRP Field Note 20). Gulu, Uganda: JRP.

Khadiagala, G. M. (2010). Boundaries in Eastern Africa, *Journal of Eastern African Studies* 4(2): 266–278.

Leopold, M. (2009). Crossing the Line: 100 Years of the North-West Uganda/South Sudan Border, *Journal of Eastern African Studies* 3(3): 464–478.

McEwen, A. C. (1971). *International Boundaries of East Africa*. Oxford: Clarendon Press.

Meagher, K. (1990). The Hidden Economy: Informal and Parallel Trade in North-western Uganda, *Review of African Political Economy* 47: 64–83.

Middleton, J. (1962). Trade and Markets among the Lugbara of Uganda, in P. Bohannan and G. Dalton (eds.), *Markets in Africa*. Evanston, IL: Northwestern University Press, pp. 561–578.

Middleton, J. (1992). *Lugbara of Uganda*, second edition. Orlando, FL: Harcourt Brace Jovanovich College.

Mukohya, V. (1991). Import and Export in the Second Economy in North Kivu, in J. MacGaffey, V. Mukohya, R. W. Nkera, B. G. Schoepf, M. M. Mavambu Ye Beda and W. Engundu (eds.), *The Real Economy of Zaire: The Contribution of Smuggling and Other Unofficial Activities to National Wealth*. London: James Currey, pp. 43–71.

NPA. (2015). *Second National Development Plan (NDPII) 2015/16–2019/20*. Kampala: National Planning Authority <http://npa.go.ug/wp-content/uploads/NDPII-Final.pdf>

NPA. (2020). *Second National Development Plan (NDPIII) 2020/21–2024/25*. <www.npa.go.ug/wp-content/uploads/2020/08/NDPIII-Finale_Compressed.pdf>

Nugent, P. and Soi, I. (2020). One-stop Border Posts in East Africa: State Encounters of the Fourth Kind, *Journal of Eastern African Studies* 14(3): 433–454.

RLP. (2004). *Negotiating Peace: Resolution of Conflicts in Uganda's West Nile Region* (Refugee Law Project Working Paper No. 12). Kampala: RLP.

Titeca, K. (2009). *The Changing Cross-Border Trade Dynamics between North-western Uganda, North-eastern Congo and Southern Sudan* (Crisis States Research Centre Working Paper No. 63). <https://core.ac.uk/download/pdf/96058.pdf>

Titeca, K. and Herdt, T. (2010). Regulation, Cross-Border Trade and Practical Norms in West Nile, North-Western Uganda, *Africa* 80(4): 573–594.

UBOS. (2014). *National Population and Housing Census 2014 Main Report*. Kampala: Uganda Bureau of Statistics.

UNHCR. (2021). *Inter-Agency: Revised Uganda Country Refugee Response Plan, July 2020 – December 2021*. <https://data2.unhcr.org/en/documents/details/84715>

4 Cross-border refugee crisis and local governments in the West Nile Region, Uganda

Satomi Kamei

Cross-border refugees and local governments

Located in East Africa, the Republic of Uganda is a small landlocked country with a population of estimated 43 million (UBOS, 2020b). With leading export commodities such as coffee, gold, and fishery products, the country's 2019 GDP per capita is USD 794 (World Bank, n.d.) while Uganda is a member state of the East African Community. Despite the compact land area, Uganda shares its borders with five other states: Kenya, Tanzania, Rwanda, the Democratic Republic of Congo (DRC), and South Sudan. There are 40 official entry/exit points along the borderline with the neighbouring states (Ministry of Internal Affairs, n.d.).

These unique geographical conditions, alongside multiple other factors, have profoundly shaped Uganda's acknowledged refugee protection policy. Cross-border migration and refugees are not anything new to this East African nation. On the contrary, Uganda has been long subjected to trans-regional movements as well as intrastate displacements of people. In recent years, however, cross-border refugees have become one outstanding subject matter for the Government of Uganda (GoU) and the international community alike. With over 1.4 million refugees from other African states, Uganda is among the world's top refugee-hosting nations along with Turkey, Colombia, and Pakistan (UNHCR, 2020). As of April 2021, the number of registered refugees from South Sudan alone is over 911,000, and they are mainly accommodated in the West Nile region of Uganda.

Given this background and decentralized governance structure in the country, this chapter examines the case of cross-border refugees and the West Nile region to reflect on how the recent refugee influxes have impacted on the local governments (LGs) in the region. It illustrates prominent issues and challenges associated with regional governance and draws key lessons that address policy implementation at decentralized levels in the discourse of state-building. At the initial stage of the crisis, refugees were mostly viewed as a huge burden and even a threat to LGs. At the same time, however, the local population generously accepts the responsibility to accommodate refugees fleeing from the civil war and violence across the border. Despite persistent hardships to date in West Nile, the LGs have begun to confront decentralized responsibilities with more confidence and increasingly demonstrate accountability in the local development discourse.

DOI: 10.4324/9781003202318-4

West Nile as a distinctive region

In Uganda's administrative context, West Nile is categorized as a sub-region positioned in the north-western corner of the country and west of the river Nile. During the precolonial period, the region went through slave-raiding by Turkish slave traders and ivory poaching by Europeans. Prior to integration into the British Uganda Protectorate in 1914, West Nile was administered as part of the Congo Free State (1894–1908), privately owned by King Leopold II of Belgium, and then as part of the Anglo-Egyptian Sudan under British and Egyptian condominium administration (Leonardi, 2020; Leopold, 2006; West Nile Web, n.d.). As hinted from these colonial transitions since the late 19th century, West Nile experienced rather distinct governance paths characterized by complex colonial power struggles.

It was only after the 1914 incorporation into the British Uganda Protectorate that West Nile became, for the first time, a part of today's Uganda. The whole West Nile region was then administered as one large district – West Nile District – while the colonial administration headquarters was placed in Arua town. Prior to Uganda's independence in 1962, Madi District, which combined the current Moyo, Obongi, and Adjumani districts, was established in 1955. Over the five decades since then, remaining West Nile District was gradually subdivided into several districts, starting from South Nile District established in 1974 and then

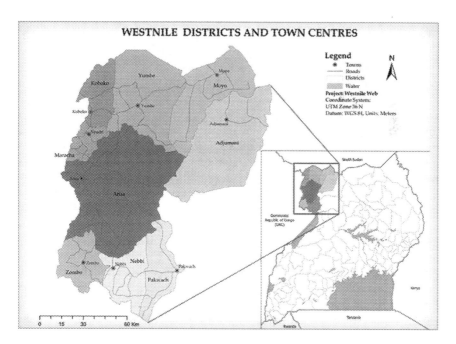

Map 4.1 The West Nile Region and Districts (prior to 2019)
Source: West Nile Web

renamed as Nebbi District in 1980 (West Nile Web, n.d.). As of Fiscal Year (FY) 2020/21, West Nile sub-regional LG has increased to 12 at district level, in addition to two municipal and one city governments.

Today, West Nile sub-region has a population estimated to be roughly three million, which is uniquely diverse with different ethnic and linguistic groups. The main ethnic groups include the Lugbara, Kakwa, Madi, and the Nilotic Alur while other ethnic groups are Ukebu, Kuku, and Nubians (West Nile Web, n.d.). Given this diversity, ethnic composition principally determines the current district boundaries. The recent creation of Madi Okollo District, out of Arua District, in 2019 is another case of ethnic districting; the former ethnic composition is mostly Madi while the latter is primarily Lugbara. Similarly, Obongi District, created out of Moyo District in 2019, is ethnically Madi Rigbo while Moyo is Madi. Through this process, the mother district of West Nile, Arua District, has been transformed into 12 districts determined primarily by their ethnic dimensions. Despite such administrative subdivisions, West Nile is uniquely characterized with its strong unity as a region.

Another interesting fact about West Nile is that the notorious former dictator, Idi Amin, who ruled Uganda from 1971 to 1979, came from the region, more precisely from Koboko area – a borderland adjacent to southern Sudan and northeastern DRC. Amin indeed recruited and promoted top military personnel from the region in the early 1970s (Leopold, 2020). As internationally condemned, Uganda suffered from horrific violence during Amin's regime and the loss of a large number of civilians killed by his uncontrolled soldiers (Leopold, 2020). This devastating historical incident has had a lasting effect on the population as well as the LGs across West Nile. Following Amin's fall in 1979, many inhabitants had to seek refuge on the other side of the border, to southern Sudan, due to the central government's retaliation against the region (Leonardi & Santschi, 2016). Peripheral West Nile was accordingly demoted and deprived of backing from the centre. It seems likely that long years of marginalization and hardships inflicted upon the population have profoundly influenced the formation of their frontier mindsets and antipathy against the current government.

Over the last few decades, Uganda has significantly reduced poverty within its state boundary. The proportion of the population, living under the national poverty line, declined from 56% in 1993 to 31% in 2006, then further down to 20% in 2013. The ratio slightly rose to 21% in 2016/2017 (UBOS, 2019). Behind this reduction was a positive economic growth recorded since the 2000s. The growth primarily resulted from favourable market prices for agricultural products, which eventually improved household income. In northern Uganda, post-conflict peace notably contributed to doubling agricultural production (World Bank, 2016). This encouraging development also benefited the West Nile region, although the local population still mainly engages in subsistence agriculture today. Additionally, in some growing urban areas, Non-Governmental Organizations (NGOs) are considered to be an important employment sector. Cross-border trade is also crucial for the sub-regional economy. Nevertheless, FY2016/17 national data on poverty distribution rank West Nile the fifth poorest among 13 sub-regions nationwide (UBOS, 2020a). Hence, the region is still perceived as one of the most deprived and disadvantaged within Uganda.

Another notable feature is that the West Nile region is bordered by South Sudan and DRC – two neighbours long struggling with intrastate upheavals and insecurity. Unsurprisingly, people often associate state borders with distress; in fact, the sub-region has periodically encountered cross-border migration and refugee inflows from adjoining fragile states. For instance, Rhino Camp Settlement, a refugee settlement located in Madi Okollo District, was originally established in Arua District in 1980 to shelter Sudanese refugees fleeing from the civil war, and today, it still houses over 120,000 refugees mostly from South Sudan. Given the ongoing insecurity in the wider region, this particular settlement has existed for the last 40 years and continued housing displaced people.

Significantly, internally displaced persons in northern Uganda were also sheltered within the same settlement at the height of intrastate disruptions. In this regard, it is important to recognize that Ugandans had to seek refuge by crossing the border into Sudan during the civil strife following the overthrow of Idi Amin in 1979 and also into Zaire during the Lord's Resistance Army's (LRA's) insurgency in the 1990s. As discussed by Leonardi and Santschi (2016) using the case of some tribal groups in northern Uganda and southern Sudan, migrations of local populations took place reciprocally across the borderlands and have been, to some extent, continuous. Moreover, it should be noted that part of the boundary between West Nile and southern Sudan, today's South Sudan, has not been legally defined and remains unsettled to date (Leonardi, 2020). Regardless of the disputed boundary, it is a trans-regional legacy for West Nile that many borderland residents on both sides share the same experiences of seeking refuge as well as accommodating refugees from either side.

Decentralization and local government structure

The last few decades have seen a consistent trend of decentralization across the globe. Sub-Saharan Africa is no exception and has become a centre of extensive endeavours undertaken since the 1990s. As far as sub-Saharan Africa is concerned, this movement was largely a result of the shifting of international aid policy focus towards good governance in the early 1990s and away from structural adjustment assistance vigorously applied across the region during the 1980s.

In the case of Uganda, the country embarked on decentralization in the late 1980s following the establishment of the government of the National Resistance Movement (NRM) under the leadership of President Yoweri Museveni (Ssonko, 2013). Despite some changes made over time, the core of the decentralization policy has remained intact as the government essentially determined it with its internal purposes (Steiner, 2006). Given this background, Uganda has been somewhat of a leader in decentralization within sub-Saharan Africa although there are varied opinions on the eventual outcomes.

Equally important is that international financial institutions and bilateral development partners also played a prominent role in Uganda's development discourse since the 1990s, having a keen interest in making the country a model of decentralized governance and poverty reduction. As a matter of fact, Uganda became the first country eligible for the Highly Indebted Poor Country (HIPC) Initiative in 1996. The initiative eventually resulted in substantial international debt relief (Nannyonjo, 2001) when the candidate fulfilled a range of conditions set by the international financiers. The conditionality predictably required governance reform agenda; the formulation of a poverty reduction strategy together with a decentralization framework (WB, 1998). Having met the conditions while demonstrating solid ownership in the process (Sasaoka, 2011), the GoU was collectively praised by the international donor community and considered as a good performer capable of complying with stringent aid requirements.

In 1993, Uganda officially embarked on the implementation of its decentralization reform, whose policy is stipulated in the Local Government Act (LGA) of 1997 and grounded in the state's constitution of 1995. In essence, the policy transfers powers and responsibilities from the centre to local levels in administration, finance, and political decision-making and thereby seeking to improve accountability, effectiveness, and ownership with local development (MoLG, 1997). Behind this ambitious objective, there exists a political commitment of President Museveni to maintain a social order and peace while promoting participatory democracy through devolution (Steiner, 2006). Principally, Uganda's decentralization is intended to realize devolution to make LGs autonomous.

Uganda's LG structure is distinctively layered. The LGA, Section 3 clarifies the structure as follows: LGs in rural districts are Local Council (LC) 5 or LC5; municipal governments as LC4 and division councils as LC3; and sub-county and town councils as also LC3. Then, parish councils are structured as LC2 and village councils as LC1 (MoLG, 1997). Thus, Uganda's LG structure consists of vertical tiers of rural councils in LC1, LC3, and LC5, which constitute a political wing, and administrative units installed in LC2 to LC5. A local council has an elected chairperson while one elected councillor represents his/her electoral area in the case of district council. On the side of administration, Chief Administrative Officer (CAO) oversees the entire operation of LG administration. The CAO is a top civil servant appointed by the central government. While Deputy CAO is also posted by the centre, the rest of LG employees are deployed by the District Service Commission.

Dimensions of border issues

Uganda shares the borders with five adjoining states. While it seems foreseeable for this landlocked country to occasionally encounter border issues along the boundary, the nature of such issues varies and evolves around particular affairs and/or incidents happening within the wider region or specific countries.

Having sent own troops to the African Union (AU) Mission in Somalia (AMISOM), the GoU demonstrated its commitment for regional stability and played a role against profound insecurity in the Horn of Africa. Triggered by Uganda's involvement in the peace keeping operation in Somalia, a major retaliation was carried out in the capital city of Kampala in July 2010. The suicide bombings killed 74 civilians at a restaurant and a club within Kampala, which used to be a peaceful city up to this incident. Somalia's al Qaeda-linked al Shabaab claimed having conducted the attacks. Following this shattering assault, tightening the security around the border with Kenya was reemphasized as necessary. Yet, the border has remained volatile despite the repeated threats of terrorism. Meanwhile, the United States State Department reported in 2019 that the GoU was increasingly concerned with security threats along the border with DRC but also that the government had not taken decisive measures (US State Department, 2019). In fact, continued upheavals in north-eastern DRC have been driving refugees into Uganda through porous border. The borderline with this fragile state is said to be particularly problematic. In 2020, a considerable rise in the number of Congolese refugees was registered (UNHCR, 2020). After South Sudan, DRC generates the second highest number of refugees, over 428,000, sheltered in Uganda as of March 2021. Border porosity and security issues linger on.

One recent unresolved case is the border with Rwanda. Having disputed on mutual supports to rebel groups to destabilize the other state (Collins, 2020), President Museveni and President Paul Kagame of Rwanda closed down Gatuna border post shared between the two states in 2019. Under a normal circumstance, Gatuna is one major transit point of transporting goods between Uganda and Rwanda while the two nationals freely cross the border for local trades. Despite the high-level meetings intermediated by Angola and DRC respectively the lingering disputes and hostility keep the border tightly closed without a decisive solution as of April 2021. Cross-border goods and human movements have been completely disrupted for the last two years.

Another critical issue emerging most recently is concerned with the COVID-19 pandemic. As a landlocked state, Uganda largely depends on land transportation of imported goods from major sea ports in Kenya and Tanzania. To mitigate potential infections that can be spread into Uganda via truck drivers and traders from the two neighbours, the GoU has taken strict measures at the border posts (Chepkonga, 2020). On the other side of Uganda also lies a long borderline with DRC. To assess preparedness to fight against the pandemic, the Parliamentary Technical Committee on COVID-19 travelled to West Nile sub-region and made a statement in May 2020 that the porous border with Congo was undermining Uganda's fight against the virus. The committee then urged the central government's attention to porous and illegal border entry points in Arua District (Parliament of Uganda, 2020). Similarly, periodic outbreaks of Ebola in DRC threats bordering districts due to the porous border between the two countries.

As these practical cases reveal, Uganda's geographical position, entangled with mostly porous and volatile borders, can expose its vulnerability in national security, sociopolitical, and economic dimensions. And, regardless of the issues confronted, state borders pose not only the centre but also peripheral LGs enormous political, social, and economic challenges in minimizing negative bearings to be inflicted upon national as well as regional security and stability. Owing to the geopolitical position, Uganda is indeed central to the trans-regional security and sustainable governance. This is significantly the exact reason why the international donor community is strongly committed to supporting the Ugandan government through development aid provision.

Historical setting and local perspectives on state borders

To make the border issues more complicated, part of the north-western borderline between the West Nile region and southern South Sudan has been long disputed without a mutually agreed demarcation (Leonardi & Santschi, 2016). As far as these border areas are concerned, the first attempt to define boundaries goes back to the early 19th century when the United Kingdom administered both what have become Uganda and southern Sudan after independence. The boundary between the two territories was first defined by a 1914 British colonial order (Leonardi, 2020). Behind the contested boundary, which was initially proposed to be amended in the future, the British colonial administration attempted to establish a tribal boundary to separate different ethnic and linguistic groups living in the west of the river Nile (Leonardi & Santschi, 2016). Although the British considered such a demarcation suitable, some tribal groups, namely Kuku, Kakwa, Madi and Lugbara, had long lived side by side and been intermingled through marriage and migrations over time (Leonardi & Santschi, 2016). Even today, local populations mingle across the borderlands. Despite the past experiences and norms set outside of Africa, it has been absolutely vital for the locals, on both sides of the West Nile region and southern Sudan, to be able to cross the boundary whenever needed, especially at the times of civil wars and insurgencies.

For those who had to escape from wars and violence for survival, the definitions of state boundaries probably do not carry much weight. In the West Nile region, a large part of the state boundary exits, in reality, without any clear fencing or physical demarcation. Hence, the local residents come and go between the borderlands for practical reasons. For them, particularly those who have relatives and friends on the other side, state borders are historical remnants from colonial supremacy and today's administrative divisions rather than political as discussed by Dobler (2016). Inquired how the local population sees state borders in Arua District, a district officer, who grew up near the border with Zaire, responded that the people generally perceived them artificial and impractical. He further points out that the locals are well aware of the fundamental relationship they have with people on the other side, sharing the same languages and cultures. These are the cases with Lugbara and Alur in Uganda and eastern DRC and also with Kakwa in Uganda and South Sudan.

As discussed earlier, the issues around state borders are becoming increasingly more complex and globalized, especially now that the COVID-19 pandemic inevitably raises serious concerns of safety and security across the borders and borderlands. From many locals' viewpoint, state borders have long remained de facto and disconnected from their cross-border movements and livelihoods. Indeed, the borders primarily remain pre-modern or "green" according to the typology debated by Dobler (2016). It might be anticipated, however, that borderland people, especially urban residents, will see it as a necessity to transform state borders to a more advanced stage. And, this is primarily to prevent potential troubles for their borderland living in today's globalized world.

Refugee influxes and Uganda's refugee policy

Uganda's geopolitical position has inevitably formed the modern history of cross-border migration and refugees from neighbouring areas. As of May 2021, the country hosts over 1.4 million refugees and asylum seekers from other African states. South Sudanese and Congolese account for 90% of them. There are 30 refugee settlements established across 11 districts and Kampala City (UNHCR, 2018). As far as West Nile is concerned, war-torn South Sudan is the country of origin for most refugees currently sheltered in the region. Due to the fierce conflict between the South Sudanese government's and its opposition forces and violence inflicted upon civilians, more than 900,000 South Sudanese, mostly women and children, have escaped to northern Uganda in recent years. According to UNHCR, an arrival of over 143,000 refugees in Uganda was initially recorded in July 2016. The total number of refugees rose to 373,000 – more than doubled – by September 2016. Then, it continued to reach 898,000 by April 2017 and hit one million by July 2017. UNHCR reported that Uganda had experienced an average of over 1,800 incoming South Sudanese refugees per day in 2016–2017. The number of refugee influxes was unprecedented and took the centre as well as peripheral LGs by surprise even though the country had confronted periodic inbound refugees in the past.

To tackle the refugee crisis urgently, the GoU and the United Nations (UN) organized the "Uganda Solidarity Summit on Refugees" in Kampala in June 2017. The summit was well represented by international humanitarian and development agencies, financial institutions, bilateral countries, NGOs, Civil Society Organizations, the private sector, and the like. Among the participants were 12 refugee-hosting LGs, including some representatives of five district governments from West Nile. While the international delegation unanimously commended the GoU for its exceptionally generous and progressive refugee protection policy, it

Table 4.1 Top 3 country of origin and number of refugees in Uganda

Year	South Sudan	DRC	Burundi	Total Refugees
2015	207,600	195,700	30,500	513,000
2016	627,900	221,900	44,200	982,700
2017	986,600	236,400	39,700	1,395,000
2018	985,000	310,000	56,000	1,370,000
2019	861,600	397,600	N/A	1,400,000
2020	887,800	420,300	49,500	1,446,000
May 2021	921,000	432,400	51,000	1,494,000

Source: UNHCR

called upon much increased supports from the global community to reinforce efforts led by the GoU alongside refugee-hosting LGs. The summit attained USD 358 million pledged by the international donor community, although the GoU intended to raise USD two billion, an estimated amount required to tackle the crisis (UN News, 2017).

In West Nile, Adjumani District was already housing South Sudanese refugees at Nyumanzi Refugee Settlement even before the surge of inflows began in July 2016. To respond to the massive refugee influxes, three additional refugee settlements, namely Bidibidi Settlement in Yumbe District, Palorinya Settlement in Moyo District, and Imvepi Settlement in Arua District, were established by early 2017 together with the expansion of Rhino Camp Settlement in Arua District. In addition to the enlarged refugee settlements, 15 health facilities, 14 schools, a water treatment plant, and 7,500 communal latrines were constructed across the settlements in FY2016/17 (UNHCR, n.d.). Regardless of these immediate actions realized mostly by international and domestic Non-State Actors (NSAs), refugees' basic needs, particularly with water-sanitation, education, and health services, continued to expand dramatically.

Uganda's refugee protection policy is fundamentally guided by the Refugee Act (2006) and Refugee Regulations (2010). The Office of the Prime Minister (OPM) indicates the country's progressive policy aspects being: open borders, non-camp settlement, equal access to government-provided social services, a chance to work, and land allocation for farming and shelter (OPM, n.d.). Moreover, the GoU articulated the Settlement Transformation Agenda (2015) to pursue self-reliance and local settlement among refugees along with social development in refugee-hosting areas (UNHCR, 2018). The agenda significantly urged refugee responses to be integrated into national development frameworks and to address needs of both refugees and their host communities.

UNHCR describes Uganda's refugee policy as providing "one of the most favourable protection environments for refugees, including freedom of movement, the right to work, own business and property, and access to public education and health services" (UNHCR, n.d.). To honour Uganda's policy implementation and cope with skyrocketing demands for public service delivery on the ground, the international donor community mobilized financial as well as in-kind supports for humanitarian needs – particularly in food security, water and sanitation, health care, and education to say the least. Refugees from South Sudan continued to cross the border and streamed into West Nile throughout 2017.

In September 2018, South Sudanese President, Salva Kiir, and opposing rebel leader, Riek Machar, finally signed a peace agreement to end the five-year civil war in South Sudan. Although two years have passed since then, over 911,000 South Sudanese still remain as refugees in Uganda as of April 2021 (UNHCR, 2021). This number accounts for 61% of the total number of refugees sheltered across the country. As for their whereabouts, approximately 85% of South Sudanese refugees are accommodated within the West Nile region, specifically in the following five districts: Yumbe housing – 238,107; Adjumani – 223,730; Madi

Okollo and Terego, new districts established out of Arua District – 188,113; and Obongi – 124,854. The national population of these five districts combined is roughly 1.75 million while over 774,000 refugees are sheltered within the districts. Considering these figures, it is apparent that hosting refugees, in accordance with the central government's progressive refugee policy, has generated immense pressures and challenges for the LGs concerned.

Impacts on refugee-hosting local governments and communities in West Nile

The refugee crisis has been unavoidably affecting the host LGs and their communities in every way. During 2016–2017, the author witnessed extraordinary incidences occurring in the host districts within West Nile. One astonishing case is recalled as evidence that border and borderland issues cannot be rightfully debated without understanding the intricate background of a given borderland. In February 2017, in a sub-county near the state border with South Sudan, one head teacher reported to his sub-county chief the following: his primary school did not conduct any lesson for the first two weeks of 2017 school year because no single child came to school despite that more than 300 children had registered for the new academic year. To a great shock, it was speculated that the local residents and their children all had fled to a refugee reception centre, disguising as refugees from South Sudan, to access food aid for incoming refugees. This particular sub-county accommodates a substantial number of South Sudanese who have self-settled given the cross-border kinship.

The year 2016 experienced an exceptionally severe drought in the region. As hinted by the aforementioned incident, the local population suffered from acute food shortages during 2017. Poor harvests and rapidly increasing demand for food by incoming refugees also led to price hikes. Strenuous livelihood conditions at the time severely affected the local Ugandans in the borderland. Food security, not only for the refugees but also for the national population, became a crucial agenda for both the centre and LGs in early 2017 onwards. Similarly, water supply became another concern. Various international and domestic partners quickly intervened to increase and equip water facilities around the refugee settlement areas.

Basic education is another prominent case where demands vastly increased and required immediate responses. Itula Sub-County, Obongi District – formerly a county under Moyo District – is a Lower LG where Palorinya Settlement lies. This particular sub-county recorded an indigenous population of 3,096 primary-school aged – between 6 and 12 years old – in 2017 while 43,761 children of the same age group were registered refugees in the same sub-county. Itula Secondary School also recorded 2,000 in student enrolment in 2017, which was a tenfold upsurge from the average number registered in previous years (JICA, 2018). To respond to these extreme situations, then-Moyo District took decisive actions, including deploying additional school teachers, while infrastructural work was mostly supported by NSAs. Since both the LGs and local communities regard education as a priority, the sector has seen a considerable improvement with the extensive investments made in recent years. However, the host LGs remain severely constrained by a chronic shortage of education funding. Capitation grant allocation, a main financial source for school operation, does not consider numbers of refugee children enrolled at schools. Similarly, refugees are granted access to public health care. A huge demand for medical services and supplies emerged as refugees continued to settle in northern Uganda. This situation has put immense pressures on health centres, other service provider institutions, and the LGs at large.

Another area, increasingly receiving more attention, is environmental degradation. Across the refugee-hosting districts, deforestation has become exceptionally problematic. Even prior to the refugee crisis, depletion of trees and degradation of wetlands were widely recognized as a serious challenge throughout West Nile. The speed of the degradation accelerated as firewood consumption rose rapidly along with the refugee settlements. Given no other practical options, refugees depend on locally available natural resources for their daily survival. Arua District, for instance, reported in 2016 and 2017 that cases of illegal logging were increasing due to a high demand of charcoal. Despite the mounting threats, environment and natural resources sector has been poorly financed, which results in a repeated failure of LGs in taking necessary measures. Only recently, however, positive changes are finally emerging because more external funds are made available for refugee-hosting districts to combat the long-overdue environmental dilemmas.

Local government as a responsible agent for refugee policy implementation

When it comes to the refugee sector, the OPM has the overall responsibility for policy guidance and overseeing refugee affairs in Uganda. It has a regional office, located in Arua town, to administer and coordinate all activities related to the refugee sector within West Nile sub-region. On the implementation side, UNHCR plays a leading role in the operation of relief activities on the ground. Thus, the OPM and UNHCR work closely to coordinate and facilitate all kinds of undertakings in line with Uganda's refugee policy.

On the other hand, Uganda's decentralized governance structure places LGs to be essentially responsible for provision of shelters and basic social services to those refugees who have settled in their designated settlements within the LG's jurisdiction. Not surprisingly, therefore, cross-border immigration and refugees are one primary source of massive struggles for peripheral LGs, given their restricted resource bases and capacity, in the discourse of regional development and governance. Along the same line, the case of refugee crisis in West Nile reveals that it is critical to take into account the decentralized governance structure and arrangements when examining policy implementation concerning cross-border refugees.

In addition to the provision of shelters and other social services, refugees are granted plots of land to cultivate agricultural products for their own consumption. Since land rights are based on customary ownership in the northern region (Zakaryan & Antara, 2018), lower LGs consult and negotiate with the land owners in an effort to make lands available for their refugees. Similarly, local councils customarily intervene to settle land disputes if any matter arises. Ironically, though, LGs often face legal cases of such disputes, which are costly and time-consuming for their constrained financial and human resources. Inbound refugees can accordingly cause a tension for host communities due to the increasing demand for limited land area. Managing land issues are, therefore, crucial mandates for LGs in realizing the national refugee protection policy.

Fundamental challenges for refugee-hosting district governments

There is no doubt that the recent refugee crisis, having resulted in over 774,000 refugee settlements across the West Nile region, has posed enormous challenges – more than ever before – in the regional development discourse. Among various impediments, the top issue undoubtedly concerns with finance for refugee responses. Despite the apparent and urgent need of service provisions, the central government barely increased budgets for host districts to expand public services for their refugee population. To begin with, the GoU's fiscal envelope is too constrained to respond to financial requirements alone. LGs' locally generated tax revenue is also extremely limited. Furthermore, Uganda's current budgeting system does not take account of the refugee population; both recurrent and development budget allocation formula is purely based on districts' national population. As a consequence, Obongi District, for example, is allocated budgets based on its native population of 53,000 even when the district hosts over 124,000 refugees. Without a legitimate and predictable resource allocation through the country system, refugee-hosting LGs unavoidably struggle in service delivery and largely remain incapable of integrating in-house refugees into their operational plans and budgets. This is quite a paradox given the fact that the refugees are considered a long-term issue, and thus, the centre emphasizes refugee-integrated planning as imperative.

Basically, the current state's budgeting system hardly allows LGs to plan contingency or newly emerging requirements beyond their predetermined budget ceilings. In this respect, it could be significantly beneficial if international aid agencies and bilateral donors enhanced provision of budgetary assistance. More predictable and reliable financial resources would enable the centre and host LGs to integrate additional necessities and costs for refugees into their planning and governance structure. For instance, the GoU has disbursed substantial amounts of the World Bank's IDA credits, financing the national programme called USMID (Uganda Support to Municipal Infrastructure Development), specifically to refugee-hosting districts to improve basic infrastructure for both local communities and refugees. Host LGs perceive this particular funding highly favourable because the funds, conditional to basic infrastructure yet largely discretionary, facilitate peripheral LGs to make their own decisions and execute necessary actions by using the country system while constructively supported by NSAs. Furthermore, LGs can directly respond to both refugees and their host communities according to locally identified and prioritized investment needs. This arrangement is correspondingly expected to enhance local ownership and accountability.

In practice, NSAs' intervention is mainly realized through project implementation and in-kind support provision. Hence, LGs cannot fully integrate external assistance into their planning, budgeting (off budget), and reporting system. Ultimately, LGs are severely dependent on external decision-making, finance, and direct intervention through often scattered project-based engagements. It is evident, however, that continuous efforts are widely recognized as vital for more effective coordination among various stakeholders – both state and NSAs – and for a better alignment to the state system.

Another dimension, which is equally critical, is the capacity of refugee-hosting LGs. As already addressed, finance is one exceptionally crucial element to determine overall LGs' management and implementation capabilities. Fundamentally, though, another undeniable reality is that the LGs, in particular the administration, must manage overall service provision at the decentralized levels. Yet, in the northern region of Uganda, peripheral LGs typically suffer from severe staff shortages, especially technical staff including those in education, health, planning, and engineering sectors. In recent years, however, staffing has been improving under the new LG structure amended in 2015. It is particularly notable that key LG positions, including Community Development Officers (CDO) and Parish Chiefs, have been upgraded and the number of deployed servants has considerably increased across sub-counties and parishes within West Nile. While the CDOs and Parish Chiefs play vital roles in relation to local communities and residents, they directly engage the refugee-hosting communities. Encouraged by the positive developments recently made in staffing, both higher and lower refugee-hosting LGs appear to continue striving for further strengthening their human resource base and management. Since various NSAs are implementing local development activities, a great deal of coordination is required among the actors involved as well. With all these demanding aspects, it becomes unquestionable that the refugee-hosting LGs are in need of continued supports for capacity strengthening from both the centre and NSAs.

On political side, concerned actors include elected council members from LC1, LC2, LC3, and LC5 under the district government structure. With over 60,000 villages across Uganda, LC1 council election was finally organized nationwide in 2018 since the last election was held in July 2001. Uganda's constitution requires council elections to be held in every five years. As LC2 is composed of village chairpersons, the current LC1 and LC2 council members were thus largely restored in 2018. Given this relatively recent development, the local residents generally hold high expectations towards their political leaders' roles in the local development and governance. Uniquely positioned between villages and a sub-county, LC2 handles imperative local issues, including land disputes, while mobilizing community members for various activities. Regardless, Parish Chief is a sole administrative servant deployed for the parish level. As a result,

Parish Chief coordinates a wide range of grassroots matters and moreover assists the council's mandates. In this connection, close coordination and collaboration between LC1/LC2 chairpersons and Parish Chief is one indispensable component to ensure smooth local development engagements, including refugee issues, at the lower levels.

In the end, the extent of commitment and efforts made by political leaders matters considerably because they are the ultimate decision-making authorities on LG affairs and are responsible for sensitizing and engaging the local population about a livelihood conducive for both Ugandans and refugees to co-exist in a non-conflicting manner. Given the roles and responsibilities to be fulfilled, sensitization and capacity enhancement of political leaders are equally necessary when favourable mindsets and commitment are lacking in some cases. Profoundly, capacity development is one outstanding challenge given that it requires continued engagements and commitment to transform not only physical abilities but also mindsets, attitudes, and norms over time.

Lessons learned from the refugee crisis and policy implementation in West Nile

Geopolitically uniquely situated in East Africa, Uganda has been long subjected to a variety of issues and challenges associated with its state borders. Among emergent affairs drawing a global attention is the refugee crisis discussed in this chapter. Uganda's refugee policy – originated from an African state – is widely acknowledged as one inclusive refugee protection model. With the largest number of refugee population experienced ever before, many local residents in peripheral West Nile still accept refugees as their responsibility. To rightfully understand these unique circumstances in the context of sub-Saharan Africa, one must reflect on border and borderland affairs by using multiple spectacles; historical, socio-political, and cultural to mention a few. The case of the recent refugee crisis in Uganda has revealed fundamental structural issues in policy implementation but also multifaceted elements that are distinctive and particular to the West Nile region.

Although Uganda's state borders are often understood to be porous, borderland residents do not take it as a problem as long as cross-border mobility remains manageable for their practical needs. Historically, trans-regional movements have been continuously carried out. In the case of West Nile, the local population distinctively possesses similar experiences as their counterparts in seeking refuge themselves on the other side of the border. In this respect, for many, borders are meant far beyond state politics and administrative boundaries. Some may be inclined to relate the borders to their own existence and survival. Against the odds, many borderland residents maintain a close ethnic and cultural link (Leopold, 2006) as well as socio-economic networks with their counterparts across the border.

In more recent years, however, people's perceptions seem to be changing; tightening cross-border movements is increasingly seen as relevant due largely to rapidly increasing threats from the pandemic as well as trans-state conflicts and terrorism. Future development on border security and associated policies, therefore, should be closely followed. In the past, the Ugandan government took varied degrees of attention and actions, depending on the nature of border issues confronted. Evidence from the past occurrences to date possibly allows us to interpret that Uganda somewhat manages the border issues at large. The government pursues its own course by cautiously calculating potential merits and demerits from the perspectives of state-building as well as wider trans-regional relationships. Uganda is accordingly inclined to strive regardless of globalized views and set norms. Thus, the country determines and leads fundamental policies and strategies. Annoyingly, though, some limitations are undoubtedly foreseen, depending on the nature and the scale of policy actions to be undertaken.

On the other hand, recognized as today's global agenda, refugee affairs certainly draw keen attentions. The recent refugee crisis has been primarily driven by intra-state conflicts and volatility within Africa. Due to the prevailing insecurity in some parts of East and Central Africa, the global community inevitably expects Uganda to play a vital role in its regional stability and peace building. In essence, refugees remain a major political and development challenge for the continent of Africa. Given that refugee migrations pose especially refugee-hosting nations enormous sociopolitical, administrative, and financial burdens, the challenge goes beyond one African state's capacity to overcome. As a consequence, global intervention becomes inevitable, as has been the case with Uganda, to respond to a wide range of humanitarian needs and coordination work for refugee responses. One important lesson learned from the Uganda case implies that a refugee-hosting government should take a strong lead in directing and coordinating the country's refugee policy implementation. Despite the solid policy framework, however, Uganda's reliance on external assistance and intervention, ironically and perhaps unavoidably, has exposed its vulnerability and limitation in coping with the scale of the recent crisis – globalized challenges initiated from the borders of fragile African states.

Given the decentralized governance structure in Uganda, the case of the West Nile region exemplifies that LGs are a key determining factor for the national policy implementation. In this relation, one fundamental lesson is that envisioned refugee protection under the national policy framework requires a wide range of commitments and coordination to be mobilized and managed locally among the host governments, non-state partners, and borderland residents. Accordingly, it should be emphasized that locally generated commitments and capacity must be reinforced, to a maximum extent, with required resources, especially predictable and reliable funding supplemented by the central government together with the international donor community. Budgetary support is advantageous in enabling host governments to integrate all public funds into and execute them more systematically through the LG's own operational arrangements. Fundamentally, additional finance and internal competency are two central requisites for Uganda to govern its policy implementation. Bilateral, multilateral donors and NSAs need to respectfully support the state system with a genuine consideration for locally embedded sociocultural values and practices. This would allow some room for the centre and LGs to determine suitable strategies and be equally accountable for decentralized policy implementation with their own will.

Peripheral West Nile, long marginalized by the centre, demonstrates more potential today to be further resilient as a sub-region and strive for remaining challenges in locally determined development endeavours. In fact, the regional districts are strategizing better and increasingly integrating refugee agenda together with prioritized needs of refugees and host communities into their operational structure. One growing concern is, however, that international supports for refugees are substantially declining recently and likely to cause host local governments further agonies. As the current global situation may imply, micro-regionalism would not effectively advance when disconnected from globalized politics and economy. Regardless of all, the world must well acknowledge that the local governments together with their rural population are genuinely striving to cope with complex cross-border challenges in peripheral borderlands in the Pearl of Africa.

References

Chepkonga, F. (2020, June 24). *East African Countries Must Develop a Centralised Policy for Disease Control and Coordinated Cross-Border Controls in Response to the Pandemic.* https://policynetwork.org/opinions/blogs/cross-border-issues-and-pandemic-containment-in-east-africa/

Collins, T. (2020, March 23). Rwanda-Uganda Conflict: Is the End in Sight? *African Business Magazine.* https://african.business/2020/03/economy/rwanda-uganda-conflict-is-the-end-in-sight/

Dobler, G. (2016). The Green, the Grey and the Blue: A Typology of Cross-Border Trade in Africa. *The Journal of Modern African Studies,* 54, 145–169.

JICA. (2018). *Study on Social Infrastructural Needs for the Refugee Hosting Communities in West Nile Sub-Region of Uganda.* Japan International Cooperation Agency [JICA], Tokyo, Japan.

Leonardi, C. (2020). Patchwork States: The Localization of State Territoriality on the South Sudan – Uganda Border, 1914–2014. *Past & Present,* 248(1), 209–258.

Leonardi, C. & Santschi, M. (2016). *Dividing Communities in South Sudan and Northern Uganda: Boundary Disputes and Land Governance.* Rift Valley Institute, Nairobi, Kenya.

Leopold, M. (2006). Legacies of Slavery in North-West Uganda: The Story of the 'One-Elevens'. *Journal of Africa,* 16(2), 180–199.

Leopold, M. (2020). *Idi Amin: The Story of African Icon of Evil.* Yale University Press, London, England.

Ministry of Internal Affairs. (n.d.). *Border Management.* https://immigration.go.ug/content/border-management

MoLG. (1997). *Local Government Act.* The Ministry of Local Government [MoLG], Kampala, Uganda.

Nannyonjo, J. (2001). *The HIPC Debt Relief Initiative: Uganda's Social Sector Reforms and Outcome.* WIDER Discussion Paper, 2001/138, United Nations University.

OPM. (n.d.). *Comprehensive Refugee Response Framework Uganda.* The Office of the Prime Minister [OPM]. https://opm.go.ug/comprehensive-refugee-response-framework-uganda/

Parliament of Uganda. (2020, May 13). *Arua's Porous Borders Undermining Covid-19 Fight.* www.parliament.go.ug/news/4620/arua%E2%80%99s-porous-borders-undermining-covid-19-fight

Sasaoka, Y. (2011). *Development and Politics in Global Governance.* Akashi Shoten, Japan (written in Japanese).

Ssonko, D. K. W. (2013). Decentralisation and Development: Can Uganda Now Pass the Test of Being a Role Model? *Commonwealth Journal of Local Governance,* 13/14, 31–45.

Steiner, S. (2006). *Decentralisation in Uganda: Exploring the Constraints for Poverty Reduction.* GIGA Work Paper, 31, German Institute of Global and Area Studies, Humburg, Germany.

UBOS. (2019). *Poverty Maps of Uganda – Technical Report.* Uganda Bureau of Statistics [UBOS]. https://www.ubos.org/wp-content/uploads/publications/02_2020Poverty_Map_report__Oct_2019.pdf

UBOS. (2020a, February 17). *Distribution of Poverty in Uganda Across Regions.* UBOS. https://www.ubos.org/explore-statistics/33/

UBOS. (2020b, May 23). *End of Month Population Projections 2015–2040.* UBOS. https://www.ubos.org/explore-statistics/20/UNHCR. (2018). *Comprehensive Refugee Response Framework: The Uganda Model.* United Nations High Commissioner for Refugees [UNHCR]. https://data2.unhcr.org/en/documents/download/63267#:~:text=The%20CRRF%20in%20Uganda%20encompasses,Self%2Dreliance%2C%20Expanded%20Solution%20and

UNHCR. (2020). *Refugee Data Finder.* www.unhcr.org/refugee-statistics/

UNHCR. (2021, April 30). *Refugees and Asylum-Seekers in Uganda.* https://data2.unhcr.org/en/country/uga

UNHCR. (n.d.). *Year-End Report.* https://reporting.unhcr.org/node/5129?y=2016

UN News. (2017, June 23). *More than $350 million pledged for refugees in Uganda; 'A good start, we cannot stop', says UN chief.* https://news.un.org/en/story/2017/06/560242-more-350-million-pledged-refugees-uganda-good-start-we-cannot-stop-says-un

US State Department. (2019). *Country Reports on Terrorism 2019: Uganda.* Bureau of Counterterrorism. www.state.gov/reports/country-reports-on-terrorism-2019/uganda/

West Nile Web. (n.d.). *The Region.* www.westnileweb.com/the-region

World Bank. (1998, March 20). *Report and Recommendation of the President of the IDA to the Executive Directors on Assistance to the Republic of Uganda.* The World Bank [WB], Washington, DC.

World Bank. (2016). *The Uganda: Poverty Assessment Report 2016.* The World Bank Group, Washington, DC.

World Bank. (n.d.). *GDP Per Capita (Current US$) – Uganda.* https://data.worldbank.org/indicator/NY.GDP.PCAP.CD?locations=UG

Zakaryan, T. & Antara, L. (2018). *Political Participation of Refugees: The Case of South Sudanese and Congolese Refugees in Uganda.* The International Institute for Democracy and Electoral Assistance. www.idea.int/publications/catalogue/political-participation-refugees-case-south-sudanese-and-congolese-refugees

5 Mobility as a culture in rural Africa

Yuichi Sekiya

The overlooked culture

It is clear from many previous studies and research surveys that the immigrant lifestyle has taken root as a culture in Africa. However, there do not seem to be many articles that clearly show this fact in the context of the current situation of various African societies. The fact that the mobility of African societies has been overlooked in research agendas may be due to the fact that it is known both diachronically and synchronically. Examples include the migration of labour from Africa to the Americas and other regions brought about by the Atlantic slave trade that lasted for more than 300 years from the 16th century, the subsequent great migration of people of black descent in the Americas, and the ongoing migration of people from Africa to the American continent for various reasons. In this chapter, I will discuss how mobility as a culture is entrenched in African societies, focusing on mobility in rural communities in three African countries.

At the outset, I will discuss the current situation where mobility as a culture has taken hold in various rural communities and is accepted as fairly common practice. Next, I will discuss the various circumstances that support the current situation of many migrant workers from rural Africa. This will be followed by a discussion of how rural communities maintain their functions while this mobile culture is prevalent. As specific examples, I will refer to relevant phenomena in Niger, Malawi, and Kenya. Then, I will discuss how mobility as a culture can be the focal point again. Finally, I will discuss future challenges for the study of rural Africa where mobility and sedentariness coexist.

Mobility as a culture in rural Africa

In the social sciences, mobility is a contemporary paradigm that explores the movement of people (human migration, individual mobility, travel, transport), ideas (communication), and things (transport), as well as the broader social implications of these movements. Mobility can also be thought of as the movement of people through social classes, social mobility or income, or income mobility. In John Urry's influential essay, mobility is divided into five types: mobility of objects, corporeal mobility, imaginative mobility, virtual mobility,

DOI: 10.4324/9781003202318-5

and communicative mobility (Urry 2007). Especially in sociology, there was reaffirmation of the mobility of society and its influence spread to anthropology. The subject of qualitative research has been the society that settles, and the people and things that move around have been kept in a black box. The importance of the reaffirmation of mobility was to realize this fact.

Urry's trial of establishing and stabilizing the mobility paradigm still seems to be controversial in the drastically changing world situation. However, by using Urry's mobility theory as a hint, I would like to point out in this chapter that the mobility paradigm is taking a turn, not only in sociology but also in anthropology. As a starting point, whereas the livelihood of people in rural Africa has traditionally been treated as static, I will attempt to reconsider the topic from a more dynamic perspective in which sedentariness and mobility coexist.

It goes without saying that much attention has been paid to the mobility of rural Africa historically. For example, research on indigenous trade and markets – already a classic in African anthropology – has shown that slaves, local products, and imported goods from outside the continent have historically been distributed through indigenous trade routes and markets in Africa. Another example is the Tenth International African Seminar that was held at Fourah Bay Collage Freetown in December 1969 under the chairmanship of Claude Meillassoux of the French National Centre for Scientific Research (CNRS). At this seminar, scholars of various disciplines discussed the development of indigenous trade and markets in West Africa. The focus of the seminar was the development of indigenous trade and markets in West Africa. Research papers and discussion covered both French- and English-speaking territories. They were organized according to the following main themes: precolonial trade and politics, trading areas and market centres, the interrelations of trade and social organization, long-distance trade and the development of specialized trading groups, the adaptation of African economies and trade to 19th century changes in the European markets on the coast, the impact of modern capitalism on African trade, and comparative review of the spheres and categories of African trade. The seminar was a breakthrough in the academic world because leading anthropologists, economists, and historians of the time gathered to discuss the results of their various studies on indigenous African trade and market networks.

As Meillassoux concluded in his introduction, the seminar was successful in renewing scientific interest in indigenous trade and markets in the region. As a result, the seminar left participants with several important findings. Firstly, it freed anthropology from its exaggerated focus on the study of apparently isolated societies resting on institutions that, in this context, appeared to be more ideal than functional. Secondly, it disclosed a history that was not limited to a few human groups but instead linked together millions of men faced with the need to adapt their institutions to new and pressing circumstances. Thirdly, it revealed the political dimensions of these contacts and the impact of the conveyance of goods and wealth across an entire continent. Finally, it demonstrated the compelling relationship between the African and European economies; this relationship was never simply one of the dualities from the outset (Meillassoux 1971).

The discussion on mobility in Africa at the international seminar held about half a century ago addressed the question of how to capture the dynamism of rural Africa, rather than mobility itself. A major academic concern was how to understand the social and cultural changes brought about by external pressures, such as social changes since the invasion of Arab societies, the slave trade by Europeans, and the subsequent colonial situation, along with the traditional ways of being. It was important that the dynamic aspects of historical change could be more clearly depicted by promoting interdisciplinary research.

However, attention to the fact that rural Africa is a highly mobile and sedentary society has become clearer from various ethnographic studies, and the worldview of the diverse people living in rural Africa has become clearer from a micro-perspective. The fact that African farmers are not only engaged in agriculture but also live in a wide network, travelling to and from cities, trading, and buying and selling at markets, has not been addressed until relatively recently.

As I will describe in more detail later, Paolo Gaibazzi (2015) discussed young village men in modern rural Gambia who are ethnically Soninke. Soninke people are well known as merchants who established trade between the Berber people of the Maghreb and the empires in sub-Saharan West Africa. Soninke people continue their traditional way of life in the present day. A contradictory and interesting finding from Gaibazzi's study on the descendants of Soninke people was that they remained in their village to support their mobility (Gaibazzi 2015). Since the colonization of Africa by the Western powers in the 19th century, urbanization has progressed, rural populations have moved into cities, and livelihoods have diversified. It is thought that people who had been engaged in only agriculture began to engage in commerce and other occupations in cities, establishing a mobility that was no different from that of traditional merchants. Therefore, I speculate that in Africa, the forms of livelihood of commercial and agricultural societies have diversified along with urbanization and that mobility has been established in these societies up to the present day. Traditionally, commercial, nomadic, and peasant societies have influenced each other to become more sedentary and mobile.

I have conducted rural surveys in three countries: Niger, Kenya, and Malawi. In these countries, young men at the peak of their careers often moved away from their village for work. I was in Niger for two and a half years for fieldwork, and I learned that several men never returned to their village from their place of work. The wife remained in the village and the man's family cared for the children. It was impossible to maintain such a family without a large family system. Today, boys work in various jobs in cities far away from their village, just as their fathers did, while girls stay in the village to take care of their family.

Migrant workers from rural Africa

The number of migrant workers in Africa is increasing due in part to urbanization and convenient transportation. It is well-known worldwide that many African migrants not only within but also outside the continent follow sea routes and shipping lines. According to the African Migration Report published by the International Organization for Migration (IOM) in 2020, the number of international migrants in Africa increased from 15.1 million to 26.6 million between 2000 and 2019; this is the sharpest increase (76%) among all major world regions. Thus, the share of international migrants in Africa relative to the total globally increased from 9% in 2000 to 10% in 2019.

In 2019, Eastern Africa hosted the largest share of all international migrants residing in Africa (30%), followed by Western Africa (28%), Southern Africa (17%), Middle Africa (14%), and Northern Africa (11%). However, relative to the total population, Southern Africa hosted the largest migrant population (6.7%), followed by Middle Africa (2.2%), Western Africa (1.9%), Eastern Africa (1.8%), and Northern Africa (1.2%). Seven countries in Africa hosted more than 1 million international migrants, including South Africa (4.2 million), Côte d'Ivoire (2.5 million), Uganda (1.7 million), Nigeria and Ethiopia (1.3 million each), the Sudan (1.2 million), and Kenya (1 million) (IOM 2020). These seven African countries have historically been geopolitical sites, transportation hubs, and, in many ways, migration centres. Although they are hubs of migrant networks, they are clearly more economically developed than their African neighbours, but their political situation is not necessarily stable and they face many challenges. Against this background, it must be said that the political and economic development of rural Africa is directly linked to the stable development of these hub countries.

Let me explain the increasing trends of migration in Africa from other aspects. Research on the important role of remittances sent by migrants in food security in African societies is emerging. Adebayo Ogunniyi of the International Food Policy Research Institute and his colleagues (2020) statistically analysed panel data covering 15 sub-Saharan African (SSA) countries from 1996 to 2015 and found that remittances had a positive effect on food and nutrition security. They also stressed that remittances are unpredictable in terms of frequency and value and only some households can access them. Additionally, in terms of the mobile phone revolution, another study reported that in nine SSA countries (Cameroon, the Democratic Republic of Congo, Gabon, Kenya, Madagascar, Tanzania, Uganda, Zambia, and Zimbabwe), the number of mobile money accounts has surpassed that of bank accounts due to the widespread use of mobile phones (Kanyam et al. 2017). Thus, along with Africa's growing immigrant population, there is increasingly widespread use of mobile phones and the Internet. However, the relationship between these two phenomena remains unclear. In general, it can be said that the impact of mobile phones and the Internet will substantially affect the mobility-based lifestyle in Africa, bringing about considerable change to the current situation (Aker and Mbiti 2010; Pesando et al. 2021). There is no doubt that the innovation of information technology will greatly impact both sedentariness and mobility in Africa.

Rural Africa, where sedentariness and mobility coexist

There is a question that naturally arises when considering the coexistence of sedentariness and mobility. How is rural Africa able to maintain its society even though mobility as a culture is so pervasive? According to the latest projections by the United Nations, SSA has the largest population growth rate. Its population is expected to double from 1,066 billion in 2019 to 2,118 billion in 2050, accounting for more than 30% of the world's population in 2100 (United Nations 2019).

Although urbanization is progressing rapidly along with rapid population growth, the basic form of livelihood in Africa is agriculture. Two-thirds of the African population relies on family farms for employment and food. These family farmers also substantially contribute to ecosystem preservation and environmental protection (FAO 2019a). In December 2017, the United Nations proclaimed the United Nations Decade of Family Farming (2019–2028), an initiative that will contribute to achieving its Sustainable Development Goals (FAO 2019b). Regardless of the extent of globalization's reach throughout the continent, the focal importance of family farming in Africa seems to be unchangeable (Sekiya 2019).

However, the current situation in rural Africa is far conducive to realizing a stable livelihood based on family farming. Men move to cities or other commercial farms as wage labourers, and women cultivate commodity crops in rural areas, but the commercial farmlands tend to overwhelm the family farms, and thus, farmers are unable to sustain their livelihoods based solely on family farming (Bryceson 2018).

Even though family farming was the mainstay of farming in the days of Evans-Pritchard's fieldwork in Azande and Nuer, the reality has drastically changed in contemporary rural Africa (Evans-Pritchard 1937, 1940). Accordingly, we need to focus more on the coexistence of sedentariness and mobility when analysing African farming villages.

Anthropology has elucidated the various lifestyles of African farmers, but it has also cast a keen eye on the social and cultural transformations that accompany modernization, urbanization, and globalization. However, although it is undeniable that the view of rural areas has been rather fixed, in reality, rural areas have been constantly connected to the outside world and have been changing in a very dynamic way. Here, I would like to refer back to the interesting ethnography by Paolo Gaibazzi. As mentioned previously, he focused on the descendants of the Soninke people who have settled in the rural areas of the Gambia and continue to make a living as traditional traders. "To the reader familiar with the region, associating Soninke men with non-migration might sound like an oxymoron" (Gaibazzi 2015: 5). Thus, Gaibazzi was hesitant to give a completely different perspective on the livelihood of the people of Sabi village, which was the subject of his research.

By following the sedentary lives of young men in Sabi, Gaibazzi analysed the social construction and ambivalent experience of rural permanence. The ethnography broadly proceeded along the age scale from boyhood to manhood and from individual to collective forms of "sitting": settling in a village, farming and rural dwelling, generating income, being unemployed and static, being the head of a household, and participating in age groups. Gaibazzi's ethnography of the Gambia is unique in pointing out the sedentariness of a people whose livelihood was originally based on mobility and commerce. However, as I argued at the beginning of this chapter, mobility has always been pervasive throughout African rural societies and is becoming increasingly common as communication and transportation networks improve. Against this background, it becomes clear that the youth of Sabi are not the only group trying to promote rural development by striking a new balance between mobility and sedentariness.

The cultural anthropological study of rural Africa has done much to reveal the dynamic aspects of the region from a microscopic perspective. However, in rural areas, the focus is inevitably on what locals are doing and how they are living. Those who have left rural areas for work and are not there when anthropologists conduct their research are inevitably placed in a black box. Their existence can be recognized indirectly through people's narratives, but it is difficult to get to know them directly.

Gaibazzi's ethnography weaves together diachronic and synchronic perspectives of the youth now in Sabi and those of the older generation who once left their village to work in their youth and returned or who are now living in the diaspora far from home. The ethnography captures the perspective of today's youth and what kind of life they will lead in the future to become full-fledged *Sabinkos* ("Sabi villagers" in the local language).

The dynamic way of life of the people of Sabi village is revealed in this way, partly due to the development of information and communication technology and the rapid progress in infrastructure and transportation networks in modern Africa. These advancements have made the connection between people in the distant diaspora and those who remain in the village closer than ever before. This is largely due to the fact that people in the distant diaspora are now more closely connected to those who remain in their villages. Nevertheless, Gaibazzi's careful analysis of the young people's narratives and fragments of various documents has revealed the dynamic aspects of Sabi village, where sedentariness and mobility coexist.

Next, I show how the coexistence of sedentariness and mobility that Gaibazzi found in the way of life of the Sabi people is a cultural characteristic that can be seen in other African farming villages. Also, I show how this coexistence can be analysed in the way of life of the rural people in the three African countries that I have studied as a field researcher, as mentioned previously.

Mobility as a culture in rural Niger

Twenty-five years ago, as a member of the Japan Overseas Cooperation Volunteers (JOCV), I was engaged in activities to promote greening and prevention of desertification in the Karey-Gorou region of the Republic of Niger. I was staying in the village of Yoreize-Koira, which was a relatively large farming village in the Karey-Gorou region with an estimated population of 2,500 at the time. The village was mainly an agricultural village of the Songhay-Zarma society, but the nomadic-sedentary community of the Peul society can be found around nearby sand dunes and fishermen called *sorko* can be found on the banks of the Niger River. The Tuareg people also occasionally visited the village (Sekiya 2019).

These communities were not only diverse but also only an hour's drive from the capital, Niamey. Many farmers made their living by interacting with the city. They sold surplus grain and commodity crops at the market in Niamey, and young people engaged in various trades in Niamey. Of course, some young people became civil servants or soldiers. In addition to this urban situation, many men went to work in neighbouring countries such as Mali, Ghana, Togo, and Nigeria. Migration to countries located mainly along the coastline of West Africa has long been practiced by the agrarian Songhay-Zarma society. The number of migrants has been reported to have further increased since the colonial era of the 19th century, when transportation became more convenient.

In 1956, the film *Les Maîtres Fous (The Mad Master)* was released. It is about the *Haouka*, which is a religious ceremony performed by farmers from Niger who move to Ghana to work. This film made the director, Jean Rouch, a famous visual anthropologist. *Les Maîtres Fous* is about poor Nigerien migrants working in various occupations within the power structure of the colonial context and in contact with Whites. They gather near the city of Accra on holidays to perform the *Haouka* ritual. In the ritual, they dress up as various colonial authorities, including administrators, soldiers, and commanders and dance around, imitating Western-style ceremonies. Although researchers have many theories about the meaning of this ritual, it is generally considered to be a resistance movement of the rulers against the ruled in a colonial situation. This film provides clear evidence that there was a Nigerien diaspora in Ghana since before the film was made (Rouch 1956). Diasporas are found not only in Ghana but also in other countries, including Mali and Nigeria, where Niger farmers migrate. Since these diasporas first appeared, they have served as a base for many farmers' livelihoods.

When I was staying in Yoreize-Koira, a woman cooked for me. Her husband had left for Kumasi, Ghana, to work for a long time and had not yet returned. I enjoyed her home-cooked meals for two and a half years, but never saw her husband. Her eldest son was in his late teens, her second son was 7–8 years old, and her third son was 3–4 years old. We all got along well. I casually asked the children, "When is your father coming back?" The reply was, "He should come back someday," but there was no definite answer. However, the father's presence was firmly felt, and they sometimes received letters and money from him. One day, a young man from another household in the village decided to go to Kumasi to work. I thought that he was probably going to rely on his relatives who had gone before him. After a year or so, the young man returned with many souvenirs. Importantly, however, the father of the children never returned. The children's mother died of an illness soon after I returned to Japan upon completing my term as a JOCV member. I do not know how their father is doing, but I recently found out through WhatsApp that the three children who had taken to me are now working in Ghana (the eldest), Benin (the second), and Cote d'Ivoire (the third).

I recently asked the second son who is living in Benin, "Even though you are working in Cotonou now, you will eventually return to your village, right?" He replied, "I don't really think about going back. I have a family here." However, soon after I connected with him, I received calls from his elder brother in Ghana and his younger brother in Cote d'Ivoire. Even though the brothers are living in separate countries, they are still connected with each other and probably continue to send money back to their home village. This was the case with the men of Sabi village described by Gaibazzi earlier.

In other words, even though people from nomadic tribes and agrarian societies are not from merchant societies, they have long been moving to the big cities of Africa to work, and many of them live out their lives there. However, their connection with their place of origin and the family is maintained by sending money and communication, and this communal connection continues unbroken. If we think of the village as the centre, we can see that villages cross-borders and form diasporas everywhere. Also, the village continues to exist in its original location and maintains connections with diasporas, and at the same time, the mobility of the villagers is firmly established.

Mobility as a culture in rural Malawi

I also visited Malawi to evaluate a development project. Malawi is among the world's least developed countries. The economy is heavily based on agriculture, and the population is largely rural. The Malawian government heavily depends on foreign aid to meet its development needs, although this need (and the aid offered) has decreased since 2000. The Malawian government faces challenges in building and expanding its economy, improving education, health care, and environmental protections and becoming financially independent amidst widespread unemployment. Since 2005, Malawi has developed several programmes that focus on these issues, and the country's outlook appears to be improving, with improvements in the economy, education, and health care seen in 2007 and 2008. I was involved in a mission to evaluate a small-scale rural development project by the Japan Overseas Cooperation Association (JOCA) in Malawi. JOCA is an NGO organized by former Japan International Cooperation Agency (JICA) volunteers. Its principal aim is logistical and other forms of support related to JICA's volunteer mission. However, it is also engaged in its own various cooperative projects, including the project in Malawi that was officially named "Malawi Farmer Self-sufficiency Aid Project for Better Livelihoods and the Self-Reliance of Farmers in Mzimba" (hereafter, the M project). It was launched in 2005 with the aim of improving livelihoods and systematically nurturing an attitude of self-help among smallholder farmers in the country. In 2009, the Japanese Ministry of Foreign Affairs agreed to fund the M project for three years. The project did not involve construction of facilities or provision of materials. Rather, it hoped to achieve its aim through its own initiatives to introduce appropriate farming methods that make use of locally available resources and to enhance communal activities. The third stage of the M project started in February 2014 and finally terminated in 2017.

The M project used the "farmer-to-farmer" methodology employed by JICA volunteers to achieve its aim with the Tumbuka in northern Malawi. Initially, the

M project involved only 586 households (approximately 2,930 people) in 31 villages. However, in the second stage, the number of households increased to 1,830 (approximately 9,325 people). In its final stage, the total number of beneficiaries was 6,499 households (approximately 32,495 people) in 113 villages (Sekiya 2019).

The activities of the M project to promote self-reliance among the farmers were very effective. However, I was concerned about the fact that the occupants of many households in every rural village were away on business, especially working men. Many had moved to South Africa as migrants and were sending money back to their village. According to Harvey C. Chidoba Banda (2017, 2018) and Elliott P. Niboye (2018), labour migration from Malawi to South Africa is a "century-old phenomenon." It dates as far back as the 1880s following the establishment of diamond and gold mines. In the period up to the 1980s, this migration took on either a formal or informal nature, whereas in the post-1990 period, it became exclusively informal and was popularly known as *selufu* in Malawi. The M project in northern Malawi was in the Mzimba district, which is one of the persistent senders of labour migrants to South Africa. Niboye sought to examine the socio-economic impacts of labour migration on families in the Mzimba district from various viewpoints, including education, health, labour supply, intra-family roles, norms, and decision-making. Among 27 villages in the Mzimba district, he examined eight that had the highest number of migrants. Field data were obtained through in-depth interviews, observation, and focus group discussions. Secondary data were obtained mainly through library research. The results revealed that overall, households that have migrant relatives in South Africa have experienced change in their welfare, including positive change in socio-economic household conditions and/or positive change in social relations and family relations. Negative consequences of labour migration on the remaining households included loneliness, especially for the spouse left at home; psycho-social problems, especially among children due to the absence of the father; and low esteem in the spouse to the extent of not being fully involved in familial matters. The migrant themselves lived in untenable working conditions, often illegally, and in most circumstances were unwelcome in the host country (Niboye 2018).

Let me return to discussing the M project. A woman who we interviewed during the evaluation survey kept her mobile phone on the roof. When asked why, she said that getting a signal in this location was easy, so she could receive calls from her husband who was working in South Africa. Because of such circumstances, M project often conducted training sessions to provide support to rural women's groups. Tomato jam making and other cash-generating businesses that the women became active in were also characteristic of the project.

Similar to Gambia and Niger, a large part of the rural working population in Malawi crosses the border into South Africa and other more industrialized countries to work. They try to maintain ties with their rural community while largely depending on their earnings in the host country. Thus, they develop a lifestyle in which sedentariness and mobility coexist.

CBOs with global mobility in rural Kenya

The next case is Kenya. Community-based organizations (CBOs) refer to voluntary and autonomous local self-help organizations with established rules and procedures of operation that are endogenous to a community. They are formed to address the needs of the community. In Kenya, CBOs can be broadly divided into income-generating or welfare groups whose main aim is to engage in wealth creation activities, and program-oriented organizations that set out to implement programmes in certain fields including health, agriculture, and environmental conservation (Kinyua-Njuguna 2013). CBOs became popular when the Grameen Bank founded by Muhammad Yunus became well known. Since becoming more widespread, CBOs have functioned to realize people-powered, participatory, and social development. They are principally based on people's purposes or objectives rather than on members' communal ties or relationships in rural Kenya. Firstly, I should clarify what kind of organization I consider a CBO to be based on several CBOs from Kenya and their characteristics. In Japan, they are officially referred to as nonprofit organizations (NPOs), and they engage in multipurpose activities. A CBO is generally defined as a public or private entity that uses public or private funds respectively to meet community needs. In developed countries, CBOs are organized primarily as NPOs; however, in developing countries, CBO activities involve many kinds of profit-making functions that promote self-help among residents. Statistically, the most popular activity of Japanese NPOs is social welfare for older persons or individuals with disabilities. In rural Kenya, there are a variety of CBOs, but a common characteristic of the many CBOs I visited is global activities that transcend national boundaries. There were CBOs that were established because of international development projects; many were formed to help the orphans and widows of HIV/AIDS victims in Kenya by carrying out diverse activities, such as providing jobs for persons with disabilities and unemployed youths, empowering women and widows of AIDS victims, and supporting AIDS orphans. Most of these activities were for profit. A unique case involved charging a fee for using a chair in the marketplace. One CBO raised funds by renting out these chairs.

Forming a CBO has both advantages and disadvantages. The advantages are that people can (1) open a collective bank account for their activities, (2) plan a project, (3) apply to receive public funds, and (4) apply for foreign funds. A disadvantage is that a CBO that is reliant on a single large donor becomes vulnerable if that donor withdraws its support. Another disadvantage for CBOs such as those in Kisumu is that organizational solidarity falters due to the overly diverse nature of the people who joined because of their interest in the initial objective. Several cases have clarified that it is still difficult for people from different backgrounds or societies to form a CBO together.

In 2012, I joined a JICA volunteer mission as an instructor for participatory development. The mission was a week-long programme for Japanese volunteers who had been sent to eastern and southern African countries that faced difficulties due to the involvement of local beneficiaries in their activities. Around 30 volunteers working in various African countries, including Kenya, Mozambique,

Ethiopia, and Malawi, gathered for a week in Nairobi to join the training program. We contacted several local Kenyan CBOs to collaborate with us in this training program. The CBOs detailed their problems and formed working groups in collaboration with the Japanese volunteers to find solutions and devise action plans. From the perspective of the CBOs, this programme provided a good opportunity to find practical solutions for problematic issues with help from various Japanese volunteers. However, the Japanese volunteers who were supported by the Kenyan CBOs devised their own activities for international development. We can therefore see that African CBOs have recently been helping Japanese volunteers in terms of international development (Sekiya 2019).

This case study on the CBOs in rural Kenya demonstrates that in rural Kenya, CBOs have been established by residents to meet the needs of health promotion, livelihood improvement, and economic revitalization. We can see that these CBOs are already working to engage in international networking and exchange. In other words, citizens are using their networks across borders to distribute goods, raise funds, and exchange human resources. When we look at rural Africa in the context of development assistance, we have been conscious only of its sedentariness and we have been thinking a priori about the relationship between the people who settle in rural areas and the aid workers who come from outside to provide development assistance. However, the reality is more dynamic, and we are reminded that those who settle in rural areas are already making a living while maintaining a network with the outside world. In other words, they have had mobility from the outset.

Mobility as a culture for structural transformation

Statistics show that 70% of immigrants on the African continent migrate to a different country than their country of origin (UNDESA 2015). It should be noted that this is a far cry from the illusion of mass migration from Africa to the European continent that has been created by the media in recent years. SSA thus has the second largest share of intra-regional migration globally, with 63% of all migrants born in SSA living in another country or area in the region in 2020. Refugees and asylum seekers comprise around one-third of all international migrants within SSA, which points to a complex array of factors, including humanitarian ones, and shapes migration movements in the region (UNDESA 2020).

However, this does not mean that the number of migrants from Africa to the rest of the continent is small. It is true that the number of immigrants to European countries and the Americas, as well as to Asian countries, is increasing year by year. It is also true that there are more immigrants from Africa in China and Japan than ever before. However, we should realize that, as the statistics show, it is overwhelmingly African migrants who have found work, formed and expanded diasporas, and entrenched sedentariness and mobility as cultural modes within the African continent. In contrast, studies on the African immigrant diaspora in Europe, America, and Asia are quite numerous and well read, whereas studies on immigrants who have moved from one African country to another are scarce or have not received much attention. Many migrants must have formed diasporas in neighbouring African countries not only for economic reasons but also because of changes in the natural environment or conflicts.

Until 2020, when the coronavirus disease 2019 (COVID-19) pandemic began, the world's migrant population was growing. Most of the immigrant population moving in and out of SSA was from within Africa. Of course, there were a few migrants from western Asia and northern Africa, but in general, African migrants form networks and diasporas in neighbouring African countries. The case of the Gambian farmers who were extending their migration network in Europe, as mentioned in Gaibazzi's ethnography, is statistically in the minority. The latest trend analysis by Sara Mercandalli and Bruno Losch (2019) shows that most migrants from rural Africa are farmers moving from rural areas to other rural areas, although in the past, there has been a large rural-to-urban influx. From a micro-perspective, the analysis shows that the reasons for migration are not only work, education, and family reasons but unfortunately also natural disasters, conflicts, and other undesirable reasons. The analysis concludes that migration or mobility as a culture is embedded in the process of structural transformation (Mercandalli and Losch 2019). Despite regional variation, historical evidence reminds us that the internal and international mobility of people goes hand in hand with productivity growth; that is, there is intersectoral transfer of labour and urbanization. Globally, people have been moving from rural areas to other places – generally cities and sometimes other countries. However, this pervasive mobility does not undermine, but rather maintains or enhances, the sedentariness of rural Africa. The rural Gambian youth featured in Gaibazzi's article seem to continue to maintain their rural Gambian identity after all.

In the case of the Niger farmers I discussed earlier, they continued to work in the diaspora to which they had been historically linked and in some cases spent their entire lives supporting their families in the diaspora. They continued to send money and keep in touch with their village of origin and maintained their diaspora networks. In the case of Malawi, the Mzimba people have built South Africa on a history of migrant immigration that has continued throughout the century. However, they have managed to remain mobile and have settled without severing ties with their rural village of origin. In terms of the history of migrant workers, it can be said that they have faced both the good and bad aspects of migration while making gradual changes over time.

The recent development of information and communication technologies has led to remarkable structural transformation in rural Africa. The case of the CBOs in Kenya illustrates this very well. Kenyan CBOs are using the latest communication technology to form international networks to raise funds, sell products, and even exchange human resources.

Interplay of the three dimensions of rural African issues

So far, we can see that rural Africa is facing structural transformation with mobility as culture and that this transformation is becoming increasingly complex and diverse. If we are to properly analyse the situation of this complex and diverse structural transformation, then keeping focus on how rural Africa maintains a balance between mobility and sedentariness in their culture is especially important. I have discussed this point to some extent in this chapter.

In the past, anthropological studies of rural Africa have focused on sedentariness and mobility separately. However, in reality, sedentariness and mobility have been coexisting in the same rural area, and few qualitative studies focus on this rather contradictory coexistence. The coexistence of sedentariness and mobility is easy to explain in words but is exceedingly difficult to realize in practice. The cases I have discussed, including the Soninke in Gambia, the Songhay-Zarma in Niger, the Tumbuka in Malawi, and the CBOs in Kenya, are not without their problems. Many of these problems cannot be easily solved, such as the decline of the rural labour force and development due to the outflow of many migrant workers, issues with the host society at the destination, unemployment and deportation, accidents during migration, and problems during remittance and transportation of goods.

With regard to the events in various African countries that have been discussed in this chapter, there is an important task for researchers who wish to deepen their understanding of the structural transformation of rural Africa today. They must depict the livelihoods and lifestyles practiced by rural communities and people in terms of sedentariness and mobility and consider how the two coexist. For example, it would be interesting to examine from the perspectives of people from the same farming village what kind of life they lead in their host country and how they maintain ties with their farming village. In addition, it would be interesting to capture a bird's-eye view of the historical ties between diaspora in the host country and the farming village of origin.

In Mercandalli and Losch's (2019) analysis of patterns, drivers, and relation to structural transformation of the rural migration in SSA, various factors were divided into three different levels (micro = individual and household; meso = a community or a region; and macro = global). They further attempted to analyse mutual interaction among the three levels. They stated that "the framework considers that the many drivers that initiate, orient, and sustain migration at micro-, meso-, and macro-levels do not operate in isolation. Instead, drivers work in combination, and their effects are intertwined in what can be called drivers complexes" (Mercandalli and Losch 2019: 25). Therefore, it is important to deepen discussion on how the same society and people maintain their livelihoods and lifestyles while confronting a variety of micro-, meso-, and macro-levels, and how the three layers intersect.

To evaluate the dynamism of the African border region, Gregor Dobler discussed about the typology of cross-border trade. By analysing the historical development of African state borders' social and economic relevance, Dobler presented a typology of cross-border trade in Africa, differentiating trade across the "green" border of bush paths and villages, the "gray" border of roads, railways, and border towns, and the "blue" border of transport corridors to oceans and airports. The three groups of actors associated with these types of trade have competing visions of the ideal border regime, to which many dynamics in African cross-border politics can be traced back. Dobler argued that the interplay between these three types of trade crucially characterizes borderland dynamics in Africa today (Dobler 2016).

Dobler's typology and his way of analysing borderland dynamics provides an effective hint for understanding the dynamic transformation faced by rural Africa. Dobler parted actors into three groups accordingly to his typology, but I would like to consider what happens if we think that the same society or people face the three types of borders in different situations of their life. With regard to what I have discussed in this chapter about the coexistence of sedentariness and mobility in rural Africa and its people, it is important to think about how the issues divided into the three levels of micro, meso, and macro will interplay and about the kinds of problems that exist, as discussed by Dobler regarding the borderlands in Africa.

For example, on a micro-level, the three Niger children that I came to know are now personally earning money, doing business in a foreign city far away from their homeland. They are sending money back and also supporting their families in the places they have migrated to, living a vibrant life. The money they send back home and the networks they build in the cities where they work are a valuable source of income and human resources for the meso-level village of Yoreize-Koira and Niger. The income and human resources contribute to the sustainable development of their rural communities. Furthermore, from a macro-level perspective, we can see how they are surviving with the coexistence of sedentariness and mobility as the driving force behind the productivity of modern African farming villages. Further research studies will be needed to continue this discussion.

References

Aker, J. C. and Mbiti, I. M. (2010). Mobile Phones and Economic Development in Africa. *Journal of Economic Perspectives*, Vol. 24, Issue 3, 207–232. http://dx.doi.org/10.1257/jep.24.3.207.

Banda, H. (2017). *Perspectives of Labour Migration from Mzimba District, Malawi, to South Africa*, Langaa Rpcig.

Banda, H. (2018). *Migration from Malawi to South Africa: A Historical & Cultural Novel*, Langaa Rpcig.

Bryceson, D. (2018). Gender and Generational Patterns of African Deagrarianization: Evolving Labour and Land Allocation in Smallholder Peasant Household Farming, 1980–2015. *World Development*, Vol. 113, 60–72. https://doi.org/10.1016/j.worlddev.2018.08.021.

Dobler, G. (2016). The Green, the Grey and the Blue: A Typology of Cross-Border Trade in Africa. *The Journal of Modern African Studies*, Vol. 54, 145–169.

Evans-Pritchard, E. E. (1937). *Witchcraft, Oracles and Magic Among the Azande*, Clarendon Press.

Evans-Pritchard, E. E. (1940). *The Nuer: A Description of the Mode of Livelihood and Political Institutions of a Nilotic People*, Clarendon Press.

FAO. (2019a). "Family Farming in Africa" on the Family Farming Knowledge Platform Web Site. www.fao.org/family-farming/regions/africa/en/ (Accessed June 28th 2019).
FAO. (2019b). United Nations Decade of Family Farming 2019–2028 Global Action Plan. www.fao.org/3/ca4672en/ca4672en.pdf (Accessed June 28th 2019).
Gaibazzi, P. (2015). *Bush Bound: Young Men and Rural Permanence in Migrant West Africa*, Berghahns.
IOM. (2020). *Africa Migration Report: Challenging the Narrative*, International Organization for Migration (IOM).
Kanyam, D., Kostandini, G. and Ferreira, S. (2017). The Mobile Phone Revolution: Have Mobile Phones and the Internet Reduced Corruption in Sub-Saharan Africa? *World Development*, Vol. 99, 271–284. http://dx.doi.org/10.1016/j.worlddev.2017.05.022.
Kinyua-Njuguna, J. (2013). *Strategic Social Marketing, Operating Environment and Performance of Community Based HIV and AIDS Organizations in Nairobi County, Kenya*, A Doctoral Thesis Submitted to the School of Business, University of Nairobi.
Meillassoux, C. (Ed.) (1971). *The Development of Indigenous Trade and Markets in West Africa*, Oxford University Press.
Mercandalli, S. and Losch B. (Eds.) (2019). *Rural Migration in Sub-Saharan Africa: Patterns, Drivers and Relation to Structural Transformation*, Food and Agriculture Organization of the United Nations.
Niboye, E. P. (2018). International Labour Out-Migration in Mzimba District, Malawi: Why Persistent? *International Journal of Research in Geography*, Vol. 4, Issue 2, 9–21. http://dx.doi.org/10.20431/2454-8685.0402002.
Ogunniyi, A. I., Mavrotas, G., Olagunju, K. O., Fadare, O. and Adedoyin, R., (2020). Governance quality, remittances and their implications for food and nutrition security in Sub-Saharan Africa. *World Development*, Elsevier, 127(C). https://doi.org/10.1016/j.worlddev.2019.104752.
Pesando, L.M., Rotondi, V., Stranges, M., Kashyap, R. and Billari, F.C. (2021). The Internetization of International Migration. Population and Development Review, 79–111. https://doi.org/10.1111/padr.12371.
Rouch, J. (1956). Les maîtres fous. *Jean Rouch* (DVD), Editions Montparnasse.
Sekiya, Y. (2019). Cultural Forms of Organization: Importance of Learning Process and Human Empowerment for Sustainable Development in Modern Africa. *African Study Monographs*, Suppl. 58, 69–92.
UNDESA. (2015). *Trends in International Migrant Stock: Migrants by Destination and Origin*, United Nations.
UNDESA. (2020). *International Migration 2020 Highlights* (ST/ESA/SER.A/452).
United Nations. (2019). *World Population Prospects*. https://population.un.org/wpp/ (Accessed April 29th 2021).
Urry, J. (2007). *Mobilities*, Polity Press.

6 Micro-regionalism in Southern Africa[1]

Yuichi Sasaoka

The necessity of regional cooperation is well recognized, but the theoretical foundations of the arguments for regionalism and regional cooperation are mainly based on European models (Bøås et al., 2003). In this chapter, the author aims to determine whether a non-European model can be established in Southern Africa as an alternative. Firstly, the African civil society and informal sector perspectives have been recognized as counterarguments to the *top-down development* approach since the 1990s. However, the concept of civil society is derived from European societies, so it has been suggested by some scholars that its application in African societies would not be valid (Chabal & Daloz, 1999). The actual structure of African civil society therefore needs to be captured. Secondly, micro-regional views have existed since around the year 2000, mainly in the *development corridors* that link Southern African states (Soderbaum & Taylor, 2001). This stream of thought was recently highlighted by the NEPAD, and the possibility of a model of regionalism promoted by a state and interstate framework thus exists. Another aspect of micro-regionalism is transnationalism, and the interpenetration of neighbouring societies is an important ingredient. We need to understand whether specific micro-regionalism is driven by state actors or NSAs and which intervention is greater. From the viewpoint of national interests, micro-regionalism can be linked to the interests of the political elite. As is often the case, the transnational civil society argument is not free from such a messy state involvement.

This chapter analyses the development corridors in Southern Africa, especially those involving Mozambique, from the viewpoint of civil society. Many development corridors occur across state borders, so arguments in regarding micro-regionalism and the management of state borders are relevant. Development corridors can link up ports, mineral resource areas, industrial estates, and forests and are also called economic corridors or resource corridors. The most prominent corridors in Africa are the Maputo development corridor (MDC), the Walvis Bay Development Corridor, and the Tri-national Dja – Odzala – Minkebe (TRIDOM) in Cameroon, the Republic of Congo, and the Republic of Gabon. MDC is considered the most successful corridor and links the Gauteng, Limpopo, and Mpumalanga provinces in South Africa and Maputo, the port city

DOI: 10.4324/9781003202318-6

and Capital of Mozambique. The author will then examine MDC and the other corridors in Mozambique.

South Africa's economic power in the Southern African region is strong. South Africa alone occupies half of the GDP of the 15 member countries of the Southern African Development Community (SADC). South Africa has cherished the idea of the Spatial Development Initiative (SDI) for a long time and has promoted micro-regionalism in Southern Africa. SDI was the encompassing vision for resource development and industrial policy along with development corridors. This idea was promoted by the South African Department of Transport and Industry under the leadership of the neoliberalist former President Mbeki and formulated following bitter lessons learned in the 1990s where SADC tended to spur traffic infrastructure policies only along the development corridors and to ignore industrial policies. MDC was one of SDIs that South Africa used to try to upgrade cooperation with its neighbour. Maputo is a good port, faces the Southwestern Indian Ocean, and is located in a very strategic place. MDC facilitates exports from South Africa and imports into Mozambique. Notably, however, the former value is 120 times larger than the latter (Bowland & Otto, 2012).

Mozambique gained independence from Portugal in 1975, and Frente de Libertacao de Mozambique (Frelimo), a former military group, became the ruling party and advocated socialism. Resistencia Nacional Mocambicana (Renamo), a former military group and opposition party, was created in South Rhodesia to collapse Frelimo when Mozambique tried to block South Rhodesian trade on the coast (Funada, 2008). After South Rhodesia became Zimbabwe in 1980, South Africa assumed South Rhodesia's role by supporting the military group, and it was then named Resistencia Nacional Mocambicana. Renamo's ruling area was the northern part of Mozambique. When the Cold War ended, Frelimo abandoned Marx – Leninism, and apartheid ended in South Africa. The battles between Frelimo and Renamo stopped, and a peace accord was reached in 1992. Following the intrastate war, Frelimo won the first election. South Africa tried to change its antagonistic position against Frelimo and started working on cooperation projects. One of the important projects was the revamping of MDC. South Africa was also involved in the civil war in Angola, which ended in 2002, 10 years longer than civil war in Mozambique.

MDC gained everybody's attention in the region due to its size and economic effects. This corridor extends 150 km and was developed by the World Bank and private financial investments (PFI), including foreign ones, based on a bilateral agreement in 1995. It is an enormous program comprising a toll road between the two countries, key infrastructure facilities, and industrial estates. MDC is considered a pioneering model in the region. However, the subsequent corridor plans did not progress steadily since there were some problems with the underlying philosophy. The origin of MDC was the agreement signed in 1897 between Portugal and the (then) Republic of Transvaal, which existed until the early 20th century. This agreement provided Mozambican labor to the gold mines in the Transvaal on a continuous basis, while Transvaal government promised to export half of its products through the MDC via the Maputo port. Mozambique was one of the countries supplying labor to South Africa, but the number of emigrant workers declined during the apartheid era. After apartheid, the number of workers suddenly increased, and about 340,000 legal emigrant workers were dispatched to South Africa in 1996 (Niemann, 1998). In the early 20th century, South Africa produced a quarter of the world's gold, and Mozambique provided 80% of the gold mining labour. MDC was a route for the steady supply of labor and gold exports transfer. Thus, the colonial-time agreement was revived as an advanced case of micro-regionalism.

The position of the MDC

Mozambique is a coastal country and has various corridor plans linking it to neighbouring inland countries. The major plans are MDC, the Beira Development Corridor (BDC), and the Nacala Development Corridor (NDC). BDC links Beira port in Mozambique with Mutare, a city in Zimbabwe, and NDC links the port of Nacala in Mozambique with Malawi and Zambia. Three corridors are positioned in Mozambique in a balanced way: MDC is located in the south, NDC is located in the north, and BDC is located centrally. Mozambique had been a Portuguese colony since the 16th century. This rule continued until Portugal was democratized in the 1970s. Mozambique had not only had a vertical relationship with Portugal but also a special relationship with South Africa, a sub-imperialist in the region (Aminaka, 2007). South Africa was quite dominant and located in the central position of the region. This sub-imperialism laid the foundation of today's interstate relations in Southern Africa. Portugal was not only a suzerain state but also a debtor country in the imperialist 19th century context. Its colonial policy attempted to sell the colony by piece: in the northern and central parts of Mozambique, chartered companies handled everything from the police to tax collection, and their budget was derived from gold industries. In the southern part, Mozambique was a colony, and Portugal had a labor agreement with the Transvaal (Denoon, 2009).

The present MDC program consists of the N4 toll road between Johannesburg and Maputo. This road was reconstructed on a build – operate – transfer (BOT) basis through a 30-year contract with a private consortium comprising South African, French, and Mozambican companies. The Maputo port was recently refurbished, and its handling cargo volumes amounted to 20 million tons in 2018. This refurbishment was entrusted to the private consortium. Along with the toll road, there is also a railway, which is administered by Transnet, a part of the railroad and port agency of South Africa. The aluminium refinery Mozal, the third largest in the world, is located 20 km from Maputo, and this consortium was financed by the Australian South 32, the Japanese Mitsubishi Corporation, the South African Industrial Development Corporation, and the Mozambican government. Maputo has become one of Africa's major industrial areas given its factories and infrastructure facilities.

Soderbaum and Taylor (2008) compared formal and informal micro-regionalism to investigate the meaning of today's MDC. Formal micro-regionalism usually means top-down implementation of the government's priority programs and its related institutional building. Furthermore, the invitation of private investment is guided by neoliberal government policies, and this genuine partnership limits part of the government's sovereignty due to the existence of bilateral agreements. Informal micro-regionalism refers to ordinary people and vendors' trade and traffic of any kind, including that occurring without the government's permission. When vendors on the MDC are excluded because of the toll road, they cross the state border over the fence using any means, putting themselves at risk and potentially sacrificing their lives. Given this situation, Soderbaum and Taylor (2008) attempted to determine who benefits from the corridor. They observed that some people were positively affected by the presence of the corridor while others were not. They noted that the economic disparities between South Africa and Mozambique determined the character of the corridor and pointed out that MDC was a *top-down development*. It thus lacked the vision of a bottom-up approach that could induce townspeople into the development process.

The purpose of SDI for South Africa was to produce economic growth and development in accordance with local potentiality, to provide stable employment for local people and the nation, and to advance regional cooperation by utilizing private investment. MDC, the first case of SDI, induced foreign investment and restricted government spending. Thus, MDC became a good example of a public–private partnership (PPP), and the positive effects were confirmed through the national economy by virtue of increased trade volumes between the two countries.

However, this program has faced many challenges. Capital-intensive factories around MDC have limited the job creation effects, and the spill-over effects of MDC into agriculture and tourism have also been limited. Informal traders tend to be shut out from the corridor, and smuggled goods from South Africa have delivered a serious blow to the local economy in Mozambique. According to an expert in industry enterprises, if you want to make a product in Mozambique, almost all the materials and even its packaging will need to be imported from South Africa (interview, 2019). Moreover, issues such as the low capacity of the railroad infrastructure, soaring prices of transportation, and imbalanced bilateral trade are considered key problems. Part of the body running MDC was intended to be decentralized from the central government to the provinces, and it has not yet been realized (Soderbaum & Taylor, 2001), but at present, for example, Mpumalanga province maintains MDC project components. The relations between South Africa and Mozambique have nevertheless developed favorably, and MDC has become a symbol of the two countries' relations.

South Africa formed the Southern African Customs Union (SACU) with Botswana, Lesotho, and Eswatini in 1910 and implemented a common tariff policy with these inland countries. Moreover, the South African Rand was used as the common currency. In the Cold War period, Malawi supported the apartheid policy, and the white South Rhodesian government itself implemented the policy. Mozambique opposed to the policy with Zambia and Tanzania following independence. However, when the African National Congress (ANC) won the 1994 elections in South Africa and abolished apartheid, a cooperation commission was established between South Africa and Mozambique. A bilateral economic forum was established in 1997, and minister-level meetings were held regularly. The trade and investment relationships between the two countries have since improved and intensified, without SACU type agreement, and Mozambican workers continue to emigrate to South Africa.

Top-down development history

MDC has influenced SDI approach in Southern Africa, and further top-down development has been facilitated since its inception. Although many SDI plans were proposed, the majority of the plans were not realized. A reason for the slow pace of implementation of SDI plans seemed to be apartheid's negative antecedents. Apartheid policy aimed to divide the living spaces of people based on the criterion of race, where black people were forced to live in the so-called homelands. The South African government has therefore felt uneasy dividing the space and promoting region-specific development in the post-apartheid period since 1994 (Robbins, 2008). Acceptable SDIs have included the Industrial Development Zones (IDZs), which invited large private investment and transborder corridors like MDG. However, in the case of the transborder SDIs such as the Walvis Bay Development Corridor, multilateral negotiations were needed in the planning stages, and the negotiations were not easy. South Africa was not incentivized to deliver products from neighbouring inland countries to its ports, and the division of labor beyond nation state has not progressed due to the slow pace of diversification of industrial and export goods in the region (Beer et al., 1999).

The most serious bottleneck of MDC has undoubtedly been the lack of communication between the various stakeholders. The South African government talked with a few dozen investors and ministry officials about this large-scale development project but did not convene consultation meetings with the local population (Mitchell, 1998). The provincial government of Mpumalanga tried to set up a comprehensive communication strategy with the local people to resolve the issues, but the meeting was postponed due to a change in leadership (ibid.). The toll charges for the use of N4 were therefore not announced to local people and informal sector vendors. Local people living along the corridor near Nelspruit, the provincial capital city, and other places were thus suddenly required to pay for use of the road on their way to schools, offices, hospitals, and shopping areas. People were embarrassed and became angry, so stakeholder consultations were held, and it was decided that a subsidy would be allocated to local people to reduce their financial burden. Shaw (1999) called this situation the *democracy deficit*.

Arguments in support of the development corridor were expressed gradually by AU, SADC, AfDB, World Bank, and the US and Japanese governments. These donors were positive about economic growth rather than poverty reduction which was the net transfer to poverty priority sectors. They subsequently felt compelled to shift course when they saw China had started to pour money into infrastructure development in Africa on a massive scale. In 2009, the Japanese government expressed interest in promoting development corridors, especially NDC, via an assistance program to Mozambique. The Japanese government and the Japan International Cooperation Agency (JICA) decided to implement ProSavana, a tropical agricultural development project, through a triangular cooperation scheme with Brazil and Mozambique, to formulate a master plan called the Project for Nacala Corridor Economic Development Strategy (PEDEC-Nacala), and to design the entire program and its components (Oriental Consultants, 2014). PEDEC-Nacala aimed to serve as the foundational strategy from which to invite appropriate development and investment into NDC, to analyse its promotive and restrictive factors, and to start a variety of project component investigations (ibid.).

JICA held a side-event seminar on the development corridor for African economic growth at the fifth meeting of the Tokyo International Conference in African Development (TICAD) in 2013. On the African side, then President Guebuza of Mozambique, the Mozambican Minister of Agriculture, the Malawian Minister of Economic Planning and Development, and the CEO of NEPAD made speeches on the importance of development corridors. Thereafter, the Mozambican, Malawian, and Brazilian governments and JICA explained NDC. The following year, Japanese Prime Minister Abe visited Mozambique with a private sector mission and emphasized the expansion of investment through PPPs. In a joint statement by President Guebuza and Prime Minister Abe, Japanese aid amounting to 70 billion yen in official development assistance (ODA) was pledged, with a focus on infrastructure, such as road, port, electricity, and industrial development, based on the strategic master plan of NDC (Ministry of Foreign Affairs [MoFA], 2014).

NDC agricultural project undertaken by Brazil and JICA received recognition as a model (Collier & Dercon, 2014), but NGOs in Mozambique, Brazil, and Japan, as well as a group of researchers, expressed concern about the expulsion of small-scale farmers from their homes. Funada (2014) explained that land deprivation had become a serious issue for farmers and environmental groups around the year 2010. She had also started a campaign around that time when she had noticed the problem with ProSavana. When she saw the working plan, there was no reference to the rights of inhabitants, the issue of deforestation, or environmental care. In 2012, Uniao Nacional de Camponeses (UNAC) issued a statement criticizing ProSavana planning and implementation method, which had tended to exclude civil society organizations (CSOs) at every stage of the development process. Mozambican farmers' associations and CSOs could participate in the meetings, but they received only monotonous responses from the government. UNAC stated that ProSavana situation had resulted from a *top-down development* policy that had not paid attention to the farmer's needs, prospects, and concerns. They denounced the initiative to relocate the community and to expropriate farmers' land to realize large-scale monoculture projects. The Japanese NGO Japan Volunteer Center (JVC) continued to sensitize public opinion on this issue. NDC demonstrates the revival of the *top-down development* that occurred in MDC.

ProSavana is an agricultural development project covering 14 million hectares (ha) along NDC in the Niassa, Nampula, and Zambezia provinces. The Japanese agricultural land was estimated to be 4.5 million ha in total in 2015. This project's prototype was an agricultural project undertaken by Brazil and Japan in Cerrado, Brazil. The Cerrado project realized large-scale monoculture commercial agriculture and enabled Brazil to become a grain-exporting country. Nevertheless, it was criticized because of the expulsion of indigenous people and the ensuing environmental degradation. Recently, land enclosure has been facilitated by the use of foreign capital through funds like the US pension fund (Vasquez, 2019). At present, small-scale farmers are at risk of being expelled from their homelands all over the world (United Nations Human Right Council, 2019). By comparison, there is no land market in Mozambique, and the population density in ProSavana project area is much higher than that in Cerrado (Horn, 2018). Large-scale development projects integrate many people's lands, and small-scale farmers may be expelled unless they become tenants. UNAC, an environmental NGO called Justicia Ambiental, and a researcher group started a campaign against ProSavana that targeted corruption scandals involving President Guebuza, Frelimo's top leaders, and foreign investors (Madeleine, 2011). They pointed out that foreign companies were colluding with local companies to obtain large-scale tracts of land. Several thousand people lost their land rights even though the government had promised these farmers that they would reap the benefits of the corridor development. This set of events also seemed to be a revival of Portugal's colonialism (UNAC & GRAIN, 2015). The plantation land that the Portuguese landlords relinquished the right in 1975 had been returned to local farmers. Under the Mozambican land law, if farmers wanted to continue cultivating their land, they could claim entitlements. However, the government condemned the land so that it could be lent it to foreign companies or foreign companies could purchase the land directly from farmers at very low prices.

Brazil's involvement in NDC seems to have been diminishing in recent times. There are several reasons for this: the decline of the international investment boom in the agribusiness sector due to lowered future commodities prices, the anti-ProSavana campaign conducted through the international cooperation of CSOs and academics, and reconsideration of the necessity of large-scale development projects (Shankland & Goncalves, 2016). Moreover, Brazil's Temer administration had been promoting land enclosure using foreign capital since 2016, and the policy direction of large-scale agricultural projects was rearranged in favor of domestic ones. Foreign companies involved in land enclosure in NDC were manifold, comprising returned Portuguese landlords, European and Mozambican companies in joint ventures, South African and Brazilian companies, Mauritian government, and a paper company with a tax haven address (UNAC & GRAIN, 2015). Mozambique's non-concessional loan share has been growing, and the debt per GDP ratio has risen to over 60%. Furthermore, former President Guebuza's non-disclosure debt issue was revealed in 2016. IMF's lending policy to Mozambique was suddenly stiffened, but the Ministry of Economy and Finance has been consulting with creditor groups to try to arrange a debt repayment schedule by putting up the future revenues of natural gas fields as collateral. However, it was suddenly announced that ProSavana project was terminated by both Japanese and Mozambican governments in July 2020, after many criticisms on the human rights violation and communication manipulation.

In a proposal by the Norwegian fertilizer company Yara in 2008, BDC was envisioned to yield agricultural production across 10 million ha. Yara is the world's biggest agribusiness company and was expecting a green revolution in Africa. BDC was discussed at the World Economic Forum (WEF) in Davos in 2009 when the then-Mozambican Prime Minister Diogo explained the importance of PPPs. In the same year, the government established a secretariat to construct industrial free zones and special economic zones and set up the Agriculture Promotion Center to facilitate PPPs. This center has the specific role of providing advice to foreign investors when they try to expropriate land from farmers. This development vision can be traced back to the South African SDI approach at the time of MDC proposal (Kaarhus, 2018). BDC starts at the port of Beira and has two main routes: the Machipanda railway line to Zimbabwe and Zambia and the Sena railway line to Malawi. However, interest from the Norwegian side has since faded although the Mozambicans have remained very positive. Soil and water quality testing conducted by Yara in 2010 for a factory site revealed that the construction costs would be very high (Kaarhus, 2018).

The Mozambique Ministry of Transport and Communications did not relinquish BDC development plan and continued to hold investment meetings in Beira. N6 road linking the Beira port and Zimbabwe has subsequently been rehabilitated using Chinese financial assistance. There are plans for Sena line to be rehabilitated, and part of the line will be double-tracked in response to the growing demand for coal transportation from Tete Province (JETRO, 2015). The Norwegian embassy has invested in agribusiness projects through BDC catalytic fund, and the United Kingdom and the Netherlands have joined the fund. The center of these activities has been Manica Province. There used to be public farming when Portugal ran the plantations during the colonial period, but this was privatized by the government in 1989. The land was mainly sold to Frelimo and government elites, and they became absentee landlords. Some Zimbabwean farmers who escaped the confiscation of white-owned farms have settled there (Kaarhus, 2018).

As demonstrated through these development scenes in the corridors, *top-down development* clearly differentiates between the beneficiary and the victim, and external resources tend to be linked to concessions for power elites through unclear channels. This composition is akin to the relationship between the actors in the center and the periphery advocated in *dependency theory* in the 1970s (Frank, 1977). While the Mozambican government has tried to introduce foreign capital and set up public institutions, the power elites and government have controlled their vested interests through joint ventures and affiliated companies with foreign capital. In a formal sense, foreign capital pays for land acquisition costs, and agreements are reached with local leaders on the usage of the land; however, farmers are often being expelled from their homeland. Who benefits from the development? This question has been asked since the initiation of MDC in Mozambique (Taylor, 2002). The acquisition process has not changed significantly over time, and as a result, civil society continues to feel excluded, and this has led to protests against the government with the help of global outsiders. Farmers and residents are usually not provided with essential knowledge about their livelihoods, works, and the right to know (Club of Mozambique, 2018).

Desirable structure of micro-regionalism

Development and intrastate political confrontations

Japan has been involved in many development activities in NDC, and the ProSavana agricultural development project is one of them. Firstly, the Nampula-Cuamba road improvement project was made possible through a yen loan, and the project for the construction of bridges on the road between Ile and Cuamba was carried out following Japanese grant assistance (JICA, 2011). Secondly, another yen loan was financed to develop and improve the cargo facilities at the port of Nacala. Mitsui & Co. and Vale are co-financing the management and operation of the coal terminals in the port. The coal is delivered by rail from the Moatize coal mine in Tete Province to Nacala, a distance over 912 km, and over 10 million tons of coking coal are shipped from Nacala to India and Japan annually (JETRO, 2018). Thirdly, the Japan Bank for International Cooperation (JBIC), policy-based financial institution, AfDB, and others have made $2.7 billion of international co-finance available for the port and railroad in the NDC. Moreover, adjacent regions have received grant capital assistance for the education and energy sectors around the NDC.

NDC programs may appear similar to the East–West economic corridor in Vietnam that links the port of Da Nang to inland countries as Japan provided the financing for the Second Mekong International Bridge; however, NDC is more reminiscent of the Eastern Seaboard Development (ESD) program in Thailand in the 1980s. This program aimed to develop a natural gas project in Siam Bay and to provide good natural ports in Laem Chabang and Map Ta Phut as alternatives to the Bangkok port so that container and other cargo could be moved between the eastern seaboard and the Bangkok metropolitan area. The Thai National Economic and Social Development Board (NESDB), the Japanese government, and JICA promoted ESD program together, and half of Thailand's development budget was disbursed for the program. The author was involved in ESD program as a staff member of the aid agency and was concerned about the environmental risks to local fisheries voiced by civil society and scholars at the time (Satake, 1992). After a quarter of the century, ESD program created a base for the second-largest industrial zone in Thailand after the Bangkok metropolitan area, and its impact on the national economy was greatly appreciated (Ariga & Ejima, 2000). Nevertheless, this unequal development pattern in Thailand seems to have led to political confrontations between urban and rural areas and coastal and inland areas, even though it is difficult to carry out evidence-based research on this. From the author's viewpoint, if the impact of development is accompanied by serious disparities among local groups, it could add a political dimension to the development. In Mozambique, serious confrontations have occurred between Frelimo and Renamo, the ruling and opposition parties respectively. Renamo's base used to be the northern and northern-central areas. The disbursement of the development budget to the northern area has been quite limited compared with that to the southern area. What matter are the development methods and their potential political impacts.

While MDC seems to have had negative effects on residents and the informal sector, NDC has threatened the livelihoods of, and materially damaged, small-scale farmers. On the other hand, the farmer groups are more organized than the informal sector groups, so they have been in a better position to make their claims heard both domestically and globally. In practice, these claims have contributed to the opening of a public hearing as well as changes to the content of the master plan (Shankland & Goncalves, 2016). Brazil side was disappointed to learn that the Cerrado formula had not found easy application in NDC. Nonetheless, the small-scale farmers' claims were not taken seriously, and the government did not respond to the claims appropriately (Funada, 2014). Indeed, it is said that over 6,000 refugees made an exodus from Mozambique to Malawi during these years. Although the Mozambican government rejected this claim, Medecins Sans Frontieres (MSF) in Malawi reported that the number of refugees grew from 2015 because military and police forces attacked and persecuted Renamo militia and supporters (MSF, 2016). Frelimo has expanded its influence through its position as the long-term ruling party, reaching the northern provinces and suppressing Renamo's power by using foreign money. Renamo has clashed with Frelimo in many places. As a result of these battles, even though limited in scale, refugees have streamed out of Mozambique to Malawi in the same way as occurred during the Cold War period.

Maravi, the predecessor of Malawi, was an enormous empire during the 16th century and included parts of Mozambique and Zambia. Maravi traded with Portugal and the Arab countries and diffused the Chichewa language through the region. Portugal purchased slaves and forced them to work on many plantations in Mozambique and Brazil, and the Chichewa language is now spoken in central and southern Malawi, Tete Province in Mozambique, and eastern Zambia. Malawi became a British protectorate at the end of the 19th century after the British took over from Portugal. In a sense, NDC could be seen as the revival of the Malawi cultural zone if the corridor is developed and trade with the surrounding areas is activated. However, if it is conducted by external actors and Frelimo and thereby excludes the local people, it will be an ironic twist in the region's history.

Mozambique was forced to stop the lending programs of IMF and others because its external debt had been growing, and untraceable financing between

Credit Suisse and the Russian Bank, on the one hand, and the public enterprise Empresa Mocambicana de Atum (EMATUN), on the other hand, was revealed in 2013. A similar scandal came to light in 2016, and IMF became very cautious. JVC & AJF (2016) explained that common elements in these scandals were the undertakings by unknown enterprises related to the intelligence agency in the Department of Defense, but President Guebuza assured lenders of government security with respect to foreign loans. It is said that unidentified borrowing accounted for 20% of Mozambique's total external debt, and the Mozambique News Agency (Agência de Informação de Moçambique) recognized that the debt repayments were already unsustainable. In addition, the government declared that the debt repayment by EMATUN was already untenable. A default was declared in January 2017. This was the second case of a default following that of Cote d'Ivoire after the highly indebted poor country initiative was applied to LICs and Africa (Wallace, 2017).

Looking back on the history of the development corridors in Mozambique, MDC was a symbol of the quickly improving relationship with its former enemy, South Africa. It seemed to be the reemergence of a colonial time agreement with South Africa, but the significant contribution to the local economy was acknowledged. Nevertheless, it was a *top-down development*, not the *bottom-up* type or one that involved citizen participation, where the voices of local people are listened to. It was also not carefully designed. BDC is also a *top-down development* and has facilitated land acquisition, though this has not been significantly progressed.

Mozambique's inland partner, Zimbabwe, has been worn down because of more than 10 years of political turmoil, and this has led to large numbers of emigrant workers moving to South Africa. As a result, the competitive power of BDC has declined sharply. The movement of goods between Zimbabwe and Mozambique has not grown steadily, with the mobility of human resources between Zimbabwe and South Africa growing instead. The ProSavana in NDC plan was abandoned, and one of the reasons is civil society's criticism on the *top-down development* approach. When its main promoter, the former President Guebuza, was suspected of being involved in bribery, the development momentum slowed down. In essence, BDC and NDC were designed to strengthen the power bases of Frelimo and its related business circles and to weaken Renamo. The Mozambican state relationships with the inland former British colonies, Malawi, Zambia, and Zimbabwe, are expected to develop over the long term – and they are desirable, but BDC and NDC deteriorated into domestic political confrontations before stable interstate relationships were realized.

Top-down by neo-patrimonial systems

The Mozambican micro-regionalism and development corridor policy has been conducted using the *top-down approach* of the power elite. This approach was steadily progressed by inviting PPPs and foreign assistance, in line with catching up global trends. It has also given rise to awkward questions regarding the limited range of beneficiaries. The power elites are concentrated among those with personal connections in the substantial one-party system, and collusion and cooperation between the party, government, and enterprises have thus been easily formed. Soderbaum and Taylor (2008) attributed the rise of the power elites that has driven development to an Africa-specific neo-patrimonial rule. The approach in MDC can be found in BDC and NDC. This begs the question: How can desirable micro-regional approaches be achieved? Is a *bottom-up approach* possible? This approach would involve and affect the *everyday lives* of Africans, with local traders and civil society members crossing the border and constructing human networks. Can this approach be incorporated as an essential component of large-scale corridor developments? The essence of the approach requires that local merchants, traders, farmers, and residents be able to voice their opinions and obtain necessary and timely information from the government, and the lives of these people are respected and their livelihoods maintained, even in the pursuit of large-scale development.

Micro-regionalism through SDI has depended on the Mozambican government's capacity to control many aspects of development by augmenting cross-border economic activities. MDC has followed the path of dependence by utilizing the existing historical corridor through which Mozambique sent emigrant workers to South African mines and mobilizing the large-scale economic power of South Africa and foreign capital. The status of state border was super-modern type and a sort of "blue border." Mozambique has promoted this development strategy and invited massive scale of wealth, but the interests of the informal sector have been ignored. NDC was started in 2010 based on an agreement between Malawi, Zambia, and Mozambique; however, relations between Malawi and Mozambique were not as intimate as those with South Africa, and demand for transportation between the two countries was also not so high. With the commitment of Japan and Brazil, President Guebuza pushed this development corridor project forward, but it resulted in land appropriation issues and the exclusion of small-scale farmers because Frelimo tried to construct a power base and interest networks on Renamo's home ground. Accordingly, Frelimo elites have been criticized by international civil society. In the process of establishing both MDC and NDC, the *everyday lives* of Africans were not considered. Some observations are given in the following.

Firstly, PPPs have some merit because they expand the financial packages for a given development plan to include aid and foreign investment. At the same time, they carry risks. Private investors can approach politicians and high-ranking officials to seek favorable conditions and the removal of restrictions, thereby paving the way for corruption. It is very hard to investigate murky public–private relations that are mingled with external financing, especially when the state controls the information. This is notable in the case of former President Guebuza, who has been linked to suspicious activities. At the start of his tenure in government, the president nominated his *friends* to some important posts so that concessions could be offered to the private sector. These people were very alert to lucrative investment opportunities for the private sector and were very loyal to him (US

AID, 2009). A part of the president's structural corruption has been made public, and a dozen of his *friends*, including his son, were arrested in 2019. The information disclosure needs to be conducted for all large-scale development projects, such as PPP and SDI, to ensure transparency in all financing deals.

Secondly, in NDC-related areas, potential "blue" corridor and SDI, land appropriation has been facilitated by buyers who have established and maintained close contact with local chiefs. This phenomenon can be considered the construction of neo-patrimonial interest systems that link the center with the local, and neo-patrimonialism is thus taking root in these local societies. This system was founded on the vision of large-scale development and the construction of human networks closer to Frelimo and suppressed resistance from small-scale farmers and CSOs to land acquisition. In opposing these activities, transnational civil society has used the words "*land grabbing*," convened meetings, produced a movie about the Cerrado project that destroyed the forests of Brazil, and alerted outside society to what has transpired. As a result, donors have come under pressure and the concepts of tenant farmer, landed farmer, and local market are emphasized in the JICA Master Plan (Hanlon, 2019). Transnational civil society, Mozambican farmer associations, and environmental groups have jointly resisted the introduction of the neo-patrimonial system in local society (Shankland & Goncalves, 2016). This movement is not limited to Mozambican civil society, however; it has been supported by a global coalition of civil societies. In a sense, in opposing the neo-patrimonial system in Mozambique, global civil society movements have united an otherwise weak civil society in Mozambique.

It is undeniable that the development corridors could have the effect of strengthening the unity of the region if the right development methods and actors are selected. Fourteen inland countries in Africa badly need these development corridors. However, there is competition regarding which routes should be selected first. In the early 2000s, an African corridor boom was anticipated given the positive economic growth rate in each country. However, Zimbabwe's economic downturn and the weakening of BDC plan took place simultaneously, and Yara decided to promote the Southern Agricultural Growth Corridor of Tanzania (SAGCOT) project linking Dar es Salaam, the capital city, with Zambia. As a result, BDC plan has been dropped from the list. The United States, the United Kingdom, and the World Bank have joined the SAGCOT project, inviting similar *land-grabbing* problems. BDC plan was promoted by Zimbabwe, and once competed with MDC, which was promoted by South Africa. NDC is alive, but the railway system is not linked closely with local folks' business, and ProSavana was abandoned.

The rise and fall of the main corridors have been affected by trends in the economy, transport, agriculture, tax policies, and public opinion. They are indeed troubling. SADC created FTA in 2008, and its member countries agreed to abolish tariffs in the region extending from South Africa to Tanzania. Some of the FTA members have delayed the process, but Zimbabwe abolished the tariffs in 2014, and Mozambique abolished the tariffs to South Africa in 2015. From a donor perspective, many conditions seem to be favorable for the construction of corridors in Southern Africa. Conventional development corridors have been resource-focused and colonial in form, where resources are moved to ports and shipped from there, and subject to external demand. It is irony that similar trend can be found in the super-modern type corridor. However, contemporary development corridors need to respond to internal demand in Africa and develop a bottom-up scheme. The bottom-up model can lead to endogenous development, but would it be able to coexist with the neo-patrimonial system? Many questions need to be answered, but the seeds of a new system have taken root in civil society's debate on NDC.

The long-term significance of micro-regionalism is without doubt, and it is essential for the development of inland countries in Africa. However, in the short and medium terms, external actor's influence tends to facilitate *top-down development* received by the governments which seek for immediate profits. The interstate relations in southern Africa have been quite improved, and economic interdependence has been constructed. The remaining issue is that the promoters of the corridors reside in the capital city, and it is deeply entrenched in African neo-patrimonialism, not paying attention to grassroots and border people. Aside from South Africa, the civil societies in the region are still weak, but the interpenetration of the civil societies needs to be facilitated as a measure of rectifying the situations.

Note

1 This chapter is based on an article of a Japanese publication, in Taga, H. and S. Igarashi, eds., *Multi-Layered Sub-Regions and New Regional Architecture in East Asia,* Keiso Shobo, 2020.

References

Aminaka, A. (2007). Historical thoughts on energy resource development in Mozambique, Africa Report No. 3, pp. 41–45, Chiba: Institute of Developing Economies (in Japanese).
Ariga, K., & Ejima, S. (2000). Comprehensive impact evaluation on eastern seaboard development plan in Thailand. *Journal of JBIC Institute,* No. 2, pp. 41–69 (in Japanese).
Bøås, M., Marchand, M., & Shaw, T. (2003). The weaveworld: The regional interweaving of economics, ideas and identities, in Soderbaum, F., & Shaw, T., eds, *Theories of New Regionalism: A Palgrave Reader,* Basingstoke: Palgrave.
Bowland, C., & Otto, L. (2012). Implementing development corridors: Lesson from the Maputo corridor, *Policy Briefing* 54, Johannesburg: The South African Institute of International Affairs (SAIIA).
Chabal, P., & Daloz, J.-P. (1999). *Africa Works: Disorder as Political Instrument,* Oxford: International African Institute, James Currey and Indiana University Press.
Club of Mozambique (2018). Administrative tribunal orders Mozambican government to release information on Pro SAVANA, by Adrian Frey, September 27. (https://clubofmozambique.com/news/administrative-tribunal-orders-mozambican-government-to-release-information-on-prosavana/) accessed September 10, 2019.

Collier, P., & Dercon, S. (2014). African agriculture in 50 years: Smallholders in a rapidly changing world. *World Development*, Vol. 63, pp. 92–101.
de Beer, G., Mmatli, R., Mahumane, A., Nyathi, S., & Soares, F. (1999). The future development of Southern African Borderlands. *Journal of Borderlands Studies*, Vol. 14, No. 2, pp. 47–66.
Frank, A. (1977). *The Sociology of Development and the Underdevelopment of Sociology*, London: Pluto Press.
Funada, S. (2008). *The Origins of "Unity" and "Division" in Contemporary Mozambican Politics: Focusing on Maua District/Niassa Province during the Liberation Struggle*, Tokyo: Ochanomizu-shobo (in Japanese).
Funada, S. (2014). Critical review on the ProSavana in Mozambique – What Japan Brazil ODA development discourse has realized? in Obayashi, N., & Sakamoto, eds, *Endogenous Development of New Born Africa – Local Residents and Assistances*, Kyoto: Shouwado (in Japanese).
Hanlon, J. (2019). Mozambique: US secret debt indictment points to Guebuza, All Africa, March 13, 2019 (https://allafrica.com/ stories/201903130176.html)
Horn, C. (2018). Accountability and ownership in Brazil's development cooperation: the case of Prosavana in Mozambique. *Journal of Public and International Affairs*, Vol. 45.
Japan Volunteer Center (JVC) and Africa Japan Forum (AJF) (2016) Ministry of Finance and NGOs regular consultation memo No.63, Question from NGOs: Debt problems in Mozambique and Yen loan credit provision policy, June 24, 2016 (in Japanese).
JETRO. (2015). *Beira Corridor Investment Meetings*, Mozambique: Johannesburg Office (in Japanese).
JETRO. (2018). Explore business chances in Nacala corridor: the dispatch of Japanese company mission, Johannesburg Office biznews, June 30 (in Japanese).
JICA. (2011). Preparatory survey report on the project for construction of bridges on the road between Ile and Cuamba in the Republic of Mozambique (open_jicare-port.jica.go.jp/615/ 615/ 615_521_12044798.html)
Kaarhus, R. (2018). Land, investments and Public-Private partnerships: What happened to the Beira agricultural growth corridor in Mozambique? *Journal of African Modern Studies*, Vol. 56, No. 1.
Madeleine, F. (2011). Indirect expropriation: the role of national institutions and domestic elites in the Mozambican farmland grab, presented at the International Conference on Global Land Grabbing, LDPI/Journal of Peasant Studies, 6–8 April.
Medecins Sans Frontieres (MSF) in Japan. (2016). Malawi: Refugees rapidly increase – What is asked for? January 27, 2016, accessed on July 20, 2019 (in Japanese).
Mitchell, J. (1998). The Maputo development corridors: A case study of the SDI process in Mpumalanga, *Development of South Africa*, Vol. 15, No. 5, pp. 757–769.
MoFA. (2014). Prime Minister Abe's visit to Mozambique (www.mofa.go.jp/mofaj/afr/af2/mz/page24_000187.html) (in Japanese).
Niemann, M. (1998). Regional Labor Migration in post-Apartheid Southern Africa, paper for the workshop: Globalisms Regionalisms of the IPSA Study Group III, New World Orders? University of Oslo, 6–8 August.
Oriental Consultants, RECS International Inc, International Development Center of Japan, Kokusai Kogyo Co, Ltd, and eight-Japan engineering consultants Inc.

(2014). Draft to Relatorio das Estrategicas do PEDEC – Versao 3. Maputo.: MPD and JICA (www.jica.go.jp/project/english/mozambique/002/index.html).

Robbins, G. (2008). Reflecting on South Africa's post-Apartheid experience with spatially informed economic development programmes, Trade and Industrial Policy Strategy Report, Pretoria: Department of Trade, Industry and Competition.

Satake, Y. (1992). Destruction of the villages and environment, in Murai, Y., ed., *Verification of Japanese ODA*, Tokyo: Gakuyo-shobou.

Shankland, A., & Goncalves, E. (2016). Imagining agricultural development in South-South cooperation: The contestation and transformation of ProSavana. *World Development*, Vol. 81.

Shaw, T. (1999). New regionalism in Africa in the new millennium: Comparative perspectives on renaissance, realism and/or regressions, paper for 3rd annual conference of the Centre for the Study of Globalisation and Regionalisation, University of Warwick, 16–18 September.

Soderbaum, F., & Taylor, I. (2001). Transmission belt for transnational capital or facilitator for development? Problematising the role of the state in the Maputo development corridor. *Journal of Modern African Studies*, Vol. 39, No. 4. pp. 675–695.

Soderbaum, F., & Taylor, I. (2008). *Afro-Regions: The Dynamics of Cross-Border Micro-Regionalism in Africa*, Uppsala: Nordiska Afrikainstitutet.

Taylor, I. (2002). The Maputo development corridor: Whose corridor? Whose development? in Breslin, S., & Hook, G, eds, *Microregionalism and World Order*, Basingstoke: Palgrave Macmillan.

UNAC & GRAIN (2015). The land grabbers of Nacala corridor: A New era of struggle against Colonial plantations in Northern Mozambique, February 2015. (www.grain.org./media).

United Nations Human Rights Council. (2019). Open-ended intergovernmental working groups on a UN declaration in the rights of peasants and other people working in rural areas (www.ohchr.org/EN/HRBodies/HRC/RuralAreas/Pages/WGRuralAreasIndex.aspx).

US Agency for International Development (USAID). (2009). Mozambique democracy and governance assessment (www.usaid.gov/mz//doc/misc/dg_assessment_2009.pdf).

Vasquez, J. (2019). Dethroning the state from Center-Stage: The advantage of financial and energy firms over foreign territories, the Brazilian case, International Studies Association, SA06 in Toronto, 30 March.

Wallace, P. (2017). African issuers scrutinized after Mozambique's bond default. *Bloomberg*, 3 February (www.bloomberg.com/news/articles/2017-02-03/default-in-mozambique-prompts-some-analyste-to-ask-who-s-next).

7 Transnational violent actors in the borderlands of the Sahel and challenges for stabilization
Any role for Japan?

Sayoko Uesu

Actors in the borderlands and war on terror

Borders had been historically perceived as a means to manage the periphery. After September 11, it becomes, first and foremost, a space of *security* and currently seen as a zone of surveillance, heterogeneity, and vigilance, built on the technology and physical infrastructures such as surveillance camera, biometrics authentication, or drones (Longo, 2018). With this strong focus on security, based on North-American and European experiences, many borderlands are now seen as areas prone to conflict, smuggling, migrants, or grey economic activities. Consequently, "actors in the periphery are not *trusted*, they are most *at risk* from outside threats, while at the same time *at risk of being a threat*" (Longo, 2018).

Globally, and especially under the "war on terror," the main instigators of threats are often associated with specific ethnicities or communities: Ahmed (2013) argued that "[the war on terror] has exacerbated the already broken relationships between central governments and the largely rural Muslim tribal societies on the peripheries of both Muslim and non-Muslim nations." Salehyan empirically demonstrated (2009) that

> ethnic groups closed to international borders are more likely to rebel. Many conflicts are characterized by contests between ethnic groups over control of the state, secession, or dispute over the lands and resources. Moreover, such geographic location allows ethnic rebels to slip back and force across the border to escape government suppression.

By examining the representation of some nomads[1] in Western media, McDonnell (2016) observed that they are perceived as (i) an existential threat to sovereignty, (ii) an assert in a military campaign, (iii) a strategy for reconciliation, (iv) an incubator of terrorism and criminality, or (v) an inseparable element of racial identity.

The increase of Violent Extremist Organizations (VEOs) and organized crimes since the mid-2000s and the collapse of Libya in 2011 have made the Sahelo-Saharan region an epicenter of the crisis. As put by Buzan (2000), the region belongs to "a set of states whose major security perceptions and concerns are so interlinked that their national security problems cannot reasonably be analyzed or

DOI: 10.4324/9781003202318-7

resolved apart from one another." Today, we gradually understand that the current crisis is a result of several multilayered and interlinked challenges stemmed from bad governance, economic stagnation, poverty, organized crime, climate change, and the extension of violence and extremism.[2]

However, many African governments were initially in denial and claimed that threats came from the external actors[3] via porous borders, who imported the Salafi-jihadism or Wahhabism to their territories. Thus, high priority is given to the Counter-Terrorism Operations (CTOs) and other measures to hardening the borders: in Mali, military operations during 2013–14 were successful and the core elements of VEOs lost their control over northern Mali. In 2014, the reorganization of French's Operation Serval to Operation Barkhane and the establishment of the regional joint force (the Sahel G5)[4] were decided in order to prevent the further spillover to neighbouring countries. However, the area of operation of VEOs has been expanding from Mali to Niger and Burkina Faso and currently to the northern parts of Ivory Coast, Ghana, Benin, and Togo in West Africa (Tisseron, 2019; ICG, 2019). Several natural parks[5] stretching over multiple borders also became the sanctuaries of VEOs.

With the unfolding of crisis, some transnational and highly mobile actors have been perceived as terrorists, traffickers, or collaborators. Initially, the Tuareg was widely finger-pointed, as its tiny fraction joined Al-Qaida in the Islamic Maghreb (AQIM) or formed Ansar Dine, an offshoot organization of AQIM founded in 2011. Then, the emergence of Macina Liberation Front (FLM) in central Mali in 2015 had singled out another transnational community, the Fulani (Fulbe or Peulh),[6] as perpetrators of violence in central Mali and neighbouring countries. In 2017, four major AQ-affiliated VEOs[7] in the Sahel had merged and formed Jama'at Nusrat al-Islam wa-l-Muslimin (JNIM). On the other hand, ISGS (Islamic State in Greater Sahara) in Mali–Niger borders has expanded by absorbing the Toloobe, a subgroup of Fulani. Since then, VEOs were concentrated in borderlands and increasingly instrumentalized the traditional intercommunities clashes over land use under the banner of jihad. The Fulani became "both the *subject* and *object* of security,"[8] and the characteristics of "threats/targets" became more complex and blurred, making it much harder to identify the main instigators and their motivations behind the propagation of violence.[9]

Today, pastoralism is now viewed more as a security issue than an economic and development issue (UNOWAS, 2018). Coupled with the question of migration, borderlands in the Sahel became the area for control and surveillance; Liptako-Gourma, a tri-border area between Mali-Niger-Burkina Faso, is seriously affected by the acts of violence from transnational and local jihadi groups, armed militias and bandits, also by the security forces involved in CTOs (ICG, 2017, 2020a; ISS, 2019).

Against such a backdrop, this chapter will focus on how a particular transnational ethnic group has been trapped in a vicious circle of violence in the borderlands: the intense CTOs and the hardening of borders haven't prevented the spread of VEOs to other regions. Instead, jihadist narratives and biased perception have been rapidly shared locally and globally, leading to another violence by VEOs and security forces. Under such circumstance, how to assist actors of fragile borderlands in the Sahel and its neighbours? International community struggles to respond to the evolving situation, though new approaches have emerged. Japan, who started providing the security assistance to the Sahel since 2013, has launched in 2019 the New Approach for Peace and Stability in Africa (NAPSA). The Sahel region still faces the numerous challenges, and the NAPSA should learn a lot from the past experiences if Japan wants to make a difference on the ground.

Spread of violence via Burkina Faso to neighbours

In contrast to Mali, Burkina Faso was not directly affected by the act of VEOs until the popular uprising in October 2014, which swept away the former president Compaoré. During his 27 years in the presidency, he intervened in several regional conflicts as a mediator, including a peace deal with the National Movement for the Liberation of Azawad (MNLA) in 2012. Behind the scenes, it is said that the country had a pact of non-aggression with AQIM, as General Diendéré (a commander of the Regiment of Presidential Security, RSP) and Limam Chaffi (the special advisor to the President) had played an intermediary role in hostage liberation in the Sahel. The departure of Compaoré and Limam Chaffi marked a beginning of the deterioration of security situation. The dismantling of RSP and a foiled coup d'état by General Diendéré in October 2015 were decisive for the collapse of the security apparatus, reinforced during the long-term dictatorship under Compaoré. Ouagadougou, Burkina Faso's capital, had experienced three attacks in 2016, 2017, and 2018, planned and executed by AQIM/JNIM in northern Mali. Yet, many researchers point out that the development of jihadi groups in Burkina Faso was foremost the result of long-term bad governance under Compaoré. Thurston (2020) assesses the current situation as "(Burkinabe) authorities made a strategic decision to cede the peripheries to (jihadi groups) and to various community-based militias."

At the beginning (2015/2016), attacks in Burkina Faso were concentrated on the very borderlines with Mali and seen as a tiny extension of VEOs operating in northern and central Mali. In late 2016, Ansaroul Islam, a small and radical grouping consisted of Fulani and Rimaibé, has emerged in Soum in the northern area. Malam Dicko, its founder, had been in northern Mali and its linkage with Kouffa has helped Ansaroul Islam's rise, as Fulani fighters of FLM and Ansaroul Islam could circulate across the border (Thurston, 2020). Since 2018, the eastern region became another operating theatre of different VEOs who try to establish a trafficking route between the coastal countries (Benin, Togo, Ghana, and Ivory Coast). In this process, ISGS in the tri-border area and Ansaroul Islam exploited the grievance of Gourmanché, who lost their means of living after the privatization of natural reserves stretched over the borderlands in Burkina Faso, Benin, and Togo. Terrorists convinced Gourmanché to attack the forest agents and security force and provide the sanctuaries in the Pama natural reserves to VEOs.

Many Fulani and Gourmanché – chefs of the village or religious leaders – were killed or kidnapped by the terrorists or arbitrarily arrested by the security forces.

By 2019, most borders (north, northeast to south, and northwest to south) became unstable. Since 2020, the northern area (Sahel region) has seen the resurge of violence, and the security forces withdrew from their military bases, which increased the number of internally displaced people. The southwest tri-border area between Mali and Ivory Coast became another area of operation of JNIM. According to Nsaibia (2020), some residual elements of Ansar Dine Sud (south), once dismantled by the Malian and Ivoirian joint security operations in 2015, began forming the cell in the forest zone stretched in borders. A southward movement of VEOs is ongoing; in northern Ghana, incursions of elements from ISGS around Tamale had been observed since the autumn of 2018. At the time of writing (June 2021), while the southern border area hasn't recorded any kind of violence by VEOs, the Ghanaian security force signalled that "bandits plan to attack Bolgatanga and Tamale."[10]

Different narratives surrounding the Fulani in the borderland

Often, an ethnic group is regarded as a single homogenous entity. Yet, rich literature shows that such notion of ethnicity was initiated by the colonial authority to rule and divide the local population and is still used to accompany the political or military missions (Doquet, 2013). Concerning the Fulbe, Dafinger (2013) points out that "colonial administration . . . created a homonized and imagined Fulbe identity vis-à-vis the colonial state" or "a new-meta-ethnicity, a trans-regional pan-Fulbeism." However, on the ground, the distinction is blurred because of the frequent migration and inter-ethnic marriages, so that a Fulani can state a Bambara or a Tuareg in another day. Historically, in the Senegal River valley, other ethnic groups assimilated to Fulani because of its clerical status (Kane, 2016). Or, in southeast Burkina Faso, "Fulbe often use the Bisa name . . . especially when dealing with the authorities" (Dafinger, 2013).

Fulani are known for having led or been involved in the major jihads in West Africa in the 18–19th centuries. By the 16th century, the Fulani in the Sahelo-Saharan region were converted to Islam through links with Arab traders in towns and Tuareg desert nomads: the conversion encouraged their shared identity, it also provided an alternative legal system (Stapleton, 2013). From the 18th century, many Fulani specialized in scholarship, and their language (Pulaar) became important to convey Islamic learning, second only to Arabic in the western Sahelo-Saharan region (Kane, 2016). While jihads in Futa Jaron (actual Guinea), Futa Toro (actual Senegal) and others were short-lived, the Sokoto Caliphate, established in 1804 by Fulani Muslim Usman dan Fodio in Sokoto in northern Nigeria, lasted for almost a century until the colonization by the British army. The Sokoto caliphate had a strong and organized military capacity and controlled a large territory from the current northern Burkina Faso (the emirate of Liptako[11]) to eastern Cameroon. It is still regarded as a prominent example of "Fulani-led Jihad" in Africa, even in actual Nigeria and Niger (Hiribarren, 2020).[12] In 1818, inspired by Sokoto's experience, a preacher and social reformer Chiekou Amadou established the Macina Empire against the Bambara Empire.[13] Nonetheless, it is important to stress that while ethnicity plays a part in old and recent jihads, such movements are not an ethnic phenomenon (Lovejoy, 2016); in the past, Muslims came from many different ethnic backgrounds, which is also the case today.

Process of Fulani's stigmatization: Jihadi narrative

This section analyses the evolution of current Jihadi narratives in the Sahel. The formal online propagandas[14] with references to the Fulani from 2015 to early 2021 are picked up. The local propagandas – the tracts or audio in local languages (Fulfulde, etc.) – are difficult to obtain and interpret, so I complemented with interviews and secondary resources to grasp their narratives.[15]

AQIM/JNIM and its likes have accumulated expertise in twisting history and geopolitics into their propaganda machine. For instance, Zenn (2020) notes that Movement for Oneness and Jihad in West Africa (MUJAO), who split from AQIM in 2011 but remained a collaborator to it,[16] claimed in their video in 2011 that they "inaugurated jihad in West Africa," and "represented the ideological descendants of Usman dan Fodio and precolonial Fulani jihadist leaders Umar Tall and Cheikou Amadou." This narrative was later picked up by Ansaru, an offshoot organization of Boko Haram and who stayed close to AQIM: it referred to Usman dan Fodio in their founding statement in 2012 and still keeps its "pan-Fulani orientation" today, especially in northwest Nigeria (Zenn, 2020). In the same way, the history of jihad in Macina resonated with the tiny fractions of marginalized young herders in Central Mali.

In retrospect, it seems AQIM had tactically manipulated the narrative so that the target of CTOs to be shifted from the much diabolized Tuareg to another community, the Fulani.[17] Even before the rise of FLM, some young Fulani, such as Bambara and Songhai and others, already took part in VEOs in northern Mali in 2011/2012. In Gao, most of them had already formed a self-defence group against Tuareg before their alliance with MUJAO. And in Mopti, a Fulani preacher named Amadou Kouffa and his followers collaborated with Ansar Dine to move south. The French intervention in January 2013 has repelled Kouffa and Fulani fighters, who went underground and resurged in 2015 as a subgroup of Ansar Dine in the centre of Mali, which was later called as FLM. FLM, initially composed of the veterans of Ansar Dine and MUJAO,[18] had skilfully flattered young herdsmen[19] that they deserved the best as the descendants of glorious jihadists of the Macina Empire. This narrative appealed to marginalized herdsmen's ego, yet the majority of the local population stayed out of this.[20]

During 2015 and 2018, some West African capitals (Bamako, Ouagadougou) and Grand Bassam (close to Abidjan) were repeatedly attacked by AQIM/JNIM. At this moment, AQIM started to put the nom de guerre "al-Fulani" in their communiqués to highlight the Fulani origin of attackers/martyrs. The first appearance of the "al-Fulani" fighter was in the communiqué (in Arabic caption on the photo of the presumed attacker) in December 2015, claiming the attack of Radisson Bleu Hotel in Bamako. Then the first attack in Ouagadougou in January 2016 and another shooting at Grand Bassam in March 2016 also included some "al-Fulani" fighters. By so doing, AQIM tried to mark as the beginning of the "Fulani jihad" in the Sahel.[21]

However, when we tried to dig further into the identity of those first fighters labelled "al-Fulani" in the Sahel, several local resources confirmed that they were not all Fulani, but other ethnicities who cohabited with the Fulani for a long time in the area.[22] At this time, it was already foreseen that the use of "al-Fulani" would rather affect the local and international security and intelligence circles,[23] so that such discrimination would further alienate young herdsmen and push them to join the jihad. It seems that AQIM had deliberately designated "al-Fulani" for major attacks targeting the major military base or facilities of foreign interests. Such practice became sparse after the attack in Ouagadougou in March 2018, as VEOs were more involved in local fightings.

From 2019, JNIM started to blame the armed groups who assaulted the Fulani villages in Burkina Faso and Mali and called to stop the "genocide" against the Fulani. Since then, with the increase of clashes between Fulani and Dogon militia, JNIM went on the protective narrative towards the Fulani and accused France as a plotter. In January 2021, according to French security specialist Wassim Nasr, JNIM indicated that they changed the policy not to disclose anymore the ethnic identity of attackers.[24] However, in June 2021, an informal martyrdom video was shared online, in which a young black African who presented himself as "Abu Dujana," a Fulani from Tamale (Ghana) and executed the suicide operation in northern Mali, called Fulani in Ghana to take up the arm. While it is difficult to verify the authenticity of such a message, it seems very opportunistic; this online video appeared shortly after when Ghanaian police issued an unexpected security alert on Tamale. Nevertheless, the local media started to carry the message and his video, which might further stigmatize the Fulani present in Ghana.

ISGS also presents itself as a defender of the Fulani community in the borderland of Mali-Niger, Contrary to AQIM/JNIM, ISGS hasn't so far highlighted the Fulani history on their propaganda, even though they actively seek to manipulate the local dynamics and fuel tensions between different communities.[25]

Another process of Fulani stigmatization: exactions by security forces and militias

Since the 2000s, with the rise of the war on terror, armies and security forces in Northwest Africa have been the recipient of technical assistance by the United States, EU, France, and other donors. Sahelian countries also expect to benefit from the establishment of the Sahel G5 force. At the same time, its armies and security forces had inherited some colonial practices: Harkness (2018) points out that the French colonial military tended to recruit from large ethnic communities (the Bambara of Mali and the Mossi of Burkina Faso) despite a quota calculated from its population figures. And the system was not suited for the highly mobile populations of the Sahara and Sahel, such as the Moors, Tuareg, and Fulbe peoples. Moreover, the intelligence services are used to keep eyes on opposition leaders since independence and improvised by the wave of asymmetric insurgencies.

In Burkina Faso, like its neighbours, President Roch Kaboré and politicians understood that threats came from Mali, and saw that the networks and supporters of Compaoré and the former RSP were behind the surge of violence.[26] Nevertheless, in 2017 and 2018, the Ministry of Interior made public a long list of suspects who joined Ansaroul Islam.[27] The list reveals many details such as name, village, profession, and their roles in the organization, which should normally be kept confidential in a small circle. While it is no secret that Ansaroul Islam was mainly composed of Fulani in Soum at the initial phase, the newly established security apparatus wrongly assumed that Ansaroul Islam had wider support among the local population.[28]

Cases of exactions by the security forces against Tuareg and Fulani had been already reported in northern and central Mali, which pushed them to join the terrorists or form the militia to protect their communities. Since May 2017, the Niger security force started associating the Malian militia, Self-Defense Group for Imghad Tuareg and Allies (GATIA), and Movement for the Salvation of Azawad (MSA)[29] in CTOs in the Mali–Niger border area. Later, both militias became associates to the French Operation Barkhane. The militias fought against ISGS, mainly composed of Fulani fighters at that time. The local dynamics, built on the complex and long-term conflicts among ethnic groups, have benefitted ISGS to attract Fulani fighters.[30] By 2018, civil society had already alerted the international community of such exactions. Still, the use of militias spread to central Mali (Dogon militia, Dan Na Ambassagou is mobilized against FLM since 2018) and to Burkina Faso (Koglweogo was mobilized for CTOs since late 2018, and the Volunteers for the Defense of the Homeland (VDP) since 2020). Dan Na Ambassagou and Koglweogo started to attack the Fulani communities as a part of CTOs, and both had committed the mass killing of Fulani in 2019. Despite the alarming messages from the international community,[31] such exactions are still reported in the Sahel.

Other narratives among the local communities

The local population has been constantly caught between the terrorists and security forces,[32] and some formed auto-defence groups to protect their communities. In this regard, the trajectory of "petit chaffori" (Ilassou Djibo), a Toloobe from Tillabery in the Niger-Mali borderland, and a close associate to Adnan Abu Walid al-Saharawi is interesting. As petit chaffori's pastoral community had been constantly marginalized by the local government and harassed by the security forces, he fought against them and was put in jail as an insurgent. He was not radicalized at the moment, yet his leadership in the Toloobe community in the Niger-Mali borderland had attracted the interest of AQIM, who included petit chaffori in the list of a prisoner exchange with the Malian government. We don't know how

Adnan Abu Walid had picked him up, but it helped Abu Walid to get the local allies and inflate the thin elements of ISGS. A Fulani herder from Tillabery told to the author that even after petit chaffori's alignment with ISGS, he is somewhat viewed as a "hero" still today in the community.[33] In Burkina Faso, Ouédraogo (2020) analyses the movement of Ansaroul Islam and conducts several interviews with the imprisoned members. He revealed that some members see the founder of Ansaroul Islam, Malam Dicko, as a "hero, leader with a lot of charisma, or social bandit who brings the social justice." Like Kouffa in central Mali, Malam's preaching appealed to the local youth who felt marginalized by the progress of economic globalization.[34]

The politically and economically marginalized communities tend to find their accounts and construct their narratives in the peripheries/borderlands; Ansaroul Islam initially had an intention to establish the Islamic emirate[35] in northern Burkina Faso, and we have seen many other cases with the rise and fall of the Islamic State. Ba Konaré (2021), a clinical phycologist/researcher/activist and a founder of Kisal Observatory, describes the process of state making and the use of Mande-centred narrative in postcolonial Mali, and how the Fulani's narrative had been excluded from it. He stresses the need to find and support "the intersection of narratives that positively resonate with Fula communities and narratives that serve great security strategies."

Several local – transnational at the same time – jihads fought during the 18–19th centuries in West Africa are almost forgotten from a global history.[36] Or sometimes, the past jihads are romanticized (Ba Konaré, 2021). Both situations will set the ground for any opportunistic interpretation by violent actors and outsiders (including media). In this regard, Akinola (2017) stresses that the role of cleric is vital in protecting the community from such violent narrative, which is the case of Sokoto.

The impact of malicious messages or fake news circulated through WhatsApp etc. should not be ignored: they incite further violence against a specific community or ask for arms to avenge their grudge.[37] While the majority of victims are Muslims, some Christians overreacted and "believed they were targeted by a new 'Fulani Jihad'" (Zenn, 2020). Also, in Ghana, when a church in northern Burkina Faso was attacked in 2019,[38] a local security consultant speculated that VEOs in Burkina Faso started to target Christians so Ghana should be prepared.

How borderlands and actors are managed and assisted

Borderlands in the Sahelo-Saharan region are perceived as "a periphery in the periphery." Nonetheless, the area has historically played a vital role in connecting the North and West African economies: Scheele (2012) vividly described the informal networks of traders and nomads in the Malian-Algerian frontier, often seen as a hotspot of disorder. While the extreme dysfunction of African borders had always been perceived as one of the constraints, borderlands and their actors are essential elements of local dynamics, supporting the regional integration.[39] In the early 2000s, there was some optimism with the emergence of "new regionalism" in West Africa, highlighting the roles of diverse non-state actors in this process (Iheduru, 2003). Foucher (2014) described that the concept of "*pays frontiers*" was conceived and promoted by former Malian President Alpha Oumar Konaré to attenuate the tensions on borders and promote the regional integration from the ground ("*par le bas*"). Once the conflicts over borders are eased or resolved, the transborder activities have flourished, as demonstrated by the cases in Mali/Burkina Faso, Mali/Senegal/Mauritania, Mali/Ivory Coast, and Nigeria/Niger.

However, with the rising instability, such local dynamics are currently being lost: despite some attempts to support the promising cross-border areas, the use of land, pasture, or water in the borderlands rarely attract government authorities' attention, in contrast to the border controls to suppress smugglings (Lentz, 2013). To complement the militarized assistance, the international community has been supporting the region by a wide range of programmes to support the "security-development nexus," such as the Integrated Strategy for the Sahel by UN and EU or the Counter-Insurgency (COIN) strategy (by the United States and France) to "win the hearts and minds" of the local population. Despite a high expectation placed on the "security-development nexus" at international fora, its concept was built on the unrealistic assumption that "improving a security situation will lead to development" in a linear way (Antil, 2020).

Thurston (2020) points out the "Decades of 'decentralization' efforts in the Sahel have . . . provided cover for centre-periphery deal-making rather than democratic empowerment." Many Sahelian governments lacked the resources to manage the peripheries and some countries opted for concluding the social pact with the traffickers or militias. For instance, Antil (2017) described that

> In Mauritania, (former President) Ould Taya stabilized the northern country by supporting the formal and informal alliances between merchants. . . . In Niger, (security institution) will not control the trafficking in the northern part: It would prevent the northern communities to rebel again, and the government has nothing to propose as alternative economic activities.

We have observed that some VEOs, intending to control the territory, have provided the basic services to the local population. Trying to transform such a grey-zone into a transparent one by the bulk of development projects look beautiful on the international conferences, but we have already put resources in a fragmented way with limited progress.

Emerging trends to assist the borderlands

Along with the changing nature of threats and vulnerabilities, international assistances have been evolved from security-focus (i.e. border control by IOM)[40] to support the local population (i.e. from de-radicalization to vocational training by UNDP), then the scope is widened to address the economic aspect in the borderlands. Recently, UNDP has launched the Africa Borderlands Centre and reiterated that insufficient attention and resources were being given to addressing the specific needs of people in the borderlands (UNDP, 2021). A new borderland project, "Trade for Peace" in Liptako Gourma, will be implemented with a financial contribution of Japan.[41] While the effectiveness of COIN has been contested, the civilian teams of foreign armies are better placed in responding to the pressing needs of the communities. For instance, the US's civil affairs team administered a topical anti-parasitic to over 1300 cattle outside of Kaedi, Mauritania, during the joint military exercise Flintlock in February 2020. We have to ask, how these functions can be transferred and built in the local authorities.

Since the outburst of crisis (or even at an earlier stage), various mediation efforts have been taking place at higher and grassroot levels.[42] The local population in Liptako-Gourma perceived that "the traditional chief or religious leader is more trusted than the local government in terms of conflict resolution" (R-CAP, 2019), and donors have been increasingly incorporated the mediation at a community level in the borderlands assistance. For instance, IOM has been working with the largest regional herder' association Bilital Maroobé Network (Réseau Bilital Maroobé/RMB in French), to develop an early alert system to pre-empt potential conflict linked with transhumance movements across West and Central Africa. And in Liptako Gourma, the local authority (Authorité de Liptako Gourma/ALG) collaborates to identify and discuss the risk and vulnerabilities of the borderland and build a relationship with the concerned governments.

How Japan perceives the instability and assists the region

Japan has relatively a limited presence and interest in sub-Saharan Africa, except for some resource-related mega investments (i.e. offshore gas development in Northern Mozambique). However, the rise of global VEOs had pushed the Japanese government to step in on the security issues in Africa. It started after the attack on the gas plant in Tigantourine in January 2013, where 40 people (including 10 Japanese engineers) were killed by a group of terrorists circulating between the Maghreb and Northern Mali. This incident was a big wake-up call for the then Abe Administration, who had a keen interest in promoting Japan's role on the strategic and global security issue.

Following the incident, the Ministry of Foreign Affairs (MoFA) announced on 29 January the new three pillars of foreign policy, consisted of "Strengthening measures against international terrorism," "Support for the stabilization of Sahel, North Africa, and Middle East regions," and "Promotion of exchange and dialogue with Islamic and Arab countries." At the Tokyo International Conference for African Development (TICAD) V in June 2013, Japan committed to providing 1.3 billion USD in development and humanitarian assistance in the Sahel.[43] In parallel, the government quickly decided to build up and strengthen the security and intelligence cooperation frameworks and networks in Africa.[44] It was a unique opportunity for Japanese diplomacy to highlight the regional dimension (bridging the Maghreb-Sahara/Sahel-West Africa, separated in terms of administration) and give more attention to francophone countries where Japanese companies started to invest in.[45] In 2016, at TICAD 6, Japan again committed to providing 120 million USD to capacity building to fight against international terrorism, including the training of 30,000 officers. Table 7.1 illustrates how Japanese assistances after Tigantourine have been concentrated in the border control and capacity building for the security sector (including the provision of Japan-made materials).[46] Financial support for organizing the Dakar Forum during 2014–2019 was rather unique among other assistances.

In contrast to the increase of security-related assistance, the numbers of Japanese expatriates and development projects have been shrinking in Niger, Mali, and Burkina Faso.[47] It is offset by the increase of grant contribution to international organizations in two areas: one is the border management (by IOM) and prevention of violent extremism (by UNDP), another is the emergency humanitarian assistance by UNHCR and others.

Japan's engagement to the Sahel went one step further in 2019: in July, Japan joined the G5 Sahel as an observer. In September, the government launched the NAPSA at TICAD 7 held in Yokohama. The NAPSA aims to address the root causes of conflict and terrorism through supporting institution building (see Box 7.1). However, at the time of writing, "the new approaches" are not entirely clear: since its launch, Japan seems to provide the same package coupling the security-related assistance (provision of materials) and financial contribution to UN's programmes. The most recent contribution will finance IOM's border control project in northern Benin (IOM, 2021). It certainly will support the local security force, but the hardening of the border cannot contain the spillover of violence, as previously described.

Providing economic opportunities is also crucial, and the NAPSA highlights the provision of technical and vocational training to train the defectors and the youths under unemployment. In this regard, the joint training by UNDP/Toyota in Libya seems realistic and promising (see Table 7.1). However, when it comes to the Sahel, many fighters were (or still are) herders, while some elements had already received a higher education under the Arabic curriculum, which will need another solution than the technical training. ISS (2020) also notes that "there is no linear connection between vocational training and future job security. And few of these programmes are set up to respond to the underlying socio-economic realities that make people vulnerable to being recruited by extremists."

Challenges and lessons learned for stabilizing the fragile borderlands

Member countries of Sahel G5 have been under a series of political and security turmoil. Mali has been again under transition after the coup in August 2020, which kicked out the re-elected in 2019 yet much-contested President Keita. Then, "a coup within a coup" (ICG, 2021) in May 2021 has led to the temporary suspension of military cooperation by France, and the gradual reduction of French's military (from current 5,100 to 2,500) by 2023. The unexpected and sudden death of President Itno Idriss Déby of Chad in March 2021, just after his

Table 7.1 Security-related assistance to Northwest Africa since 2013

	Descriptions of security-related assistance since 2013
Sahel G5	
Mali	2014 Provision of materials and capacity building to Bamako National Police School 2015 Grant for purchasing vehicles for security forces 2016 Provision of materials for Police and Justice 2018 Grant for purchasing X-ray and other materials for International Airport 2019 Provision of materials (CCTV etc.) to penal institutions
Niger	2016 Provision of wireless communication materials and wireless vehicles to connect regional government and departments 2020 Provision of Japan-made materials (4x4, pick-up tracks etc.)
Burkina Faso	2013 (UNDP) Grant to the Project for Supporting the Consolidation of the Rule of Law and Access to Justice for the Poor Population 2018 Provision of security-related materials 2020 Provision of Japan-made security-related materials (4x4, pick-up tracks etc.) 2020 (UNDP) Preventing the violent extremism and Rebuilding the community 2021 (UNESCO/Dakar) Grant to the Project for "Supporting social stability through education and vocational training for out-of-school youths following the security and health crises in the Sahel and Eastern regions of Burkina Faso"
Mauritania	2013 (UNDP) Research on the proliferation of SALW, Capacity building for justice depts. 2016 Provision of Japan-made airport security materials 2019 Provision of vehicles for border control between Mauritania and Senegal
Chad	2019 Provision of security-related materials
Multi-countries (Sahel)	2013 The Project for Strengthening Criminal Justice and Law Enforcement Capacities in the Sahel Region (Sahel G5 + Senegal, Nigeria) 2013 (UNDP) Stabilization of Peace and Good Governance in the Sahel (G5 countries) 2014 (IOM) Capacity building of border polices between Mauritania/Mali, build coordination framework between border polices and local population 2014 (UNDP) Human Security and Rebuilding the communities in the Sahel (Mali, Burkina Faso, Chad and Niger) 2020 (UNDP) Assist G5 Sahel member countries and MINUSMA in Liptako-Gourma 2020 (UNDP) Capacity building for PKO School in Bamako (EMPABB), MINUSMA, ECOWAS and G5 Sahel 2021 (UNDP) Trade for Peace regional project (Borderlands Project) in Liptako Gourma
West Africa	
Ivory Coast	2015 Capacity building for COMNAT (National Commission to fight against the circulation of small arms etc.)-ALPC etc. 2016 Provision of Japan-made security-related materials (biometric authentication system etc.)
Senegal	2014 - 2019 Financial contribution to the Dakar Peace and Security Forum (co-organzed by Senegal and France)
Nigeria	2020 (UNDP) Reconstruction and Peace-building in Northeastern Nigeria
Benin	2021 (IOM) Reinforcement of border control management in northern Benin
Multi-countries	2013 The Project for Strengthening Criminal Justice and Law Enforcement Capacities in the Sahel Region (approximately (Sahel G5 + Senegal, Nigeria) (Training course implemented by Ministry of Justice and JICA) 2020 (UNDP) PKO School in Bamako (EMPABB), MINUSMA, ECOWAS and G5 Sahel
Maghreb/	
Algeria	2013 (UNODC) Capacity building for Justice and Law enforcement
Tunisia	2013 (UNDP) Capacity building for security institutions 2014 Provision of CCTV to airport for effective border control 2019 Provision of security-related materials (face recognition system etc.) for effective border control
Morocco	2015 Provision of high-performance CCTV to Casablanca international airport
Libya	2021 (UNDP-Toyota, agreed on 2018) Capacity building for car maintenance and customer services skills in Toyota Libya's dealerships in Tripoli, Benghazi, Misrata, and Zlitenunder, under the "Stabilization to Recovery Transition (START) in Libya"

Source: MoFA ODA Database (compiled by author)

Box 7.1 Japan's contributions for Africa – peace and stability

Build stable and reliable institutions and enhance governance
- Support development of institutions such as electoral management and administrative system
- Train 60,000 people in the areas of justice, police, security maintenance, and otsnhers
- Provide security equipment such as border control equipment (X-ray)
- Strengthen judicial cooperation through UN Congress on Crime Prevention and Criminal Justice (Kyoto Congress)

Support initiatives led by Africa toward stabilization of conflict areas
- Strengthen capacity building through 15 Africa Peace Keeping Operation (PKO) Training Centers
- Enhance capability development through UN Triangular Partnership Project for Rapid Deployment of Enabling Capabilities Support and encourage Africa's initiatives through Africa's mediation and arbitration led by AU and Regional Economic Communities (RECs) such as the Intergovernmental Authority on Development (IGAD)
- Participate in Sahel Alliance as an observer; strengthen cooperation with like-minded countries such as Germany (in the Sahel), the UK, and France
- Support institution building and human resource development for conflict prevention and sustaining peace through UN Peacebuilding Fund, technical assistance, and others

Provide humanitarian assistance to refugees, IDPs, youths, and others
- Promote the humanitarian-development nexus, providing emergency and humanitarian aid to refugees, IDPs, and host communities (including food, emergency relief goods, water and sanitation, health care, and protection) and support for self-reliance (in such areas as education, employment promotion, health, and community infrastructure)
- Prevent radicalization of youths through support for civil society and communities; strengthen vocational training and create job opportunities for youth.

Source: MoFA (2019)

much-contested re-election, has triggered the weakening of the state. The country is under transition, and the army will have to contend with many rebels inside and outside the country in this process.

With all these factors at play, a further weakening of the Sahel and neighbouring countries will have repercussions on other borderlands in the region. In addition to the tri-border area between Mali-Burkina Faso-Ivory Coast, several natural parks and a northern part of Ghana, another borderland between northwest Nigeria and the Sahel is also under stress. According to an expert of the Sahel,[48] the intensification of military operations in Liptako-Gourma has pushed some Toloobe to seek refuge in the area between Liptako-Gourma and Sokoto. In this process, the sense of stigmatization has been shared between geographically divided Toloobe and Djelgodi and pushed them to unite against the common enemy (local security forces, France, etc.). Eventually, there is an attempt to mediate with those subgroups. The recent reappearance of Ansaru in northwest Nigeria in late 2019 is also problematic, as their propaganda calls for Fulani, Hausa, etc. to join the rank.[49] Moreover, the fractions of Boko Haram and ISWAP are said to be present since late 2019 (ICG, 2020b), recruiting the Fulani involved in banditry, which could reinforce a tactical collaboration with highly mobile fighters (Zenn, 2020). On the other hand, in northern Benin, de Bruijne (2021) notes that "a Fulani Ruga (a traditional leader) . . . revealed complete disillusionment with the perceived stigmatization and marginalization of his ethnic group in the area," yet there is still hope that "no clear alignments between local community tensions and VEOs" for the moment.

How can the NAPSA respond to the unfolding crisis?

Against such a backdrop, Japan needs to consider how "the new approaches" can support the evolving local challenges. In the Sahel, Japan has been privileging the official bilateral relation and the use of international organizations, and the NAPSA foresees assistance to strengthen or complement the government capability, especially at the local government level. However, government services are mostly absent in the conflict-prone borderlands, and government agents are not trusted by the local population. The NAPSA highlights the role of prevention, mediation, and arbitration, and in the Sahelian context, a more flexible cooperation framework with the NGOs or civil society close to the local communities is encouraged, besides the formal mechanism (AU, etc.). In addition, setting up the space and bringing a wide range of actors for regular dialogue and exchange will be useful, as the small-scale version (or Ver. 2.0) of the Dakar Forum.[50]

And last but not least: as the Islamic State Central frantically claims the rapid expansion of "IS West Province"[51] and "IS Central Province," the United States and its allies see a growing threat of "IS" in Africa. Currently, there is much focus on the progress of "IS" in northern Mozambique, and the regional military operation will take place, assisted by the United States, France and other partners. At the same time, local researchers and civil society are cautious enough and try to understand the local dynamics and different narratives behind the increase

Notes

1 He analysed mostly the nomads in Sudan, Afghanistan, Mali, and Niger.
2 Many scholars are reticent to describe the terrorists in the Sahel and their motifs in a simplistic manner as "Islamic extremist" (ISS, 2015; ICG, 2016, 2017).
3 It refers mainly to the preachers and fighters from the Middle East and Gulf States but also to their neighbours. For instance, local media indicated the existence of some extremist West African preachers who freely circulate the region, as stipulated by UEMOA and ECOWAS for the free movement of people in the region.
4 The Sahel G5 Joint Force became operational in 2017.
5 With the expansion of AQIM and its affiliates, the Park W (Niger-Burkina Faso-Benin) has been considered as a sanctuary for various VEOs including Boko Haram and ISGS. The recent southward movement of ISGS and JNIM has made the forest zone in Comoé (Burkina Faso-Ivory Coast) and the W-Arli-Pendjari (WAP) complex (Niger-Burkina Faso-Benin) another sanctuary for VEOs.
6 The Fulani is a vast pastoral community of 3–4 million spread from West to Central Africa. Many of them are now sedentarized and engaged in various economic activities. This chapter focus on the marginalization of Fulani herdsmen in the Sahel, elites are well presented in political scene in Mali and other countries. Macky Sall (President of Senegal) and Buhari (President of Nigeria) are of Fula origins.
7 AQIM, Ansar-Dine, al-Murabitun and FLM.
8 Longo described (2018) the actors in the periphery as such.
9 Ba Konaré (2021) noted that in central Mali, "presenting oneself as being jihadist-adjacent as an immediate effect of tapping into terrorism's strength in instilling fear, and making oneself appear more menacing."
10 www.garda.com/crisis24/news-alerts/491751/ghana-heightened-security-likely-in-upper-east-region-and-northern-region-through-the-end-of-june-due-to-security-threat. Another source indicates that there is an increase of JNIM and ISGS elements in the area.
11 A short history of the emirate in Liptako (actual Dori and surrounding area in northern Burkina Faso) gets very little attention (Ouédraogo, 2020). Irwin (1981) collected the oral history about the jihad and political system in Liptako and its relation to the Sokoto Caliphate. According to Hampâté Bâ (1994), Liptako was never conquered by the army of Usman dan Fodio, but a pious local king placed his Kingdom (of Liptako) under the religious leadership of Usman dan Fodio.
12 Boko Haram had tried to capture the legacy of the past empires in West Africa. For instance, Shekau, a leader of Boko Haram since 2009 (killed in May 2021), tried to restore the like of Kanem-Bornu empire (or "Kanuri Caliphate"), and it was only in 2014 that he started mentioning on Usman dan Fodio (Zenn, 2020). In the Lake Chad region, while some Fulani joined Boko Haram or ISWAP, others formed a militia to fight against VEOs.
13 "Djelgodgi" (actual Djibo in Burkina Faso) constitutes the historical region and kingdom of the Fulani in Soum province (MENASTREAM, 2017), established well before the jihads in 19th century. According to Zenn (2020), as

Djelgodji was a part of the Macina Empire in 19th century, Kouffa tried to extend FLM'influence into Burkina Faso via Malam Dicko's Ansaroul Islam.
14 Which are distributed through the authorized media outlet.
15 In general, such propaganda aims to attract new elements. However, in the Sahel, VEOs recruit mainly through the social networks (family ties) or local proselytism (distributing the tract or audio in local languages), so its impact on recruitment seems limited, compared to Europe or other regions. Pérouse de Monclos (2017, 2018) dismisses that the virtual analysis of online messages and videos would only lead to misunderstanding the fundamental nature of VEOs and its threats.
16 MUJAO was successful in attracting a lot of sub-Saharan "black" Africans, in contrast to AQIM, mainly composed of North Africans and Tuareg, etc. MUJAO later formed Al-Murabitun with Signers in Blood Battalion in 2013. Over the leadership issue, a small component headed by Adnan Abu Walid al-Saharawi split from Al-Murabitun and formed ISGS in 2015. During the field surveys, sub-Saharan Black African fighters are still referred as MUJAO by local population and security/intelligence officers. It seems that the affiliation to global terrorist organization (AQ or IS) has less importance for local population.
17 A specialist of the Sahel analysed that the cadres of AQIM in northern Mali sought to protect themselves and their zone from the CTOs, so started to dispatch the local African fighters (Fulani, etc.) to execute the major attacks (interview in Dakar, November 2015).
18 The absorption of some Fulani fighters from MUJAO enabled Kouffa to create networks with the Fulani in Niger and Burkina Faso (Thurston, 2020). According to ICG's reports, some subgroups of Fulani-Toloobe (mainly in Niger, the cleric grouping known to having led the jihads in the 18th–19th centuries), Sidibe (Mali) or Djeldoji (Burkina Faso) – are involved as fighters (Hansen, 2019).
19 Kouffa has a modest background. He accuses France and its allies, local authorities (National Assembly, army, marabouts etc.), and states that "petits gens" (farmers, herdsmen, fishermen, or blacksmiths) in the area are good (Bourgeot, 2020).
20 Interview with a researcher/activist in Tokyo, June 2016.
21 During 2015–2016, Boko Haram/ISWAP had also mentioned that their "al-Fulani" fighters became martyrs during the suicide attacks in Ndjamena. While there was no coordination between VEOs, such coincidence has also marked the rise of "al-Fulani" jihadists in West Africa, especially in the intelligence and security circle.
22 This was corroborated by the senior politician and researchers of Fulani origin, native in Central Mali (interview with a local researcher/activist in Tokyo, June 2016). Here again, we should recall the subjective nature of ethnicity in West Africa.
23 For many local Fulani in the Sahel, they don't identify themselves with the reference to "al-Fulani," as Fulani is normally used in non-francophone countries (in French, they are called Peulh). So, it may appeal to the clerics with Islamic knowledge or terrorism experts (especially on the Middle East) who are familiar with the use of nom de guerre in Arabic.
24 Twitter dated 15 January 2021. The reason is unknown, yet it may be related to the recent attempts of dialogue and temporary truces between jihadists and rival communities.
25 The narrative of ISGS/ISWAP is framed by the official media outlet of IS Central.
26 Interview with a senior analyst and a mediator in November 2017 at Dakar.
27 The lists were posted online and widely disseminated by the media and SNS.
28 Interview with the local higher rank official in November 2017 in Burkina Faso.

29 GATIA was composed of the Imghad fraction of Tuareg and MSA was formed of another Tuareg-adjacent pastoralist ethnic group, Daoussahak, the dissidents of MNLA (Thurston, 2020).
30 For details, see Grémont (2019) or Thurston (2020).
31 For instance, in 2020, the French President publicly warned the Sahel G5 member countries to stop exactions against the Fulani.
32 For details, see R-CAP (2019) on Liptako Gourma and Hadberg, S. et al (2019) on Burkina Faso.
33 Presentation by a Fulani/Nigerien from Tillabery, in November 2017 at Dakar.
34 We focus much on the grievance of Fulani herdsmen in this chapter; at the same time, Dafinger (2013) notes that "Fulbe herders (in southwest Burkina Faso) repeatedly expressed a profound feeling of injustice," and "ethnicity mainly serves as the rhetorical frame for the local discourse over perceived injustice."
35 Malam Dicko referred to "Djelgodji" in their first claim for the attack in Nassoumbou in 2016 (MENASTREAM, 2017).
36 Lovejoy (2016).
37 Interview with a European expatriate resident in Burkina Faso for years, January 2019. The senders of such messages are Fulani in the northern part, but they just ask for arms, never wage jihad.
38 The attack targeted a priest, seen as an informant by VEOs.
39 From an institutional aspect, regional integration has been promoted by AUC/AU, ECOWAS, and UEMOA, and ECOWAS enacted a free movement of person and goods in 2000, after the EU's model. The African Union (AU) Border Program (AUBP) has contributed to effective border management in Africa, first by helping demarcation of African borders and by developing cross-border communities' activities, primarily in West Africa (Okumu, 2011).
40 Boyer (2019) points out that different interventions in the area of security, development, and protection in Niger have contributed to "make (the space) a contention and blocking space for people on the move."
41 The project aims to strengthen peacebuilding and social cohesion by deepening economic integration through increased cross-border trade, fostering mutual understanding between border communities, strengthening food security, improving livelihoods, and increasing income opportunities, particularly for women and youth.
42 In the Sahel, French NGO Promédiation and Swiss NGO Center for Humanitarian Dialogue are involved in different fronts.
43 (i) Install CCTV (closed-circuit television, or surveillance camera) in airports and cross-border facilities for the enhancement of surveillance capacity, (ii) contribute to medium- and long-term regional stability through development and humanitarian assistance to eight Sahel countries (Chad, Niger, Mali, Mauritania, Cameroon, Nigeria, Burkina Faso, and Senegal).
44 Capacity building of 2,000 people and provision of equipment, etc. for counter-terrorism in North Africa and the Sahel region.
45 In general, Japanese investments in Africa are largely concentrated in resource-rich East and Southern Africa (South Africa, Mozambique, Kenya, etc.).
46 Before Tingatourine, assistance for the security sector was quasi-inexistent, except for Ivory Coast. The table shows the major assistances (grant) by MoFA, and other cooperation frameworks by security and intelligence institutions are excluded from the list.
47 Japan International Cooperation Agency (JICA) manages to run a couple of social development projects (i.e. construction of the school, agriculture) in the Sahel.
48 Online meeting in November 2020.

49 Zenn (2020) indicates that Boko Haram had already intended to build networks in northwest Nigeria (Katsina and Niger State) to raise funds from banditry around 2015, as Shekau prepared the video (unreleased) titled "Message to Fulanis."
50 We should avoid creating another international diplomatic show that brings nothing on the ground.
51 Since 2018, some of the attacks had been oddly claimed by ISWAP, whose foothole is located around the Lake Chad. While there were any credible information supporting their eventual linkage of collaboration between ISWAP and ISGS, the new communication strategy of the IS Central now combines the different small local groupings into a single "Province" (West Africa Province/combining ISGS and ISWAP, and Islamic State of Central Africa Province (ISCAP)/combining Eastern Democratic Republic of Congo – Northern Mozambique) as if those physically distanced groupings were controlling the vast territory under the banner of "IS."

Bibliography

Ahmed, A. (2013). *The Thistle and the Drone: How America's War on Terror Became a Global War on Tribal Islam*, Washington, DC: Brookings Institution Press.

Akinola, E. O. (2017). 'Resistance through Islamic clerics against Boko Haram in northern Nigeria', *African Security Review*, 26:3, pp. 308–324, DOI:10.1080/10246029.2017.1294092

Antil, A. (2017). "Les trafics au Sahel: produits, impacts politiques et gestion des espaces périphériques", in *L'Afrique du Sahel et du Sahara à la Méditerranée*, dir. by Choplin, C., Mareï, N. & Pliez, O. Neuilly-sur-Seine: Atlande.

Antil, A. (2020). 'Le G5 Sahel et le concept de "sécurité-développement"', in *Recherches Internationales*, No. 117, Janvier-mars 2020, pp. 59–74.

Ba Konaré, D. A. O. (2021). *National Narratives of Mali: Fula Communities in Times of Crisis*. Lanham, MD: Lexington Books.

Bourgeot, A. (2020). "Le Djihad Armé d'Amadou Koufa (Mali Central)", in *Recherches Internationales*, No. 117, Janvier-mars 2020, pp. 95–116.

Boyer, F. (2019). Sécurité, développement, protection. Le triptyque de l'externalisation des politiques migratoires au Niger. *Herodote*, 1, pp. 171–191.

Buzan, B. (2000). "The logic of regional security in the post-Cold War world", in *The new regionalism and the future of security and development*, eds. by Hettne, B., Inotai A. and Sunkel O., pp. 1–25. London: Palgrave Macmillan. https://doi.org/10.1007/978-1-137-11498-3_1

Dafinger, A. (2013). *The Economics of Ethnic Conflict: The Case of Burkina Faso*. Martlesham: James Currey.

de Bruijne, K. (2021). "Laws of Attraction: Northern Benin and Risk of Violent Extremist Spillover", CRU Report, Clingendael – the Netherlands Institute of International Relations.

Doquet, A. (2013). "L'ethnie: Fantasme occidental et réalités culturelles", in *La tragédie malienne*, dir. by Gonin, P., Kotlok, N. and Pérouse de Montclos M-A., pp. 159–181, Paris: Vendémiaire.

Eland, I. (2013). *The Failure of Counterinsurgency: Why Hearts and Minds Are Seldom Won*. Santa Barbara, CA: Praeger.

Foucher, M. (2014). *Frontières d'Afrique: Pour en finir avec un mythe*. Paris: CNRS Editions.

Grémont, C. (2019). Dans le piège des offres de violence. Concurrences, protections et représailles dans la région de Ménaka (Nord-Mali, 2000–2018). *Hérodote*, 172, pp. 43–62. https://doi.org/10.3917/her.172.0043

Hadberg, S., Kibora, L. O., Barry, S., Cissao, Y., Gnessi, S., Kaboré, A., Koné, B. and Zongo, M. (2019). "Sécurité par le bas: Perception et perspective citoyennes des défis de sécurité au Burkina Faso". Uppsala: Uppsala University.

Hansen, S. J. (2019). *Horn, Sahel and Rift: Fault-Lines of the African Jihad*. London: Hurst & Co., Ltd.

Harkness, K. A. (2018). *When Soldiers Rebel: Ethnic Armies and Political Instability in Africa*. Cambridge: Cambridge University Press.

Hiribarren, V. (2020). 'Afrique. La mémoire vivante du califat d'Ousmane Dan Fodio'. interview by Pierre Prier in Orient XXI. https://orientxxi.info/magazine/afrique-la-memoire-vivante-du-califat-d-ousmane-dan-fodio,3549

Iheduru, O. C. (2003). 'New Regionalism, States and Non-State Actors in West Africa'. in *The New Regionalism in Africa*, eds. by Söderbaum, F., and Grant, J. A. pp. 47–66. Aldershot: Ashgate.

Institute for Security Studies (ISS). (2020). "Vocational Training to Prevent Terrorism Can Be Counterproductive." https://issafrica.org/iss-today/vocational-training-to-prevent-terrorism-can-be-counterproductive

International Crisis Group (ICG). (2016). "Central Mali: An Uprising in the Making?", Dakar/Brussels: ICG.

International Crisis Group (ICG). (2017). "The Social Roots of Jihadist Violence in Burkina Faso's North", Dakar/Brussels: ICG.

International Crisis Group (ICG). (2019). "The Risk of Jihadist Contagion in West Africa", Briefing N°149, Dakar/Brussels: ICG.

International Crisis Group (ICG). (2020a). "Burkina Faso: Stopping the Spiral of Violence", Africa Report No. 287, Dakar/Geneva: ICG.

International Crisis Group (ICG). (2020b). "Violence in Nigeria's North West: Rolling Back the Mayhem", Africa Report No. 288, Abuja/Brussels: ICG.

International Crisis Group (ICG). (2021). "Mali, a Coup within a Coup", Q&A/Africa.

International Organization for Migration (IOM). (2021). COMMUNIQUE DE PRESSE BENIN: Le Système des Nations Unies appui le Gouvernement du Bénin pour une gestion intégrée des frontiers. https://benin.un.org/sites/default/files/2021-06/COMMUNIQUE%20DE%20PRESSE_COUVERTURE%20MEDIATIQUE_Final1.pdf

Irwin, P. (1981). *Liptako Speaks: History From Oral Tradition in Africa*, Princeton, NJ: Princeton University Press.

Kane, O. O. (2016). *Beyond Timbuktu: An Intellectual History of Muslim West Africa*, Cambridge, MA: Harvard University Press.

Lentz, C. (2013). *Land, Mobility, and Belonging in West Africa*, Bloomington, IN: Indiana University Press.

Longo, M. (2018). *The Politics of Borders: Sovereignty, Security, and the Citizen After 9/11*, Cambridge: Cambridge University Press.

Lovejoy, P. E. (2016). *Jihad in West Africa During the Age of Revolutions*, Athens, OH: Ohio University Press.

McDonnell, N. (2016). *The Civilization of Perpetual Movement: Nomads in the Modern World*, London: Hurst & Co. (Publishers) Ltd.

Ministry of Foreign Affairs of Japan (MoFA). (2019). 'TICAD7: Japan's Contributions for Africa'. www.mofa.go.jp/region/africa/ticad/ticad7/pdf/ticad7_torikumi_en.pdf
NSAIBIA, H. (2020). "In light of the Kafolo attack: The jihadi militant threat in the Burkina Faso and Ivory Coast borderlands". Armed Conflict Location & Event Data Project (ACLED).
Okumu, W. (2011). "Border Management and Security in Africa." www.researchgate.net/publication/308983535_Border_Management_and_Security_in_Africa
Ouédraogo, B. K. (2020). *Sociologie des violences contre l'Etat au Burkina Faso: Question nationale et identité*. Paris: L'Harmattan.
Pérouse de Monclos, M.-A. (2017). "Boko Haram: A jihadist enigma in Nigeria". in *Understanding Boko Haram: Terrorism and Insurgency in Africa*, eds. by Hentz, J. J., and Solomon, H., pp. 19–40. London: Routledge.
Pérouse de Monclos, M.-A. (2018). "Djihad et vidéos de propaganda: le cas Boko Haram". *Politique Etrangère 3:2018*, pp. 171–183.
R-CAP. (2019). "Analyse préliminaire des risques, des vulnérabilités et des actifs de résilience dans la region du Liptako-Gourma", UNOWAS/OECD/OCHA/UNICEF.
Salehyan, I. (2009). *Rebels Without Borders: Transnational Insurgencies in World Politics*. New York: Cornell University Press.
Scheele, J. (2012). *Smugglers and Saints of the Sahara: Regional Connectivity in the Twentieth Century*. Cambridge: Cambridge University Press.
Stapleton, T. J. (2013). *A Military History of Africa, Volume One, the Precolonial Period: From Ancient Egypt to the Zulu Kingdom*. Santa Barbara, CA: Praeger.
Thurston, A. (2020). *Jihadists of North Africa and the Sahel: Politics and Rebel Groups*. Cambridge: Cambridge University Press.
Tisseron, A. (2019). "Menace jihadiste: Les Etats du golfe de Guinée au pied du mur". Note d'actualité 55. Paris: l'Institut Thomas More.
UNDP. (2021). 'Partnership for Peace and Stability in Africa Takes Center Stage at the Second Edition of AFRI CONVERSE 2021'. https://www.africa.undp.org/content/rba/en/home/presscenter/articles/2021/partnership-for-peace-and-stability-in-africa-takes-center-stage.html
UNOWAS. (2018). 'Pastoralism and Security in West Africa and the Sahel: Towards Peaceful Existence'. UNOWAS issue paper. Dakar: UNOWAS.
Zenn, J. (2020). *Unmasking Boko Haram: Exploring Global Jihad in Nigeria*. Boulder, CO: Lynne Rienner Publisher, Inc.

8 Insecurity in the Horn of Africa and the role of IGAD

Rie Takezawa

Security regionalism

Regional organizations are indispensable in order to address regional response for common problems among nation states. Despite the proliferation of various regional organizations in Africa, Intergovernmental Authority on Development (IGAD) is unique in having its focus on regional security, where other regional organizations are more economically oriented.[1] This is due to the characteristics of the security situation in the Horn of Africa.

Although the Horn of Africa has limited level of insurgency linked to terrorist groups compared to that of West Africa, the fact of regional countries supporting terrorist groups must not be ignored. Also, the security situation of the Horn is distinct from other sub-regions of the continent in having severe internal conflicts caused not only by ethnical or religious factors but often intensified by weak borders, state rivalries, and cross-border elite alliances.

In Somalia, terrorist group Al-Shabab continues to fight against the government and security forces, regularly carrying out attacks on the civilian population and sporadic attacks in neighbouring countries. Also, Al-Shabab has been involved in rivalry of regional countries as a non-state violent actor. There are reports that the opposition parties in Kenya support Al-Shabab aiming to raise criticism towards the inability of security management of the current government. Furthermore, reportedly Eritrean government has supported the group with a hostile motive to destabilize the Ethiopia-Somalia border area to disbenefit Ethiopia.

The region has also witnessed one of the longest wars on the continent. The war in Sudan since that lasted for over 20 years which led to the independence of South Sudan in July 2011. However, since 2013, South Sudan has faced severe internal instability of its own and IGAD has facilitated the peace deal between the rival political groups led by President Salva Kiir and Riek Machar in 2018. IGAD is currently supporting the implementation phase. As the Horn of Africa's regional body, IGAD has faced a wide range of tasks in addressing transboundary threats from desert locusts to violent extremism.

This chapter examines the evolution of IGAD's role over the years given the characteristics of the instability in the Horn of Africa and Japan's approach towards IGADs efforts.

The characteristics of instability in the Horn of Africa

The Horn of Africa is often described as Africa's "hotspot." Since the 1960s when the regional countries gained independence, not only has it witnessed intrastate violence and conflicts in Somalia, Sudan, South Sudan, Ethiopia, and Eritrea, but it has also experienced secessionist movements, terrorist attacks by none-state actors and piracy. Moreover, it has been hit by the worst drought and famine on the continent and also has been the scene of two of Africa's longest wars.

Although insecurity in Africa is often caused by multilayered and inter-linked factors and is difficult to define a particular cause, this section aims to shed light on various plausible explanations and arguments shaping the instability in the Horn of Africa. The various factors shaping the security situation of the Horn of Africa are the geopolitical aspect, borderlands issue, none-state actors, state rivalries, and foreign investment.

Geopolitics

When considering the factors of a long-standing regional instability in a region, one of the most traditional approaches is the geopolitical approach. In the case of the Horn of Africa, Clapham (2017) and Markakis (2011) distinguish between the highland which is fertile enough for arable farming, the highland periphery that bare characteristics of a tropical climate which is a suitable environment for plantations and the lowland periphery which suites pastoralism. They describe the "pastoralist zone" as being a land where conflict is inherent due to competition over limited resources. In other words, the regional dynamics of the Horn is fundamentally shaped by interactions between different ecological zones. The regional countries have different ecological characteristics, Ethiopia's highland periphery, the tropical dimension in Sudan, South Sudan, and Uganda and the lowland dimension including the vast expanses of dessert in Sudan, Somalia, and parts of Kenya.

Clapham (2017) explores how the Horn's topography gave rise to the Ethiopian empire, the sole African state to survive European colonialism. Its impact on its neighbours is remarkable and "Ethiopia has almost invariably served as the prism through which outside powers have viewed the region."

While such explanation provides some understanding to the long-standing instability in the region, it is a starting point in analysing the characteristics and its factors of the security situation in the region. For example, it is true to some extent that the instability of Somalia can be attributed to the lack of resources given their low-land feature but does not provide explanations for the rise of terrorism and piracy acts or the fragmentation of national regions due to the conflict between the central government and regional government. Another example is Ethiopia, which is located across the highlands but faces multiple internal security difficulties including conflicts, secessionist movements, and mass internal displacements.

Borders and borderlands

Goodhand (2018) argues that development policy makers tend to suffer from "borderland blindness" as the nation state remains the central unit of analysis and intervention, there is a policy gap when it comes to questions of borders and borderlands. According to the World Bank report "From Isolation to Integration: The Borderlands of the Horn of Africa" (2020), "A 'borderlands' perspective challenges policy makers to reconsider the nature of conflict, development, and state building". The borderlands of the Horn of Africa have long been synonymous with economic, social, and political marginalization; entrenched poverty; conflict and violence; forced displacement; and environmental degradation, spilling across national boundaries. The reach of the state is weak, and livelihoods rely on a combination of informal, illicit, and criminal strategies.

However, in a recent analysis of borderlands in the Horn of Africa, Feyissa and Hoehne (2008) argue that borderland can also go beyond material or financial benefit for residents.[2] It can even be utilized as a political resource. For example, it can be a means to transborder political mobilization, sanctuary for rebels who strive to alter national structures of power, and the strategic co-option of borderland inhabitants by competing states.

Such analysis gives understanding to the long-standing and recurrent issues of insecurity in the region such as legal and illegal trade, arms proliferation, intergroup conflict, security challenges, land conflicts, competition over resources, trafficking (human, children, women), spreading of drugs, and large displacements. Interestingly, such issues are often results or causes of a larger/wider conflict or insurgency which is discussed in the following section.

In February 2021, the United Nations Development Programme (UNDP) launched the Africa Borderlands Centre (ABC) in Kenya. The centre is a new initiative aimed at providing research, policy analysis, and programming dedicated to East Africa's borderlands.[3] The ABC will also work with borderlands influencers and leaders to co-create "innovation challenges," aimed at transforming security, economic, and environmental vulnerabilities in the borderlands into opportunities for inclusive development.[4] IGAD will also provide integrated and holistic approach to the launched centre. At its launching ceremony, the executive secretary mentioned that

> When goods do not cross borders, soldiers will. In other words, integrated trade is one of the best deterrents of conflict. For us at IGAD and the communities we work with in cross-border areas, we firmly believe that sustainable state-building must fully and deliberately account for and accommodate borderland areas.[5]

None-state actors

Although the Horn of Africa has not seen as a hot spot of insurgency linked to terrorist groups compared to that of West Africa, the fact that terrorist activities are deeply rooted in regional history and politics must not be ignored.

The evolution and expansion of terrorist and insurgent organizations in the Horn of Africa is intensified by underdevelopment and armed conflicts. Violence and oppression by government and security agencies have fuelled political and economic grievances of the local population, making it easier for non-state violent actors to conduct their activities. Conflicts and crises in the region provide a great opportunity for terrorist organizations, including Al-Shabab and IS, to penetrate and expand. It should be noted that the social unrest caused by the ongoing spread of the new coronavirus could facilitate the expansion of Al-Shabab, Al-Qaida, and IS.

In addition, it is becoming obvious in recent years that terrorist activities and insurgency recur in countries and regions where they were once swept away. It is due to the lack of sustainable stability in the regional political and security situation. The governments and security agencies in the region do not have the capacity or resources to monitor and control the vast border areas and are unable to deter non-state violent actors' cross-border movements and network. Hence, the issue of the return of fighters of terrorist organizations in the region and dealing with cross-border terrorist and extremist organizations requires mechanisms for coordination, information sharing, and joint operations among the neighbouring countries, as well as international support.

Al-Qaida and other Jihadi movements have been active since the 1990s in the Horn of Africa. In 1998, the East African branch of Al-Qaida carried out a terrorist attack against the US embassy in Nairobi and another attack against the US embassy in Dar es Salaam. Somalia has been without a functioning central government for more than 20 years, creating safe haven in which non-state actors, in particular Jihadi terrorist organizations could easily move and establish their training camps.

There are various theories about the origins of Al-Shabab, but it could have originated from a group of youth who had fought in Afghanistan and established a camp in the northern Somalia in 2003, among the Islamist forces in the country that had previously operated as the Islamic Courts Union. The organization's activity was accelerated in 2007, when the establishment of Al-Shabab was announced.

Although Al-Shabab took control of large parts of the central and southern Somalia in 2008, it was counterattacked by the Somali Transitional Government, AMISOM, and Ethiopian forces, and withdrew from Mogadishu in August 2011. It then became even more outnumbered following Kenya's deployment to Somalia in October 2011 and withdrew from major cities in the southern and central regions. In recent years, it has lost a series of senior leaders, and since 2015, it has been weakened by withdrawing from cities it had long occupied (United Nations Security Council, 2015).

On the other hand, terrorist attacks in Mogadishu and neighbouring countries continue to be active. The series of bombings in Kampala, Uganda in July 2010 killed 76 people. In Kenya, more than 60 people were killed in the September 2013 attack on a shopping mall in Nairobi and about 150 people were killed in the April 2015 attack on a university in the eastern province of

Garissa. Al-Shabab is said to have used the Dadaab refugee camp in northeastern Kenya (of which the Kenyan government announced the closure in May 2016), where many Somali refugees were housed, as an operational hub, and there are indications that the attack on the Nairobi shopping mall was planned at the refugee camp.

Al-Shabab's fighters are not only Somalis (people who speak Somali and share Somali culture) and Somali nationals but also foreign fighters from neighbouring countries and the West. In addition, support from Somali diaspora has also been confirmed. In March 2010, the United Nations reported that in August 2009, Al-Shabab launched a campaign on the Internet to seek financial support from Somalis around the world, and raised more than $40,000 in two weeks (United Nations Security Council, 2010). In addition, there are various large and small Somali communities in Europe and the United States. In particular, a considerable number of Somali nationals from the United Kingdom are said to be participating in Al-Shabab.

In other words, people, goods, and money are flowing into Al-Shabab across national borders, and the organization has the intelligence, logistics, and combat capabilities to carry out terrorist attacks outside the country. In March 2008, the US government under the Bush administration designated Al-Shabab as a Foreign Terrorist Organization (United States Department of State, 2008). Also, in April 2010, the UN Security Council's "Sanctions Committee in Resolutions 751 and 1907" designated Al-Shabab as a target of sanctions for directly or indirectly threatening the peace and stability of Somalia (United Nations, 2010).

The Al-Shabab has also been involved in the regional rivalries and politics of neighbouring countries. There are reports that the opposition parties in Kenya support Al-Shabab aiming to raise criticism towards the inability of security management of the current government. It was also reported that Eritrea has been harbouring Al-Shabab fighters and indirectly providing them with weapons and financial aides (United Nations Security Council, 2011, 2012). As a non-state violent actor, Al-Shabab is utilized by regional countries and political entities to realize their political objectives.

State rivalries and cross-border elite alliances

De Waal (2015) argues that politics in the region operates much like a market. Leaders operate on a business model, securing funds for their "political budgets" which they use to rent the provisional allegiances of army officers, militia commanders, tribal chiefs, and party official. This political marketplace erodes the institutions of government and reversing state-building and it is fuelled in large part by oil exports, aid funds, and western military assistance. Moreover, de Waal argues that in the Horn of Africa, elite alliances operate across borders. Political entrepreneurs survive only if they can secure material resources and receive funding from external patrons, which they use to purchase political support.

Others also make similar arguments. Berouk (2011) explains that the regional countries "took advantage of every local tension or conflict to support rebel movements in neighbouring states." Furthermore, he states that there is a principle of "my enemy's enemy is my friend" extending throughout the Horn of Africa. Cliffe (1999) also points out that the "opponents of existing regimes all receive some support from governmental or other forces in other countries of the region." Healy (2008) analyses that "the states of the region all act as enablers and multipliers of conflict to the detriment of their neighbours."

For example, in the mid-1990s, Sudan was characterized as a state sponsor of terrorism, and Ethiopia, Eritrea, and Uganda had a common policy to contain and confront it with US support (Healy, 2008: 39).

Characteristics

In conclusion, we can analyse that the Horn of Africa is distinct from other regions of the continent given the rivalries between regional countries states and cross-border elite alliances. However, like other African nations, the root causes of insecurity in the Horn of Africa can be attributed to internal structural challenges such as state fragility, governance vulnerability, poverty, democracy issues, economy and resource management, and foreign interventions (Berouk, 2011). Hence, the impact of border-related and cross-border challenges are multiplied or continues to pose threat to the region.

Evolvement of IGAD

Despite the challenging multilayered and inter-linked security challenges as mentioned previously, the region has not been paralysed. And even though state rivalries are one of the contributing factors to the long-standing regional insecurity, in 1986, six regional countries (Djibouti, Ethiopia, Kenya, Somalia, Sudan, and Uganda) made an agreement to establish Intergovernmental Authority on Drought and Development (IGADD). The region was hit by life-threatening drought, one of the deadliest on the African continent and there was a critical need for an organization to facilitate a common approach towards the common problem.

At the time, the region was affected by the cold war. Ethiopia was strongly supported by the USSR, while the United States sponsored Sudan and Somalia. Interestingly, the member states launched IGADD with a non-political objective and focused on tackling the challenges.

Over the years, insecurity in the region continued to intensify, and after the end of the cold war, the great powers gradually weakened their influence on the continent forcing the African countries to deal with the security challenges by themselves. In March 1996, the regional countries decided to revitalize IGADD and task it with mandates centred around peace and security such as conflict prevention and resolution.

The launch and evolvement of IGAD developed security regionalism in the Horn of Africa driven by its serious security challenges. After the cold war, regional organizations emerged as key stakeholders of international peace and security. Today, IGAD is a permanent regional organization its secretariat in Djibouti, and its peace and security section based in Ethiopia.

Performance of IGAD in ensuring security

The institutional mission of IGAD is to become the regional organization for the promotion of peace, prosperity, and integration by assisting and complementing the efforts of member states to achieve through increased cooperation (a) food security and environmental protection; (b) promotion and maintenance of peace, security, and humanitarian affairs; and (c) economic cooperation. The key objective of the organization is the peaceful settlement of interstate and intrastate conflicts through dialogue and maintenance of regional peace and security.

Healy (2009) argues that the peace and security mandate of IGAD emerged in 1996 in the context of a broad international consensus that regional organizations should contribute to the management of conflict and the maintenance of international order.

From the perspective of institutional mechanism, the IGAD holds a division overseeing the peace and security area based in Addis Ababa, Ethiopia. Such peace and security architecture can be contextualized with reference to the African Union's and United Nation's peace and security architecture. However, there is no specific office that is mandated with peace processes, but instead, IGAD Special Envoys are often appointed along with a support team.

The case of Sudan

IGAD led peace talks in Sudan was pursued in two phases. The first phase covers IGAD's intervention in Sudan through its standing committee on peace. In 1997, IGAD initiated a diplomatic and political offensive to revive the peace talks in Sudan by appointing the then President Daniel Arap Moi of Kenya as a Special Envoy to the Sudan peace process. The IGAD peace process under Kenyan leadership was successful in bringing the parties to the dialogue but was unable to produce significant gains.

IGAD's mediation initiative began again in October 1997 and the parties drafted and signed a Comprehensive Peace Agreement (CPA) in Nairobi on 9 January 2005. Borchgrevink and Lie (2009) analyse that although the CPA did not resolve all the problems, it represented a significant step forward in ending one of the longest wars on the globe.

The case of Somalia

IGAD's engagement in facilitating the Somali peace process began in 1998. IGAD summit of March 1998 called for an end to the proliferation of competing initiatives that served to undermine the peace process in Somalia. However, with the outbreak of conflict between Ethiopia and Eritrea in May 1998, Eritrea was soon reported to be arming the Aideed faction and Ethiopia began its assistance to its allies in Somalia.

In 2004, IGAD led mediation initiatives made a breakthrough in Somali peace process in facilitating the establishment of the Transitional Federal Government. The Somali warring factions and civil society signed the Nairobi Agreement which pave the way for the adoption of the Transitional Federal Charter, with a five-year transitional period of the government. In 2006, an AU-approved IGAD Peace Support Mission to Somalia (IGASOM) involving 8,000 troops at a cost of $335 million in the first year was also dispatched.

The signing of the Sudan and Somali peace agreements in the mid-2000s gave the impression that IGAD was playing a significant role in mediating regional conflicts.

The case of South Sudan

South Sudan declared its independence in July 2011, after the protracted civil wars with Sudan. However, on December 15 2013, violent conflict broke out between rival political groups led by President Salva Kiir and Rick Machar resulting in mass internal displacement and deaths.

On December 27, IGAD convened an emergency meeting of the Assembly of Heads of State and Government (summit) and was agreed that IGAD shall mediate between South Sudan's warring parties. In addition, three envoys from Ethiopia, Kenya, and Sudan were chosen in order to start the mediation process immediately.

The first round of peace talks took place in January 2014 in Addis Ababa, Ethiopia. The discussion focused on immediate ceasefire and the cessation of agreement was signed between the parties of the conflict on the same month. However, the agreement failed to meet its objective and fighting continued. There are arguments that the regional rivalries and lack of institutionalization within IGAD limited IGAD's mediation efforts (International Crisis Group, 2015). The parties of the conflict were unwilling to respect the agreement, and even though there were seven more round of peace talks, they were all unsuccessful in realizing cessation.

Given such failure, the "IGAD+(plus)" consisting of the African Union, the United Nations, China, EU, the United States, the United Kingdom, Norway, and IGAD was launched in March 2015. Since the parties of the conflict were unwilling to respect the peace agreement, pressure from the international community was considered necessary. In August 2015, the "Compromise Peace Agreement" was signed.

However, Machar returned to Juba in 2016 leading to breakout of violence. The agreement was then revitalized by IGAD in September 2018 as the Revitalized Agreement on the Resolution of the conflict in the Republic of South Sudan with the support from IGAD Special Envoy for South Sudan Ambassador Ismail Weiss, and IGAD+ was signed in Addis Ababa. The accord was brokered by Sudan's President Omar al-Bashir and Uganda's President Yoweri Museveni.

The agreement outlines a comprehensive roadmap to peace for South Sudan, including an 8-month pre-transitional period, followed by a 36-month transitional period leading to a national election in 2022.

Conventional projects and foreign assistance

Although peace processes are the most visible activities of IGAD, IGAD carries out various conventional operations and also launched mechanisms in order to address the midterm and long-term security challenges of the horn. As an example, two projects will be examined.

The Conflict Early Warning and Response Mechanism (CEWARN) of IGAD was established in 2003, with its secretariat in Addis Ababa and has been one of the key IGAD projects to date.[6] The concept of conflict early warning emerged globally in the 1990s as an instrument of preventive diplomacy. According to IGAD, therefore, CEWARN was tasked with using early warning methods to enhance security and develop peace infrastructure on the regional level. Before conflict early warning emerged globally in the 1990s as an instrument of preventive diplomacy, pastoralist conflict was treated as a low priority.[7] The objective is to "receive and share information concerning potentially violent conflicts as well as their outbreak and escalation in the IGAD region."[8] This based on the notion that timely interventions are more effective than waiting for potential conflicts to develop into full-scale crises. Since its launch, CEWARN has developed step by step into an early warning system for monitoring pastoral conflicts.

CEWARN covers selected areas, or clusters. For example, the Karamoja cluster (covering Kenya, Uganda, Ethiopia, and Sudan) and the Somali cluster (the borderlands of Kenya, Ethiopia, and Somalia) has been its focus. The CEWARN secretariat work with lower level institutions down to the district level and in each country, a national research institute is also involved, overseeing the information collection and as employers of the local level field monitors. While the clusters still cover only a limited part of the Horn of Africa, there has been a steady growth in the scope of the programme and in the inclusion of further member states.

USAID and GTZ have been the main funders of CEWARN. For the Rapid Response Fund, a multi-donor basket fund has been set up, with contributions from Austria, Denmark, the German GTZ, Italy, Sweden, and the United Kingdom.

To date, CEWARN is continuing to evolve and IGAD has analysed some of its challenges. Similar to other conflict prevention efforts on the continent, measuring the success of CEWARN has been a difficult task. There is no universal standard or criteria for measuring conflict prevention even though many analyses regarding the failure of conflict prevention exist. In other words, CEWARN is likely to gain attention only when a large-scale conflict occurs, and not during peace time even though it is a well-earned success of CEWARN.

The IGAD Capacity Building Program against Terrorism (ICPAT)[9] was launched in 2006, given the decision of the Heads of State of IGAD Member States meeting in 2002. Its aims are to build national capacities for combating terrorism and to promote regional security cooperation. The office is located in Addis Ababa, and the programme cooperates with local thinktanks. Its main areas of activities are (i) enhancing legal capacity; (ii) optimizing interdepartmental cooperation; (iii) enhancing border control; (iv) training, information sharing, and best practices; and (v) promoting strategic cooperation.

ICPAT has received financial support from Canada, Denmark, Italy, the Netherlands, Norway, Spain, Sweden, and technical support from the United Kingdom. Some IGAD officials mentioned during an interview that the activities are rather focused on intelligences sharing than actual capacity building and are donor-driven.[10] The interviewees further explained that ICPAT's role is to serve as an institution for training and capacity building of the IGAD member states rather than developing IGAD itself as the intelligence-gathering body.

IGAD as a political tool

Despite IGAD's efforts and various achievements over the years, member countries have used IGAD as a tool to realize their motive against another conflicting member country. This is evident in the case of Ethiopia and Eritrea, the two countries experienced a deadly war since 1991. It can be analysed that Ethiopia refused to transfer the chairmanship of IGAD for ten years since 2008 in order to marginalize Eritrea from other regional countries until the normalization of relations in 2018, after which Ethiopia gave up its chairmanship.

The Agreement Establishing IGAD stipulates that the Chairmanship of IGAD must rotate annually among the eight member states (i.e. Djibouti, Eritrea, Ethiopia, Kenya, South Sudan, Somalia, Sudan, and Uganda). Just like any other contemporary regional, continental, and international organizations, the principle of "Rotation and Equitable Representation" is also applied in IGAD. The IGAD member states differ in size and economic conditions, but they are all equal and entitled to equal responsibility and participation in the affairs of the organization.

When examining the case of Ethiopia's chairmanship, the principle had been violated for ten years. It can be argued that given the regional environment at the time, Ethiopia was the only member country at the time with the will and capacity to hold the chairmanship and was unbale to pass it on to other member countries. However, this section aims to examine the reasons from the perspective of regional political dynamics.

Ethiopia assumed the Chairmanship of IGAD for a one-year term in June 2008.[11] Ethiopia, invoking all types of excuses, has been deliberately preventing the IGAD Heads of State from holding their annual Ordinary Summit as the election for the chairmanship is a standing item on the agenda of the Ordinary Sessions. But, whenever it has an agenda item that serves its political and diplomatic agenda, Ethiopia has never shied away from calling Extraordinary

Summits,[12] which most of the time took place on the sidelines of the AU Summits Ethiopia Refuses to Abdicate IGAD Chairmanship.[13]

However, after Ethiopia and Eritrea signed a peace agreement in 2018 which put an end to two decades of conflict, Ethiopia gave up the IGAD chairmanship. Ethiopian Prime Minister Abiy Ahmed, who took office in April 2018 and promoted democratic evolution in the country, decided to accept that the contested land Badame was Eritrea's territory.[14] They decided to resume diplomatic, transport, trade, and communication ties that had been frozen for two decades.[15]

The challenges

In essence, thought IGAD has been useful in mediating conflicts of the region, there is no evident criteria or systematization of IGAD involvement in peace processes and a certain ad hoc native can been seen. For example, IGAD sought no major role in some of the most serious conflicts in the region such as the Ethiopia–Eritrea conflict, Northern Uganda conflict and the Darfur conflict.

One may argue that IGAD led mediation depends on the preference of member countries or is affected by the international community. On the other hand, one may argue that a certain level of flexibility and ownership is left to IGAD in the decision whether to adapt a mediation or not. Interestingly, some IGAD officials mentioned to the writer during an interview that there are cases where IGAD was unable to handle the mediation despite the will of the regional countries and IGAD itself due to the lack of human resources and funding.[16] The peace processes have been heavily depended on external resources and that extra-regional countries and partner groups have been integrally involved. The consolidation and capacity building of IGAD led mediation remains to be a task in the insecure region. However, it must be noted that although peace processes are the most visible activities of IGAD, IGAD carries out various conventional operations in order to address the midterm and long-term security challenges of the horn.

Japan's assistance to IGAD

Japan's assistance to IGAD is an example of Japan's peace building effort in Africa. However, the assistance to IGAD is significant as it aims to directly address the instability in the Horn of Africa, whereas most of Japan's peacebuilding support aims at prevention and recovery of conflicts through achieving quality economic growth but.

Japan's peacebuilding policy

Despite the differing definitions of peacebuilding among governments and donors, the conceptual basis of peacebuilding is that "peacebuilding involves a range of measures targeted to reduce the risk of lapsing or relapsing into conflict by strengthening national capacities at all levels for conflict management, and to lay the foundations for sustainable peace and development."[17] Though actors working on peacebuilding have their own interpretations of the concept and developed their own strategies, it may be understood broadly as providing seamless support in various phases, from conflict resolution to reconstruction and development.

To date, Japan's approach to peacebuilding has been unique in the sense that its contribution has focused on post-conflict nation-building and conflict prevention in peacetime[18] mainly through realizing "Quality Growth."[19] The Japanese government emphasized the importance of quality growth in the Development Cooperation Charter, revised in October 2015, stating that "in order to resolve the poverty issue in a sustainable manner, it is essential to achieve economic growth through human resources development, infrastructure development and establishment of regulations and institutions as well as the growth of the private sector."[20]

The fact that Japan's peacebuilding policy focuses on economic growth is evident by looking at Japan's development assistance implementor JICA's peacebuilding policy. In February 2011, JICA reviewed its Thematic Guidelines on Peacebuilding. One of the key revisions was that the assistance for peacebuilding shares the same objective with conventional development assistance, which is to contribute to development. Thus, sectors of assistance for peacebuilding are almost common with other development assistance, such as infrastructure, education, health, and agriculture.[21]

The case of South Sudan

Japan has supported IGAD's initiative to revitalize the Agreement on the Resolution of the Conflict in South Sudan. In 2018, Japan decided to provide a new assistance package of $34 million for South Sudan through its partnership with IGAD to facilitate the High-level Revitalization Forum in which it is a platform for peace talks among the conflict. Since, it has supported the IGAD South Sudan office in realizing the peace process. Japan is the largest donor to the office, and without Japan's support, it will not be able to sustain its activities as other donors were unwilling to support IGAD's mediation initiative. Up to date, Japan has continued to support the peace process of South Sudan through IGAD.

The case of South Sudan can be seen as a test case for Japan's more integrated approach to peacebuilding in Africa and also a unique peacebuilding case where Japan has contributed through both its contribution to the UNPKO, development assistance and support through regional organization. To respond efficiently and effectively to South Sudan's enormous peacebuilding needs, various peacebuilding-related actors including the Japan Self Defense Force (JSDF) have collaborated on realizing peace building in the country. Given the request from UN Secretary General Ban Ki-moon, the Japanese government decided to dispatch the JSDF engineering unit to South Sudan. They were mainly engaged in road construction and other infrastructure projects in and around Juba from January 2012 to May 2017. Even under restrictions of the JSDF's military activities overseas, the engineering sector in South Sudan was one where Japan could contribute with its former engineering experience from UNPKO in East Timor and Cambodia, etc. Although after the U.N. Security Council adopted Resolution 2155 in May 2014, the primary mandate of the U.N. Mission in the Republic of South Sudan (UNMISS) became the protection of civilians during nation building, the engineering unit continued its engagement through engineering operations that prioritize civilian protection such as road construction which is critical for humanitarian access.

As for Japan's contribution in the conventional development assistance sector, Japan International Cooperation Agency (JICA) has engaged in bilateral cooperation with the government of South Sudan after its independence in 2011, with the aim of contributing to the consolidation of peace in the country. However, strategically, JICA's support mainly focuses on contributing to the country's long-term development. Particularly, JICA's assistance emphasizes the development of social and economic infrastructure, the diversification of industries, the improvement of basic services, governance building, and security.

Given such peacebuilding approach of Japan, it is significant that it is providing continuous significant support towards the peace process of South Sudan.

The challenges of IGAD and the way forward

As discussed previously, although IGAD has been useful in mediating conflicts of the region, there is no evident criteria or systematization of IGAD involvement in peace processes and a certain ad hoc native can been seen. However, the launch and evolution of IGAD developed security regionalism in the Horn of Africa driven by its serious security challenges and has been useful to some extent in addressing regional challenges.

Today, the Horn of Africa is facing one of the most severe security challenges in its history. Although a tentative peace deal has been agreed between the rival political groups led by President Salva Kiir and Riek Machar in South Sudan, the implementation of the peace deal is lagging greatly in schedule, gradually raising the possibilities of relapse into conflict. The Sudan currently has a transitional civilian-led government which replaced the regime led by former President Omar al-Bashir after nearly 30 years of his power and will be holding an election in 2022. Ethiopia holds conflict in the norther Tigray region with alleged human rights violations and genocide by the government military.

Furthermore, as Middle Eastern states are increasing its influence in the Horn of Africa, a new geopolitical paradigm is emerging and rivalries among the United Arab Emirates and Saudi Arabia on the one hand and Turkey and Qatar on the other hand may fuel instability in the region. This is already evident in Somalia as the central government and regional government are fragmented with influence from both parties. There are already talks within IGAD to serve as a platform in facilitating a common policy among regional countries towards the intervention from the middle east. If such effort materializes, it will pave a new way for IGADs role as a regional organization in addressing security risks of the Horn of Africa.[22]

Notes

1 In this chapter, "Horn of Africa" denotes the geographical area comprising the seven member states of the Intergovernmental Authority on Development (IGAD): Djibouti, Eritrea, Ethiopia, Kenya, Somalia, Sudan, and Uganda.
2 The everyday operation of borderland regions is driven primarily by asymmetrical conditions on either side of the border (i.e. safety and security, living expenses, employment prospects, economic regulation, political repression, physical infrastructure (including hospitals)).
3 The Regional Bureau Africa (RBA) team in New York provides overall strategic oversight, guidance and quality assurance, management support and broader regional analysis, including on global issues. At the regional level, the Regional Service Centre and sub-regional platforms provide integrated and holistic support to RBA Country Offices and regional partners, such as the African Union Commission and the Regional Economic Communities, across all UNDP's areas of work. www.africa.undp.org/content/rba/en/home/about_us.html
4 www.africa.undp.org/content/rba/en/home/presscenter/pressreleases/2021/the-africa-borderlands-centre--reimagining-africas-borderlands-a.html
5 https://igad.int/executive-secretary/2619-igad-executive-secretary-at-the-launch-of-undp-africa-borderlands-centre
6 www.igadregion.org/cewarn/
7 IGAD [2021] CONFLICT EARLY WARNING IN THE HORN: JOURNEY
8 www.igadregion.org/cewarn/
9 www.igadregion.org/icpat/
10 Interview by author to IGAD officials carried out in February 2019 in Djibouti.
11 12th Ordinary Summit of the Organization held in Addis Ababa, on 14 June 2008
12 Member states have also the right to request the holding of extraordinary sessions in between the regular ones.
13 https://tesfanews.net/ethiopia-refuses-to-abdicate-igad-chairmanship/
14 Some argue that the historical rivalry and hegemonic competition between the ruling elites of Ethiopia and Eritrea at the time were the main causes of the conflict. Therefore, the cause of the conflict disappeared when Abiy who is from a different ethnicity and political party came to power. Even more, President Isaias of Eritrea and Prime Minister Abiy had the same enemy in common, the dominant political party of Ethiopia Tigray People's Liberation Front (TPLF) until Abiy assumed office.
15 However, there are arguments that not much of the discussion at the time has been materialized. There were talks for borders to remain open and enabling citizens of the two countries to travel freely, but this only lasted for a limited amount of time.
16 Interview carried out to several IGAD senior officials in Addis Ababa Ethiopia, July 2019.
17 U.N. Secretary-General's Policy Committee (2007), United Nations Peacebuilding Support Office. "Peacebuilding & the United Nations." www.un.org/en/peacebuilding/pbso/pbun.shtml.
18 This is largely due to restrictions on JSDF activities outside Japanese territory. In this sense, working within constraints, Japan has developed a unique peacebuilding policy over time, which differs from that of the United States and other countries that play leading roles in peacebuilding.
19 Prime Minister ABE unveiled the "Free and Open Indo-Pacific" concept in his keynote address at TICAD VI in Kenya in August 2016. Japan aims to provide nation-building support in the area of development as well as politics and governance, in a way that respects the ownership of African countries. However, there are criticism towards the concept to be too centred around Asian countries and

coastal countries which may lead to marginalization of inland countries. www.mod.go.jp/en/d_act/exc/india_pacific/india_pacific-en.html
20 Ministry of Foreign Affairs of Japan. Development Cooperation Charter (Provisional Translation) February 10, 2015. www.mofa.go.jp/policy/oda/page_000138.html
21 It is estimated that more than 4 million South Sudanese, approximately one-third of its total population, have been displaced.
22 Interview carried out to several IGAD senior officials in Addis Ababa Ethiopia, February 2020.

Bibliography

Berouk, M. (2011) 'The Horn of Africa Security Complex', in Sharamo, R. and Berouk, M. (eds.) *Regional Security in the Post-Cold War Horn of Africa*, Monograph 178, Pretoria: Institute for Security Studies.

Borchgrevink, A. and Lie, J. H. S. (2009) *Regional Conflicts and International Engagement on the Horn of Africa*, Oslo: Norwegian Institute of International Affairs.

Clapham, C. (2017) *The Horn of Africa: State Formation and Decay*, London: C Hurst & Co Publishers Ltd.

Cliffe, L. (1999) 'Regional Dimensions of Conflict in the Horn of Africa', *Third World Quarterly*, vol. 29, no. 1, pp. 89–111.

De Waal, A. (2015) *The Real Politics of the Horn of Africa: Money, War and the Business of Power*, Cambridge: Polity Press.

Feyissa & Hoehne (2008) *Resourcing State Borders and Borderlands in the Horn of Africa*. available at https://www.eth.mpg.de/pubs/wps/pdf/mpi-eth-working-paper-0107.pdf

Goodhand (2018) *The Centrality of the Margins: The political economy of conflict and development in borderlands*, Working Paper 2 "Borderlands, Brokers and Peacebuilding: War to Peace Transitions Viewed from the Margins."

Healy, S. (2008) *Lost Opportunities in the Horn of Africa How Conflicts Connect and Peace Agreements Unravel*, A Chatham House Report, London: The Royal Institute of International Affairs.

Healy, S. (2009) *Peacemaking in the Midst of War: An Assessment of IGAD's Contribution to Regional Security*, Working Paper no. 59, London: LSE.

International Crisis Group (2015) *South Sudan: Keeping Faith with the IGAD Peace Process*.

Markakis, J. (2011) *Ethiopia: The Last Two Frontiers*, Sufflok: James Currey Ltd.

United Nations Security Council (2010) Letter dated 10 March 2010 from the Chairman of the Security Council Committee pursuant to resolutions 751 (1992) and 1907 (2009) concerning Somalia and Eritrea addressed to the President of the Security Council (S/2010/91).

United Nations Security Council (2011) Letter dated 18 July 2011 from the Chairman of the Security Council Committee pursuant to resolutions 751 (1992) and 1907 (2009) concerning Somalia and Eritrea addressed to the President of the Security Council (S/2011/433).

United Nations Security Council (2012) Letter dated 7 October 2016 from the Chair of the Security Council Committee pursuant to resolutions 751(1992) and 1907(2009) concerning Somalia and Eritrea addressed to the President of the Security Council, (S/2012/545).

United Nations Security Council (2015) Report of the Secretary-General on Somalia, (S/2015/331).

United States Department of State (2008) Designation of al-Shabaab as a Foreign Terrorist Organization, February 26, www.state.gov/.

9 The hardening of African borders in the Era of growing security threats and the global War on Terror

Aimé Raoul Sumo Tayo

In the 1990s, some scholars predicted the withering away of borders and thus nation-state as the unique political structure of modern times (Wilson & Donnan, 2012). Ohmae (1996) and O'Brien (1991) have suggested that globalization will eliminate borders. In Africa, until the eve of the 2000s, some scholars had predicted the withering away of boundaries. For example, Mbembe (1999) had noted a dynamic of *deterritorialization* of borders, and Bennafla (2003) had argued the risk of territorial disintegration of some African states due to the combined effect of security crises, the weakness of the State, the revival of primary identities, and the rise of informal economies.

Like Asiwaju (2012), more optimistic scholars had revealed the devaluation of the barrier function of African borders. Evidence has shown the contrary (Wilson & Donnan, 2012), and it appears that the idea of a borderless world was wishful thinking (Debray, 2010). The reality is that since September 11, borders have been erected as front lines to protect States from undesirable individuals, ideologies, and goods to the extent that the trend towards wall construction is picking up again (Amilhat Szary, 2015). Nevertheless, September 11 is said to have a marginal impact in Africa (Ackleson, 2012). Whereas the continent has witnessed a proliferation of *Teichopolitics* (Rosière & Jones, 2012), of which walls and trenches are the most common form. These new mechanisms of hardening borders on the continent came in addition to the old ones. The latter intended to fix the borders within the framework of a conflict or fight against immigration.

This work will focus on these mechanisms of partitioning space on the continent, the forms they take, and the securitization processes that led to their implementation. It proceeds by categorizing their different morphologies and a typology based on the justifications and uses of these mechanisms. This study relies on primary sources, like documents from security and administrative archives and interviews with local actors in some borderlands of Central and West Africa. Academic works, reports from local NGOs, and newspapers will allow us to go beyond Central and West Africa.

The content analysis of these data shows that these mechanisms of partitioning space take the form of stricter access policies, the construction of physical barriers, and the establishment of reticular boundaries. The justification discourses reveal binary constructs between "us" and "others," as well as the expression of disagreement and militarization of the contiguousness that results. Beyond the discourses, a functional analysis of these border highlighting devices makes it possible to identify defensive borders against the enemy, whether jihadist or illegal migrant.

Theoretical and conceptual framework

This work relies mainly on neo-realistic approaches to security to explain the hardening of African borders. Indeed, in an anarchic international system and the absence of a common superior, states ensure their sovereignty and security in the face of external threats (Waltz, 1988). The security dilemma explains this approach with an action-response model in which the optimization or expansion of a state's military capabilities to strengthen its security leads to insecurity in third countries (Buzan et al., 1998). Faced with the limits of conventional controls governance, States sometimes choose to shield their borders. For Ritaine (2009), border hardening appears to be "an asymmetric response to the perception of an asymmetric peril." Therefore, the wall is a means of exercising state sovereignty in a context of an unbalanced balance of power.

On the other hand, transnational models present the mechanisms of hardening of borders as a method of optimization by the states, the objective is to select the desired elements likely to enrich its material capacities, and upstream, to reject undesirable people who would be a ball to its competitiveness (Beaulieu-Brossard & David, 2013). In addition, securitization theories allow us to seize the performative (Waever, 1995), politics (Buzan et al., 1998), and normative (Trombetta, 2010) dimensions of border hardening schemes in the framework of border security which refers to border control, border management, border monitoring, and border protection.

In effect, there is a global process of securitization of immigration policies and the "hardening" of borders through various closure systems to prevent un undesired flows (Rosière & Jones, 2012). This dynamic consists of physical walls and strict border control to prevent crossing borders (Pettersson, 2020). It also consists of reinforcing laws and regulations on migrations and controlling the transnational movement of peoples and goods, the ultimate objective being to detect and prevent the entry of unwanted persons, animals, vegetal, and goods (Okumu, 2011). Fences and walls are considered the "most emblematic artefact of teichopolitics" (Rosière & Jones, 2012). More recently, in Africa, some states are hardening their borders in a context where regional security mechanisms like the Economic Community of Central Africa State (ECCAS) have failed to deliver security (Kewirh, 2020). Building border walls, in this context, is one of the most aggressive strategies adopted by States to secure their borders (Carter & Poast, 2015).

Walls refer to the political divider with fixed masonry foundations. However, they also refer to the control method, discourse, and legislative provision (Vallet & David, 2012). These policies belong to several registers. These can be the administrative register with the control and visa systems; the military register with the laying of mines; the physical register with pits, fences, and checkpoints with a strong symbolic dimension or not (Damiani, 2013). Usually, physical barriers along national borders are called "walls." However, the support for those physical obstacles consists of various materials like sheet metal, cement blocks, fencing, and barbed wire (Pettersson, 2020). Border walls and the other elements of the hardening of borders are reputed to be violent (Jones, 2016). That is why building walls and fences are usually associated with stigma (Rosière & Jones, 2012).

Forms and characteristics of African border walls

Hardening borders can take various forms, symbolic and legal, or material forms such as walls, fences, and borders posts. Jason Ackleson classifies the post-September 11 teichopolitics in two categories: firstly, constructing walls and vehicle barriers and using the military and law enforcement resources. Secondly, there are "virtual" bordering measures such as biometrics and the "smart borders" and transborder cooperation on immigration and non-territorial border control (Ackleson, 2012).

Legal and symbolic hardening of African borders

One of the border functions is screening to regulate the movements of persons and goods. Since September 11, this border function has taken a vigorous security dimension. Borders also have a filter function since they prevent border crossing and gate function because they prevent border passage in certain places. Border have also panopticon function since they monitor inside or outside a defined area (Pavlakovich-Kochi, 2011). These various functions are fundamental for African states facing cross-border crime and insecurity (Andrés, 2008). For Ghana, for example, the main security issues are the smuggling of goods, drug and human trafficking, money laundering, refugee influx, and animal movement (Sosuh, 2011). The securitization of these various threats usually begins with speech acts by which these issues are considered an existential threat that needs exceptional measures and actions. The uprising of jihadism in Mali, for example, has led to the revocation of the 6 May 1964, Convention on the Establishment and Movement of Persons between Mali and Cameroon under which citizens of the two countries were free to establish themself in the other country.

Also, hardening the border can result from a process of othering. It has to do with the purported territorial control (Paasi, 2011). Border closure is part of the securitization discourse (Newman, 2012) and practices. In effect, security considerations have led to the "hardening" or "reterritorialization" of borders since September 11 (Ackleson, 2012). Since then, African States have reinforced the screening at their border, especially at airports and harbour where border security technologies such as X-ray and mobile scanners have been installed. Ghana, for example, has issued a Personal Identification Secured Comparison and Evaluation System to monitor and profile passengers at its mains entry points. Like many other countries of the ECOWAS, the country has issued a Biometric Passport (Sosuh, 2011).

Similarly, the Islamic Republic of Mauritania reinforced its border control infrastructure to face migration and terrorism threats and decreed an official exclusive entry point with its neighbours (Frowd, 2014). The International Organization for Migration (IOM) has helped many African countries as Soudan, Mauritania, and Zimbabwe, acquiring its Personal Identification and Registration System for their border management (Frowd, 2014). This use of Anthropometry helps to promote the movement of some and stop those of others. The resulting plurality of borders generates new forms of government of populations through their biometric census and the traceability of the movements of foreigners (Blanchard et al., 2010).

In the same vein, border hardening is usually the first state response to the Public Health Emergency of International Concern. Cameroon, for example, has regularly closed its borders to specific flows to avoid the importation of certain diseases. During the 2014 Ebola epidemic, the Cameroonian authorities took a series of measures, including a ban on entry for people coming from high-risk areas, sensitization of the population, and, above all, strengthening epidemiological surveillance at the country's ports of entry.

More recently, the COVID-19 global pandemic has accelerated the historical processes of "bordering the world" (Brunet-Jailly & Carpenter, 2020). Due to the pandemic, African countries have mostly suspended flights to their territories. Like other countries in the world, they issue travel advisories. Very early, the reaction consisted also of surveillance and disinfection at ports and airports (Smart & Smart, 2012). Some countries have introduced a 14-day quarantine to those entering their territories. Others have even closed their land and maritime borders. Nigeria, for example, has closed and militarize its border to enforce the restriction on movement at its land border with Benin (Eselebor, 2020). African countries have also taken measures related to transnational trade such as mandatory testing, truck sanitization, limitation of crew members in trucks, creation of transit testing area, for example, the global objective being to reduce movements of peoples and just allowing emergency and essential supplies (UNECA, 2020).

These *teichopolitics* also consisted of tightening visa access as instruments of control. For example, on 18 March 2021, the Cameroonian government suspended entry visas to Cameroon at various airports for 15 renewable days. Cameroon's consular services abroad had also taken the same measure. Between June and October 2020, visa delivery was accompanied by a COVID-19 negative test requirement dated less than four days. The nature of the threat leads to the establishment of networked borders.

Networked borders

Closed borders can also be dematerialized. They form networked borders in which stakeholders carry out security checks *upstream* and *downstream* of the border. As a result, the border has lost its linearity as it is dispersed (Amilhat Szary, 2015), and the relationship to margins becomes individualized (Bourdelais, 2008). The pre-clearance system allows for upstream identity checks. There is a delegation of screening to airlines that scan the passports at the departure. These are analysed during the duration of the trip, thus stretching the space-time of border crossing (Amilhat Szary, 2015). The acquisition of surveillance technology has allowed smart borders to develop around accumulating data and information on various flows. This system element allows a shift of control upstream because local services collaborate with the countries from which the flows of people and goods come. The Joint Port Control Unit at Tema Harbour in Ghana works with their foreign counterparts to track container movements to fight against drug trafficking, counterfeiting, and other illegal goods (Sosuh, 2011).

Hard borders in Africa also take the form of health barriers that organize the circulation of the invisible identifiable, including germs, seeds, and other microscopic organisms or suspended particles (Amilhat Szary, 2015). In order to fight against the spread of animal and human diseases, the countries put in place quarantine and other administrative measures. Historically, countries have placed health documents for travel, individual health passports, and cordon sanitaire (Smart & Smart, 2012) when facing a Public Health Emergency of International Concern. The recent rapid spread of the Ebola epidemic in West Africa, starting from the original Guinean outbreak, as early as November 2014, is partly due to the intensity of cross-border mobility favoured by the free movement regime of the Economic Community of West African States (ECOWAS)(Loungou, 2015). In this context, borders hardening can be a pragmatic approach to managing a virus-related epidemic that can benefit from the speed and ubiquity of transportation systems (Trouwborst et al., 2016).

Epidemics have always played out borders (Bourdelais, 2008). More recently, the pandemic of COVID-19 has favoured the expansion of smart borders used to filter essential from the optional and redefined biopolitical balance between State and society (Goeury & Delmas, 2020). Due to precarity and vulnerability, border closure was inefficient in the African context since local populations created alternate routes (Eselebor, 2020). The sense of powerlessness that stems from this may explain the use of material forms of border hardening to reassure people in the face of a significant threat, the objective being, at least, to give the impression of taking it into account (Neisse & Novosseloff, 2010).

Material forms of border hardening in Africa

The material structures of border hardening in Africa differ from one country to another and sometimes from one to another section of the border. These can be concrete, barbed wire, trenches, or sand walls between Morocco and Western Sahara. The sand wall is three-m-high and 3-m wide embarkment (Bäschlin & Sidati, 2012). It is a defence system built around walls and support points every 1.5–2 km and in which about 40 soldiers with light artillery station. Beyond these human elements, minefields, barbed wire at strategic points, and radars reinforce the wall. In the second level, rapid intervention brigades support the front line for 120,000 soldiers mobilized to monitor the wall (Quétel, 2012).

Some of these walls have a significant underground part. Egypt built a ten-foot-high wall at the border with the Gaza strip to fight against Palestinian flood into its country (Ackleson, 2012). The construction of tunnels leading to Rafah prompted Israel to reinforce this wall, with Egypt's blessing, with an 8-m-high steel plate wall that plunged 14 m deep. The wall is topped with barbed wire and complemented by sirens (Quétel, 2012).

The hardening of African borders has also taken the form of trenches, as in a Nigeria–Cameroon border section. Initially, the Cameroonian military engineering construction was limited to army barracks as support to force protection. As of 2015, this was extended to the rest of the border section, which served as a front line with Boko Haram Jihadi to shape the physical operating environment. These trenches of 3 m wide by 2 m deep have a purely tactical purpose as they are filled with water during the rainy season and prevent massive and brutal jihadist incursions from Nigeria.

Some of these walls are electrified, at least in some sections. The Kenyan Wall to counter Somali Al-Shabaab jihadist consist of a concrete wall ringed with electric barbed wire and trenches, observations posts, and electronic surveillance cameras (Touchard, 2018). At its borders with Zimbabwe and Mozambique, South Africa has developed intermittent electric fences. It is the same with the electric fence at the border between Botswana and Zimbabwe (Touchard, 2018).

Hardening borders can also be made through fences, as is the case in the Spanish *presidio* of Ceuta and Melilla (Allain, 2001). In Melilla, there is a 10.5-km-double-metal fencing of 3.5 m high for the outer fence and 6 m for the inner. These fences are equipped with barbed wire and technologies such as video cameras and reinforced with border patrols (Ferrer Gallardo, 2007). The Ceuta and Melilla barriers were built between 1997 and 1998 and reinforced in 2005 after a massive onslaught of illegal immigrants, notably with the installation of an anti-intrusion system, a defence system with tear gas, and networks of steel cables that prevent the approach of the barriers (Ritaine, 2009).

Justification for the hardening of African borders

Africa is not a homogenous entity, and there is significant heterogeneity in the justifications for the hardening of the continent borders. However, from the speech analysis in the various securitization process and the observation of daily functioning of the border security management, defensive and migration considerations are at the core of the hardening of African borders.

Civilization versus barbarism: borders coming back

Defensive walls were thought old fashioned. However, with contemporary insurrections, there is a demodernization of war and a return to fundamentals with the hardening of borders as "walls of civilization against others, barbarians" (Quétel, 2012). The rhetoric of justification reflects this perception of borders hardening.

For example, the trench construction on a section of the Cameroon–Nigeria border to fight against Boko Haram was preceded by acts of securitization by Cameroonian authorities. President Paul Biya (2016) used the lexicon of stigmatization, indignation, detestable, and abominable to demonize the insurgents in various speeches. The various labels used by the Cameroonian president are part of the construction of a dividing line between good grain and tares, normal and pathological, and acceptable and unacceptable (Guibet Lafaye, 2016). The first explanation of attacks has always been the Jihadist desire to question the Cameroonian way of life. President Biya (2017) used this Manichean and disresponsibilizing software in his opening speech at the Extraordinary Summit of the Conference of Heads of State and Government of the Central African Peace and Security Council, declared:

> The reality is simple. On one side, there are our forces, defenders of a modern and tolerant society which guarantees the exercise of human rights, including that of religion, as well as representative democracy. On the other side, namely Boko Haram and similar movements, there are partisans of an obscurantist and tyrannical society which has no consideration for human dignity. You would agree with me that these two models of society are absolutely incompatible and, hence, compromise is absolutely impossible."

In this context, the trench's construction proceeds from a certain sacralization of the border as an instinctive reaction to an existential risk (Debray, 2010).

The walls of disagreement

The construction of a border wall sometimes expresses an absolute blockage in the negotiations, but also, paradoxically, it can be a means of pressure (Allain, 2001). Many African border walls are unilateral and sometimes contested borders. Somalian officials, for example, have urged the border population to prevent the completion of the Kenyan border fence on the motive that it encroaches into the Somalian territory.[1] Similarly, the sand wall between Morocco and Western Sahara demarcates a border following the Moroccan perspective in a conflict that has lasted since 1975. It results from a lack of agreement, thus confirming that a wall is sometimes the result of an absence of a border. So, the Sand wall perpetuates a fait accompli, or at best, freeze the situation with a view of a subsequent settlement (Neisse & Novosseloff, 2010). Nevertheless, the Moroccan Sand Wall derives from the impossibility or refusal of negotiations with the other. The situation stems from what Ritaine (2009) calls "the militarization of contiguity."

The hardening of borders is very often the result of economic asymmetry. In southern Africa, for example, the wall between Botswana and Zimbabwe is designed to protect the former from the economic and social collapse of the second (Ritaine, 2009). In effect, in 2005, Botswana has built an 813 km fence at its border with

Zimbabwe to fight against illegal immigration (Rosière & Jones, 2012). Botswana is an underpopulated country with good economic growth and political stability, quite the opposite of its neighbour Zimbabwe, more peopled, poor, corrupt, and then ruled by an old reptilian dictatorship. Botswana authorities found in 2003 that 125,000 Zimbabweans entered the country legally each month and did not return home after their visas expired. In addition, foreigners were accused of stealing and spreading AIDS (Quétel, 2012). In this context, hardening the border stems from a process of securitization in which contiguity is erected as a risk, and the barrier then positions itself as a security solution (Ritaine, 2009).

Beyond discourse, the contradictory perception of walls

Official speeches do not always reflect the reality of the motivations that led to border hardening, especially the construction of walls. In the wall between Botswana and Zimbabwe, for example, Botswana's authorities said it was a matter of combating the spread of diseases. However, the Zimbabwean authorities were not fooled: the 4-m-high wall did not have its given vocation. That explains probably why their reaction to this unilateral construction had been: "Botswana is creating a new Gaza Strip" (Quétel, 2012). The same is true of the sand wall, which the Moroccan authorities justify today with the persistence of illegal immigration (Neisse & Novosseloff, 2010).

Some countries do not first assume the construction of walls at their borders. That is the case with Equatorial Guinea that has begun the unilateral construction of a wall on its 189 km border with Cameroon. The Equatorial Guinean authorities have long denied the existence of this wall. It was the case in May 2020, for example, when the Minister of Foreign Affairs and Cooperation received the Ambassador of Cameroon.[2] The construction has stopped since Cameroon accuses Guinea of encroaching on its territory. Officially, it is a wall against immigration because Cameroon is accused of being the gateway to illegal migrants of West African.[3] The same, because of its oil boom, Equatorial Guinea has been the destination of young Cameroonians looking for a job. The highest authorities in Equatorial Guinea, who were most likely victims of Cameroonian crooks, were hostile to the presence of these neighbours in their country. President Obiang himself said: "In Equatorial Guinea, there are two types of crime: Nigerian nationals carry out the bloody crime; another is pernicious, it does not shed blood, but its effects are more traumatic, it is the work of Cameroonians."[4] Nevertheless, other security considerations seem to be the main reason for constructing a wall because most attempts to overthrow President Teodoro Obiang have passed through this border, the most recent being the attempt of some 30 men to overthrow the Malabo regime in December 2017 and which led to the closure of the border for six months.[5]

The analysis of the discourses justifying border-tightening policies is relevant to understanding the dynamics underway in Africa. However, these speeches can have an instrumental dimension. Therefore, it is necessary to go beyond discourse and analyse the practices and functions of these policies.

Functions of border hardening

There are three types of border hardening devices: front lines, fences and walls, and closed straights. As far as front lines are concerned, they are rare because of the condemnation of the use of force in bilateral relations (Rosière & Jones, 2012).

Defensive border walls

The strategic and geopolitical situation can explain a physical barrier at the border. In this case, it has a military-security function (Carter & Poast, 2015). Since prehistoric times, men have erected obstacles such as piles of rocks to defend the entrance to their cave from intruders (Quétel, 2012). In Africa, walls have historically been a tool for securing borders. During the precolonial period, people used vegetal fortification to protect their villages (Seignobos, 1980). In the 13th Century in Great Zimbabwe, people used a stone-walled barrier to protect their villages (Van Waarden, 2011). In the Lake Chad Basin, anthropologists have identified defensive structures in lands dating back to the Peritchadian area, such as the ditch surrounding the vast Zilum site and dates to the 1st Millennium BC (Langlois, 2020).

During the colonial period, many defence walls were built across Africa. For example, the Italians built a 270 km barbed wired line at the Libya-Egypt border in 1931 to fight against the Libyan insurgents and prevent them from using Egypt as a safe haven. Also, France built a 45 km line along the Tunisia–Libya border to prevent any hostile activity by Italy. During the decolonization wars, the French army built a barbed-wire fence at the Algeria–Morocco border in 1956 (Touchard, 2018). In the same vein, two physical barriers, the Morice Line and the Challe Line were built between Algeria and Tunisia to counter Algerian National Liberation Army (Carter & Poast, 2015).

There had been a front line between Ethiopia and Eritrea. Today, there is a front line of 2,720 km between Morocco and Western Sahara. Constructing this wall has to do with the Spanish colonization of the Sahara and the will of Morocco to recover this territory in the name of historical rights. Its construction began in 1980 and 1987 totalled 2,720 km. Building the wall was to limit the assaults of the Polisario Front, which, after defeating the Mauritanian army, launched incursions to the north (Quétel, 2012). The Sand Wall, therefore, has an initial military purpose: "protect the strategic objectives of Western Sahara and Southern Morocco; to intercept the attack columns of the Sahrawi People's Liberation Army (APLS) to inflict as many loses as possible" (Touchard, 2018). This wall was built when the highly mobile and speed Sahrawi troops in all-terrain vehicles gained tactical victory over Mauritania and were already occupying El Ayoun, Smara, Bojador's Moroccan town Daklila (Bäschlin & Sidati, 2012).

Wall against the jihadist

Hardening borders, especially building walls, can be explained by the global war on terrorism and the State's feelings of fear and vulnerability facing terrorist networks (Koehn, 2018). The hardening of African borders can be seen as an exceptional measure to fight this against terrorism and protect the society (Buzan et al., 1998), as "extraordinary threats call for extraordinary measures (Schwell, 2014). For example, Kenya is building a 700-km-long wall at its border with Somalia to curb Al-Shabab terrorist attacks on its territory. This initiative comes after regular attacks, one of which was the one at a university in Garissa, on 2 April 2015, which caused the death of 147 people, casting doubt on the government's ability to protect its citizens (International Crisis Group, 2015).

In the Lake Chad Basin, the jihadist group Boko Haram has used trenches to protect its sanctuaries. At Kanamma, for example, the group had strengthened the site's defences with trenches, camouflages, and sandbags (Mohammed, 2018). Similarly, in counter-insurgency, states are building primarily tactical border trenches. It is the case of the trench on the Nigeria–Cameroon border, which served as a front line against Boko Haram's jihadists after dismantling all the garrisons of the Nigerian army of the north-eastern border strip. The construction of these trenches follows the first Boko Haram suicide attacks on Cameroonian territory. Very early, it appears that all the suicide bombers were prepared in Nigeria and deployed to the border from which they reached Cameroonian cities via by-pass routes on the axes such as Djimini-Blabli-Manawadi-Gouderi-Vouvere-Kolofata, Djimini-Goumouldi-Saradjé-Bamé-Kolofata, or Iza-Ashigashia-Kirawa Nigeria-Kerawa Cameroun-Mora-Djoude-Makalingai.

The trench construction also follows the jihadists' lightning, brutal, and sometimes night-time attacks on advanced posts of the Cameroonian army on the border. The insurgent used to take advantage of the thick morning fog to infiltrate stealthily and discreetly, as was the case during the Kolofata attack of 12 January 2015. The use of armoured vehicles by the jihadists, on these occasions, had created a situation of imbalance that had had a negative psychological impact on Cameroonian soldiers who were then equipped with small-calibre ammunition to which Boko Haram's armoured vehicles were invulnerable. The situation associated with this feeling of helplessness was so worrying that the army's high command feared that this would impact the fighting ardour of the soldiers in the future. Therefore, the trench construction on the front line between Cameroon and Boko Haram responds to tactical considerations.

Hard borders and migrations in and out of Africa

Another reason for hardening African borders and constructing security walls is the fight against trafficking and illegal migrations (Touchard, 2018). In effect, there is a worldwide dynamic of securing immigration. At the symbolic level, hardening policies consist of the rise of anti-migration discourses articulated between four significant axes, socio-economic where immigration explains unemployment and the welfare state crisis. It is also a question of highlighting the loss of sovereignty and internal and external security regarding the security axis. An identity axis highlights the risk of loss of national identity and an inevitable invasion impacting demography. Finally, we have a political axis linked to xenophobic and racist discourse, sometimes for electoral purposes (Tsoukala & Ceyhan, 2002). Economic disparities between two neighbouring States can also explain the wall at its consequences on migrations and the movement of goods. This physical barrier is for economic security (Carter & Poast, 2015).

The previous trend is also present in the countries of the north, which perceives immigrants as criminals, financial and social fraudsters, terrorists, troublemakers, or unassimilable persons. Migrants are generally perceived as threats to the security of the State, society, security, and identity (Tsoukala & Ceyhan, 2002). Before constructing the wall with Zimbabwe, border communities in Botswana were complaining about crime rise (Donaldson & Pratt, 2005). In the same vein, South Africa has built a wall fence at it borders with Mozambique (491 km) and Zimbabwe (225 km) for anti-migration purpose. This dynamic confirms the assertion that barriers appear on wealth discontinuity (Rosière & Jones, 2012).

The functions of these walls are dynamic over time. For example, the internal fence's function, which constitutes a veterinary cordon that divides Namibia into two halves, from west to east, has changed through time. It was constructed during the colonial period and officially intended to prevent epizootics from northern into central Namibia. Nevertheless, it "represented a culmination of the boundaries that the experiences of apartheid, colonialism, and war had imposed on Namibian society" (Miescher, 2012). In the 1970 and 1980s, the fence was used for the South African military's defensive purpose to prevent Namibian nationalists from entering the colonial heartland. Since independence, the fence is used for veterinary and security purposes. Therefore, a dynamic and factual reading of border hardening policies in Africa needs to be adopted.

Also, policies of hardening African borders sometimes stem from multifaceted pressures from extra-regional partners, including the European Union, for example, which, as part of its migration policy, outsources its borders by signing agreements with countries like Morocco and Niger. In effect, although some African State, like Niger, sees migrations as an economic opportunity, they hardened their borders in exchange for European Union financial assistance. These modalities of government on distance allowed the portability of borders of the European Union and led to the hardening of certain African borders.

Recommendations

On the margins of the dynamics of cross-border cooperation to fight against contemporary security threats in Africa, there is paradoxical dynamics of hardening state borders. These partitioning spaces consist of stricter access policies, the construction of physical barriers, and reticular boundaries. The discourses of justification reveal a binary construction, "us" versus "others," and the expression of disagreements and the militarization of the contiguousness that results. Beyond the discourses, a functional analysis of these border highlighting devices makes it possible to identify defensive borders against the enemy, whether jihadist or illegal migrant.

It is generally accepted that hardening borders respond to a need to reassure populations in the face of a significant threat (Neisse & Novosseloff, 2010). Therefore, the dynamics of re-borderization in the face of public health emergencies of international concern stem from the development of borders as frameworks of sovereignty and responsibility in the face of a very little-known threat. Rather than exclusive sovereignism, contemporary dynamics of border hardening as a reaction to multifaceted threats refer to a form of neo-sovereignism in which the State becomes "an inescapable and instituting relay of a global public service" (Allain, 2001; Gros, 2020). The result is imperative to control and regulate the movement of people, goods, and services across national borders (Lamptey, 2013) within the framework of border security (Brunet-Jailly & Dupeyron, 2007). Thus, the border plays an essential role in regulating institutionalized violence.

The conclusions reached by this work invite us to move away from the Manichean reading that open borders are good and those closed, bad. This opposition is not pertinent since each border is open and close simultaneously under the influence of concomitant processes (Amilhat Szary, 2015). The idea of a borderless world is seductive and is part of the age of time. Nevertheless, borders must be reaffirmed as a framework of sovereignty and responsibility, and above all, State should make intelligent use of them because, in small doses, the border can be a remedy. In high doses, it could be a deadly poison.

Border hardening schemes are relatively effective in the short term. In Western Sahara, for example, the sand wall is effective since it dulled the Polisario's military potential significantly and diminished its members' morale (Touchard, 2018). However, in the long run, the effectiveness of walls is always limited as they constitute short-term responses to long-term problems. This mechanism isolates problems instead of solving them (Neisse & Novosseloff, 2010). Hence, it is imperative to address the root causes of these policies because they are expensive to build and maintain.[6]

This imperative is even more critical because, in the medium term, hardening borders quickly prove counterproductive. Moreover, the various mechanisms of tightening borders create by-passing strategies and create a specific mentality and behaviours among residents (Allain, 2001). Also, in the register of by-passing logics, the barrier between Botswana and Zimbabwe is regularly torn off (Quétel, 2012). The same is true of the trench on a section of the Cameroon–Nigeria border. Due to the nature of the soils, erosion and landslides allow minor group incursions to be possible in the long run. It was seen in Tuski near Bondéri in August 2018, where groups of two or three Boko Haram fighters used a ladder to cross the trench.

Therefore, it is imperative to strengthen the capacity of border management stakeholders in Africa. In effect, border hardening policies only really work with an efficient checkpoint, allowing borders to play their control function fully (Ritaine, 2009). The operations of a checkpoint are articulated between three elements, including the material element, the human element, and the technological element (Razac, 2013). However, in most African countries, except ports and airports, checkpoints do not effectively play their roles because of the derisory material element, the corrupted human element, and the absence of technological element. For example, border control agencies are partly responsible for border porosity on the Ghana-Togo border because of their corruption (Agbedahin, 2014). They also lack infrastructures, well-trained human resources, and facilities for border security (Sosuh, 2011). More serious, African boundaries are not well protected, with some control post located at the first central town, sometimes 50 or more kilometres from the border itself, as in Mali (Mechlinski, 2010).

In addition to the need to address the root cause of border hardening in Africa, it is essential to pay attention to the harmful effects of these policies on the environment and people's human rights. Walls have consequences not only for humans but also for animals: "by curtailing migrations and other movements, by fragmenting populations and by causing direct mortality, for instance through entanglement" (Trouwborst et al., 2016). In the case of Cameroon, the effects of the trench on animals of Waza Natural Park trenches have not yet been evaluated. States also need to consider the detrimental effects of border hardening on local economies.

Notes

1 https://allafrica.com/stories/202008240705.html retrieved on 4 January 2021
2 www.guineaecuatorialpress.com/noticia.php?id=15485 retrieved on 3 March 2021
3 www.dw.com/fr/la-guin%C3%A9e-equatoriale-suspend-la-construction-dun-mur-%C3%A0-la-fronti%C3%A8re-avec-le-cameroun/a-54008132 retrieved on 3 March 2021
4 Jeune Afrique/l'Intelligent, n° 2319 du 19 au 25 juin 2005
5 www.asodeguesegundaetapa.org/guinea-ecuatorial-proyecta-construir-un-muro-en-la-frontera-con-camerun-agencia-lusa/ consulté le 3 mars 2021
6 The 300 miles fence along Botwana's border with Zimbabwe cost 3,5 million dollar (Donaldson & Pratt, 2005). In the same vein, the construction of the berm has cost 40% of Morocco GDP (Jankowski & Zenderowski, 2018).

Bibliography

Ackleson, J. (2012). The Emerging Politics of Border Management: Policy and Research Considerations. In Wastl-Walter, D. (Ed.). *The Ashgate Research Companion to Border Studies,* Ashgate Research Companion (pp. 245–261). Farnham: Ashgate.

Agbedahin, K. (2014). From Control to Parasitism: Interrogating the Roles of Border Control Agencies on the Ghana – Togo Border. *African Security Review, 23*(4): 370–380. https://doi.org/10.1080/10246029.2014.955864

Allain, J.-C. (2001). Introduction. *Guerres mondiales et conflits contemporains, n° 201*(1): 3–6. www.cairn.info/revue-guerres-mondiales-et-conflits-contemporains-2001-1-page-3.htm

Amilhat Szary, A.-L. (2015). *Qu'est-ce qu'une frontière aujourd'hui ?* Paris: Presses Universitaires de France.

Andrés, A. (2008). West Africa Under Attack: Drugs, Organized Crime and Terrorism as the New Threats to Global Security. *UNISCI Discussion Papers, 16(16)*.

Asiwaju, A. I. (2012). The African Union Border Programme in European comparative perspective. In T. M. Wilson & H. Donnan (Eds.), *A Companion to Border Studies, Blackwell Companions to Anthropology* 19 (31–46). Chichester: Wiley-Blackwell. https://doi.org/10.1002/9781118255223.ch4

Bäschlin, E., & Sidati, M. (2012). Western Sahara – Territoriality, Border Conceptions and Border Realities. In Wastl-Walter, D. (Ed.)., *The Ashgate Research Companion to Border Studies*, Ashgate Research Companion (549–565). Farnham: Ashgate.

Beaulieu-Brossard, P., & David, C.-P. (2013). Le blindage des frontières selon les théories des Relations Internationales: Contribution et dialogue. *L'Espace Politique. Revue en ligne de géographie politique et de géopolitique, 20,* Article 20. https://doi.org/10.4000/espacepolitique.2637

Bennafla, K. (2003). *Le commerce frontalier en Afrique centrale – Acteurs, espaces, pratiques*. Paris: Karthala.

Biya, P. (2016). Message to the Nation on the Occasion of the End of 2015 and New Year 2016, available at www.prc.cm/fr/actualites/discours/1611-message-du-chef-de-l-etat-a-la-nation-a-l-occasion-de-la-fin-d-annee-2015-et-du-nouvel-an-2016 retrieved on December 6, 2019.

Biya, P. (2017). Speech at the Extraordinary Summit of the Conference of Heads of State and Government of the Council for Peace and Security in Central Africa (COPAX), available at www.prc.cm/en/news/speeches-of-the-president/1168-speech-by-h-e-paul-biya-president-of-the-republic-of-cameroon-at-the-opening-ceremony-of-the-extraordinary-summit-of-the-conference-of-heads-of-state-and-government-of-the-council-for-peace-and-security-in-central-africa-copax retrieved on May 5, 2021.

Blanchard, E., Clochard, O., & Rodier, C. (2010). Sur le front des frontières. *Plein droit, n° 87*(4): 3–7, available at www.cairn.info/revue-plein-droit-2010-4-page-3.htm

Bourdelais, P. (2008). L'épidémie créatrice de frontières. *Les Cahiers du Centre de Recherches Historiques. Archives, 42*: 149–176. https://doi.org/10.4000/ccrh.3440

Brunet-Jailly, E., & Carpenter, M. (2020). Introduction to the Special Issue: Borderlands in the Era of COVID-19. *Borders in Globalization Review, 2*: 7–11. https://doi.org/10.18357/bigr21202019960

Brunet-Jailly, E., & Dupeyron, B. (2007). Introduction: Borders, borderlands, and porosity. In E. Brunet Jailly (Ed.), *Borderlands: Comparing Border Security in North America and Europe*. Ottawa: Les Presses de l'Université d'Ottawa | University of Ottawa Press. http://books.openedition.org/uop/159

Buzan, B., Wæver, O., & Wilde, J. de. (1998). *Security: A New Framework for Analysis*. Boulder: Lynne Rienner Publishers.

Carter, D., & Poast, P. (2015). Why Do States Build Walls? Political Economy, Security, and Border Stability. *Journal of Conflict Resolution, 61*. https://doi.org/10.1177/0022002715596776

Damiani, I. (2013). Ferghana: Les étapes d'une matérialisation frontalière entre intention et réalité. *L'espace Politique, 20*. https://doi.org/10.4000/espacepolitique.2651

Debray, R. (2010). *Éloge des frontières*. Paris: Gallimard.

Donaldson, J. W., & Pratt, M. (2005). Boundary and Territorial Trends in 2004. *Geopolitics, 10*(2): 398–427. https://doi.org/10.1080/14650040590946665

Eselebor, W. A. (2020). Seme Border, Nigeria: Safety and Collective Vulnerability. *Borders in Globalization Review, 2*(1): 46–49. https://doi.org/10.18357/bigr21202019861

Ferrer Gallardo, X. (2007). Border Acrobatics between the European Union and Africa: The Management of Sealed-off Permeability on the Borders of Ceuta and Melilla. In Brunet-Jailly, E. *Borderlands: Comparing Border Security in North America and Europe*. Governance Series (pp. 75–93). Ottawa: Univ. of Ottawa Press.

Frowd, P. M. (2014). The Field of Border Control in Mauritania. *Security Dialogue, 45*(3): 226–241, available at www.jstor.org/stable/26292342

Goeury, D., & Delmas, A. (2020). Bordering the World as a Response to Emerging Infectious Disease. The Case of SARS CoV-2. *Borders in Globalization Review, 2*: 12–20. https://doi.org/10.18357/bigr21202019760

Gros, F. 2020. Des sagesses anciennes à la virophilosophie contemporaine. In Lazar, M., Plantin, G., Ragot, X. *Le monde d'aujourd'hui: Les sciences sociales au temps de la Covid*. Paris: Presses de Sciences Po.

Guibet Lafaye, C. (2016). "Approche critique des sociologies de la radicalisation". Communication au Forum de la DAP, "Radicalisation violente, engagement et désengagement". Paris, France: Ministère de la justice.

International Crisis Group. (2015). "Al-Shabaab's Kenyan Ambitions," Commentary/Africa, April 15, available at www.crisisgroup.org/africa/horn-africa/kenya/al-shabaab-s-kenyan-ambitions retrieved on January 4, 2021.

Jankowski, B., & Zenderowski, R. (2018). The Walls in the Global Village. *Border and Regional Studies, 6*(2): 103–115. https://doi.org/10.25167/ppbs54

Jones, R. (2016). *Violent Borders: Refugees and the Right to Move*. London: Verso.

Kewirh, K. J. (2020). Rethinking Regional Security in Central Africa: The Case of the Central African Republic. In *International Journal of African Renaissance Studies-Multi-, Inter- and Transdisciplinarity, 15*(2): 115–133. https://doi.org/10.1080/18186874.2019.1671774

Koehn, P. (2018). *Transnational Mobility and Global Health: Traversing Borders and Boundaries*. Abingdon: Routledge. https://doi.org/10.4324/9781351124409

Lamptey, A. A. (2013). Rethinking Border Management Strategies in West Africa: Experience from the Sahel. *Kofi Annan International Peacekeeping Training Centre Policy Brief*, n° 12.

Langlois, O. (2020). Insécurités anciennes au sud du bassin tchadien: Les lueurs de l'archéologie. In E. Chauvin, O. Langlois, C. Seignobos, & C. Baroin (Eds.), *Conflits et violences dans le bassin du lac Tchad. Actes du XVIIe colloque international du réseau Méga-Tchad*. (91–108). Paris: IRD éditions. https://hal.archives-ouvertes.fr/hal-03026315

Loungou, S. (2015). L'épidémie d'Ebola en Afrique de l'Ouest. Une mise en perspective des répercussions démo-géographiques, politiques et économiques. *L'Espace Politique. Revue en ligne de géographie politique et de géopolitique*, 26, Article 26. https://doi.org/10.4000/espacepolitique.3467

Mbembe, A. (1999). Les frontières mouvantes du continent africain. *Le Monde diplomatique*, 548: 22–23. www.monde-diplomatique.fr/1999/11/MBEMBE/3418

Mechlinski, T. (2010). Towards an Approach to Borders and Mobility in Africa. *Journal of Borderlands Studies*, 25/2: 94–106. https://doi.org/10.1080/08865655.2010.9695764

Miescher, G. (2012). *Namibia's Red Line: The History of a Veterinary and Settlement Border*. New York: Palgrave Macmillan.
Mohammed, K. (2018). The Origins of Boko Haram. In C. Levan & P. Ukata (Eds.), *The Oxford Handbook of Nigerian Politics* (pp. 582–604). Oxford: Oxford University Press. https://doi.org/10.1093/oxfordhb/9780198804307.013.42
Neisse, F., & Novosseloff, A. (2010). L'expansion des murs: Le reflet d'un monde fragmenté? *Politique étrangère, Hiver, 4*: 731–742, available at www.cairn.info/revue-politique-etrangere-2010-4-page-731.htm
Newman, D. (2012). Contemporary Research Agendas in Border Studies: An Overview. In Wastl-Walter, D. (Ed.), *The Ashgate Research Companion to Border Studies*, Ashgate Research Companion (pp. 33–47). Farnham: Ashgate.
O'Brien, R. (1991). *Global Financial Integration: The End of Geography*. Boston: Cengage Learning EMEA.
Ohmae, K. (1996). *End of the Nation State: The Rise of Regional Economies*. New York: Touchstone.
Okumu, W. (2011). Border Management and Security in Africa. *Concordis Briefing, 4*(4), 1–18.
Paasi, A. (2011). A Border Theory: An Unattainable Dream or a Realistic Aim for Border Scholars? In Wastl-Walter, D. (Ed.), *The Ashgate Research Companion to Border Studies, Ashgate Research Companion* (pp. 11–31). Farnham: Ashgate,
Pavlakovich-Kochi, V. (2011). *Cross-Border Cooperation and Regional Responses to NAFTA and Globalization*. In Wastl-Walter, D. (Ed.). *The Routledge research companion to border studies* (pp. 503–526). Farnham: Ashgate.
Pettersson, J. (2020). Higher Fences and Wider Nets? Global Trends in Bordering Policies. *UI Paper, 2*. http://urn.kb.se/resolve?urn=urn:nbn:se:uu:diva-405155
Quétel, C. (2012). *Histoire des murs*. Paris: Perrin. https://doi.org/10.3917/perri.quete.2012.01
Razac, O. (2013). La gestion de la perméabilité. *L'Espace Politique. Revue en ligne de géographie politique et de géopolitique, 20*, Article 20. https://doi.org/10.4000/espacepolitique.2711
Ritaine, É. (2009). La barrière et le checkpoint: Mise en politique de l'asymétrie. *Cultures & Conflits, 73*: 15–33. https://doi.org/10.4000/conflits.17500
Rosière, S., & Jones, R. (2012). Teichopolitics: Re-considering Globalisation Through the Role of Walls and Fences. *Geopolitics, 17*(1): 217–234. https://doi.org/10.1080/14650045.2011.574653
Schwell, A. (2014). Schwell, Alexandra: Compensating (In)Security: Anthropological Perspectives on Internal Security. In M. Maguire, C. Frois & N. Zurawski (Eds.), *The Anthropology of Security. Perspectives from the Frontline of Policing, Counter-Terrorism and Border Control* (pp. 83–103). London: Pluto Press.
Seignobos, C. (1980). Des fortifications végétales dans la zone soudano-sahélienne (Tchad et Nord-Cameroun). *Cahiers ORSTOM. Série Sciences Humaines, 17*(3–4), pp. 191–222, available at www.documentation.ird.fr/hor/fdi:00992
Smart, A., & Smart, J. (2012). Biosecurity, Quarantine and Life across the Border. In T. M. Wilson & H. Donnan (Eds.), *A Companion to Border Studies*, Blackwell Companions to Anthropology 19 (pp. 354–370). Chichester: Wiley-Blackwell. https://doi.org/10.1002/9781118255223.ch20
Sosuh, M. M. (2011). *Border Security in Ghana: Challenges and Prospects*. Africa Portal; Kofi Annan International Peacekeeping Training Centre (KAIPTC), available at www.africaportal.org/publications/border-security-in-ghana-challenges-and-prospects/

Touchard, L. (2018). Of Walls and Men: Securing African Borders in the 21st Century. *Focus stratégique*, No. 85 bis.

Trombetta, M. J. (2010). Rethinking the Securitization of Environment: Old Beliefs, New Insights. In T. Balzacq (Ed.), *Securitization Theory: How Security Problems Emerge and Dissolve*. Abingdon, UK: Routledge.

Trouwborst, A., Fleurke, F., & Dubrulle, J. (2016). Border Fences and Their Impacts on Large Carnivores, Large Herbivores and Biodiversity: An International Wildlife Law Perspective. *Review of European, Comparative & International Environmental Law*, 25(3): 291–306. https://doi.org/10.1111/reel.12169

Tsoukala, A., & Ceyhan, A. (2002). Contrôle de l'immigration: mythes et réalités. *Cultures & Conflits, 26–27 | automne 1997*. 6.

UNECA. (2020). *Facilitating Cross-Border Trade Through a Coordinated African Response to COVID-19* [Working paper], available at https://repository.uneca.org/handle/10855/43789

Vallet, É., & David, C.-P. (2012). Introduction: The (Re)Building of the Wall in International Relations. *Journal of Borderlands Studies*, 10.

Van Waarden, C. (2011). The Origin of Zimbabwe Tradition Walling. *Zimbabwean Prehistory*, 29: 54–77.

Waever, O. (1995). Securitization and Desecuritization. In R. D. Lipschutz (dir.), *On Security* (pp. 46–87). New York: Columbia University Press.

Waltz, K. (1988). The Origins of War in Neorealist Theory. *Journal of Interdisciplinary History*, 18. https://doi.org/10.2307/204817

Wilson, T. M., & Donnan, H. (Eds.). (2012). *A Companion to Border Studies*, Blackwell Companions to Anthropology 19. Chichester: Wiley-Blackwell.

10 Porous boundaries and anisotropic mobility

Migration and cross-border trade between Nigeria and Japan[1]

Hisashi Matsumoto

African borders in the New Pangea Era

The Alaba International Electronic Market is one of the biggest markets in Lagos, the largest commercial city in West Africa. This market has evolved since the 1970s, with the growing popularity of music amplification in Nigeria. Many merchandises sold here are second-hand products imported from abroad. In the Harvard Design School Project on the City, Pierre Belanger et al. (2001) call this market "Pangea," the ancient supercontinent that had existed before continental drift. In the figure titled "Alaban Pangea" (Belanger et al., 2001: 704), this market is surrounded and connected to various countries and cities. The Alaba market is linked not only to African cities like Cotonou, Accra, and Abidjan but also to those beyond the continent, such as Moscow, Sanpaolo, Dubai, Singapore, Taipei, and Seoul. Commodities were bought in these cities and sent to the Alaba market through road networks and transport corridors to ports and airports. The Alaban Pangea symbolizes contemporary African borders. With imagined borders, African states share their boundaries not only with each other but also with states in other continents, including those in East Asia.

This chapter examines the migration between Nigeria and Japan, triggered by cross-border trade between these two countries. Instead of focusing on a single direction flow, I will examine the bilateral migration of Japanese and Nigerians and consider interrelationships of the multiple actors involved.

Over the past century, the flow of people and commodities between Africa and East Asia began to interest scholars. In particular, the phenomenon called "China-in-Africa" has drawn international attention, and many studies have examined the migration of Chinese people to African countries (Hsu, 2007; Kernen, 2010; Khan Mohammad, 2014; Gukurume, 2019; Liu, 2019). Simultaneously, the flow of African people to China is also remarkable. Guangzhou, Guangdong Province, in particular, has one of the largest concentrations of Africans in East Asia, which has also been studied (Bodomo, 2010; Haugen, 2012; Lyons et al., 2013). Many of these African and Chinese are more or less involved in cross-border trade, dealing with and distributing East Asian products to African markets.

While Africa's porous borders indicate the vulnerability of its states, the borderland and trans-region approaches reconsider its contribution to sociocultural

DOI: 10.4324/9781003202318-10

networking (see Introduction). Certainly, cross-border activities can enable the participants to construct new links among themselves (Dobler, 2016).

Previous studies on cross-border trade between Africa and East Asia attribute East Asian economic success in Africa to their cultural ethics and identities, such as Confucianism or social networks based on ethnicity (Bräutigam, 2003; Gadzala, 2010). However, such studies regard cultural value and ethnic identity as a given nature and ignore inequality in the sociopolitical environment for cross-border trade. For instance, Kate Meagher (2012) criticizes the neo-Weberian perspective on the cultural determinants of East Asian network's success and African's failure. She concludes that such discourses validate labour exploitation and obscure the role of states. In his study on the competition between Cameroonian and Chinese traders, Ute Röschenthaler (2016) indicates that Cameroonian traders are subject to unfair competition. Their feeling of unfairness came from "home disadvantage" created by their own government, while Chinese traders have advantages not only at home but also in Cameroon.

Such inequalities among the actors are the outcome of the anisotropic nature of border-crossing activities. "Anisotropic nature" refers to the properties of things, which change depending on their directions. In the case of cross-border trade, the direction of flow of people and commodities influences the degree of porosity. Thus, border crossing activities transform their nature according to the direction of crossing. Those who pass through a national boundary face an inquiry into who they are and what they are doing. The social status and cultural identities of those who engage in cross-border activities can change depending on the sociopolitical system in border control.

Instead of focusing on either Chinese or Africans moving between the two regions, some studies have focused on the relationship between them (Röschenthaler, 2016; Haugen, 2011). These studies attempt to consider phenomena surrounding migration beyond the cultural and identity debate of either ethnic group. Therefore, this paper focuses on the migration between Nigeria and Japan and examines a series of cross-border activities by multiple actors connecting the two countries and consider their mutual relationships.

Cross-border trade and Japanese expatriates heading to Nigeria

If we consider the flow of people between Japan and Africa, studies on Africans living in Japan have progressed since the 2000s (Kawada, 2005; Wazaki, 2009; Matsumoto, 2014, 2017, etc.). However, there is little interest in examining migration in the opposite direction, that is, Japanese people moving towards Africa. Although studies by Sumio Aoki (1993, 2000) and Takashi Okakura and Katsuhiko Kitagawa (1993) highlight the history of this migration before World War II during the reign of the Japanese Empire, no study focuses on more recent periods since the decolonization of African states.

There may be a lack of interest in Japanese migration to Africa owing to its overwhelmingly small numbers. According to the Annual Report of Statistics on

Japanese Nationals Overseas (Table 10.1), as of October 2017, approximately 1.35 million Japanese nationals left Japan to live abroad. Among these, 7,591 Japanese lived in Africa, accounting for only 0.6% of Japanese nationals overseas. By region, it has the lowest concentration of Japanese nationals after Antarctica.

Figure 10.1 summarizes the population trends of Japanese living in Nigeria since 1972. If we consider their numbers since 1990, the highest was in 1993, at 342. In particular, after 1999, when the fourth republic was inaugurated, the number remained less than 200. However, going back, there were more Japanese residents in the 1970s and the 1980s than after the 1990s. Between 1978 and 1984, more than 900 Japanese resided in Nigeria. The maximum number

Table 10.1 Population of Japanese Nationals Overseas according to region (October 2017)

Region	Long-Term Stay	Permanent Resident	Total
Asia	3,61,695	31,581	3,93,276
Oceania	53,793	69,686	1,23,479
North America	2,59,675	2,36,561	4,96,236
Middle America	10,528	3,713	14,241
South America	7,866	70,894	78,760
West Europe	1,49,606	67,443	2,17,049
East Europe & FSU	8,722	1,528	10,250
Middle East	9,146	1,909	11,055
Africa	6,756	835	7,591
Antarctica	33	0	33
Total	8,67,820	4,84,150	13,51,970

Source: Annual Report of Statistics on Japanese Nationals Overseas (Ministry of Foreign Affairs of Japan, 2018)

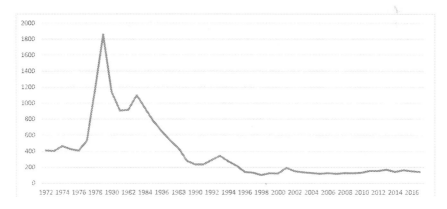

Figure 10.1 Population trends of Japanese living in Nigeria (1972–2017)

Source: Annual Report of Statistics on Japanese Nationals Overseas (Ministry of Foreign Affairs of Japan, 1973–2018)

was noted in 1979 with the numbers reaching 1,855. Among them, only two Japanese lived with as permanent residents, while the remaining 1,853 were long-term residents.

In the 1970s, owing to the soaring crude oil prices, Nigeria rose as a giant market. According to Kweku Ampiah (1997), Japanese investments in Nigeria are rarely oriented towards raw materials. Rather, Nigeria's economic boom attracted many Japanese companies as a large market for their products, thus Japanese nationals were sent here as expatriates. In his memoir, one Japanese retired expatriate who stayed several times in Lagos wrote of his experience in the mid-1970s:

> At that time, the market was booming, so "if you bring it to Nigeria, you can sell anything". . . . From Japan, steel, vehicles, electric appliances, etc. were exported one after another, and you could not make a reservation for the shipment of vessels. . . . Since it was in a situation where "if you move around the town, your business is rolling," so I too ran around from morning to sunset every day.

Trading companies and manufacturers invested in Nigeria and dispatched a large number of expatriates. Large-scale projects were formed, such as the construction of the Lagos thermal power plant by Hitachi, Ltd., and the oil refinery by JGC. According to an informant who stayed in Lagos during the 1980s, over 100 Japanese workers inhabited prefabricated houses constructed at a project site. This residential area had softball grounds and provided Japanese food prepared by Japanese cooks.

These expatriates with their families formed the Japanese Association, the umbrella organization for Japanese living in Nigeria. The Association has its secretariat at the office of the Japan External Trade Organization in Lagos, the federal capital of Nigeria till 1991.

From the late 1970s to the early 1980s, the Japanese Association grew vibrant. Every year, the association would rent a banquet hall in Lagos, host the end-of-year party for its members who gathered with their families from other cities, such as Kaduna and Port Harcourt. The members formed teams according to their residential area and held a "song battle," a popular year-end event in Japan. The members of the association would spend a few months in preparation and enthusiastically join in this event.

Many expatriates were accompanied by their wives and children, and thus, the Japanese Association opened an elementary school for its children. The wives formed women's associations under the Japanese Association with the ambassador's wife hosting meetings at the official residence.

The number of Japanese residents in Nigeria increased during the Second Republic era (October 1979 to December 1983). Later, the 1983 coup d'état instated the military rule by Muhammadu Buhari, which was replaced by another coup d'état with the reinstating of Ibrahim Babangida's rule in 1985. Owing to this turmoil, Nigeria's economic situation deteriorated in the 1980s, and several Japanese companies withdrew operations, which led to the decline in the Japanese population in Nigeria.

An informant who was stationed in Lagos during the late 1980s said that, the main task of trading company representatives, then, was "rescheduling." With the economic downturn, payments from Nigerian clients became arrears, thus, Japanese expatriates living on a day-to-day basis were forced to readjust repayment terms. This causes Japanese companies to plan the withdrawal from Nigerian market. However, it clearly upset the Nigerian government officials who worried about increasing unemployment. Consequently, the Japanese expatriates left Nigeria in a "fly-by-night" scenario, under the pretense of a business trip or vacation and asked the local staff to carry out the winding-up formalities. The Japanese school closed in the late 1980s, owing to the fewer number of students, now including only the children of the embassy staff and schoolteachers. Finally, the Japanese Association, which had once formed a thriving expatriate community, declined with the worsening business environment in Nigeria.

The capital was relocated from Lagos to Abuja. Consequently, the Japanese embassy moved to new capital in 2000. Among the members of the Japanese Association, many diplomats and international organization staff now reside in Abuja. Since Lagos remains the commercial hub of Nigeria and West Africa, most Japanese expatriates still live there. However, considering the security concerns in Nigeria, almost all expatriates are male workers who are on assignment. As of September 2019, there were approximately 60 members in the Japanese Association. Of these, about 30, living in Lagos, are active members of the association.

Reverse flow: Nigerians heading to Japan

Since late 1980, economic depression and political instability have caused Japanese companies to withdraw from Nigeria, thus causing a serious decrease in the Japanese population there. From over 1,000 in the early 1980s, the number of Japanese people in Nigeria decreased to less than 300 in the later part of the decade. However, cross-border trade of Japanese products continued under different trade networks with different actors.

While Nigerians lost their purchasing power because of the economic depression, their demand for imported commodities increased. As Dobler (2008: 410) noted,

> Consumption, and the quest for consumption, has become one of the major modes of integration of young Africans into a global society, and consumption choices have become an important means to express personal identity in relation to the wider world

The desire for imported commodities led to an economic transformation in the terrain of consumption. Since the late 1980s, imported second-hand goods, locally called *Tokunbo*,[2] became popular and spread to markets in Nigeria, and thus, these "imported second-hand goods that were condemned as 'scrap' gradually became the norm" (Adebayo, 2015: 86). This encouraged some Nigerians to participate in cross-border trade, and they headed to destinations including East Asia, especially Japan.

The migration flow of Japanese towards Nigeria and the reverse flow of Nigerians towards Japan follow a symmetrical trajectory (see Figure 10.2). As I have shown in the previous section, the number of Japanese residents in Nigeria has declined since the mid-1980s. It has remained below 200 since 1996. In contrast, the number of Nigerians in Japan has increased since 1990. According to Statistics on Foreign Residents in Japan (formerly Statistics on the Foreigners Registered in Japan),[3] the number of Nigerians in the country with a legal resident status increased from 193 at the end of 1990 to 1,315 in 1992. As of the end of 2018, 3,245 Nigerians were living in Japan, of which, 77.8% (2,526) were adult males.

However, this does not mean that there were no Nigerians visiting Japan before the 1990s. The statistics show the number of foreign nationals staying in Japan on December 31, of each year. Therefore, foreign residents who are not in Japan, then, are not included in the data. Alternately, Immigration Control Statistics, another data set compiled by the Immigration Services Agency, shows the total number of foreigners entering and leaving Japan each year. According to these statistics, there were about 1,200 Nigerians on average, arriving in Japan with short-term visas annually through the 1980s. The lowest was 760 in 1987, while the highest was 1,598 in 1985. By the mid-1980s, the number of Nigerians leaving Japan was almost the same as the number of those entering. However, since the end of the 1980s, the latter number exceeded the former. The largest gap occurred in 1991, when the number of Nigerians entering Japan reached

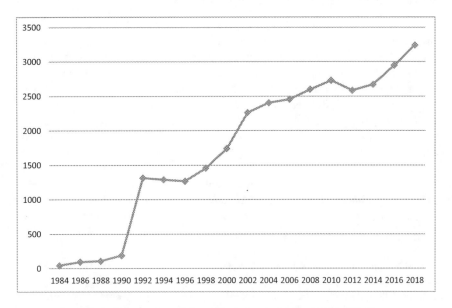

Figure 10.2 Population trends of Nigerians living in Japan (1984–2018)

Source: Statistics on Foreign Residents in Japan (Immigration Service Agency of Japan, 1985–2019)

2,290, while the number of Nigerians leaving Japan was 920. The difference is 1,370. Those who enter Japan do not necessarily coincide with those leaving Japan because short-term visa permits them to stay for three months, and thus, some immigrants may stay until the next year. However, the large gap between the number of arrivals and departures indicates an increase in Nigerians who remain in Japan for longer than their visas permit.

Even though both Nigerians in Japan and Japanese in Nigeria cross the same border for economic purposes, these two subjects of migration enjoy different social status due to immigration policies of the destination country. Japanese people heading to Nigeria are granted business visas as expatriates of Japanese companies and can stay in Nigeria with a resident permission. On the other hand, many Nigerians can obtain visas only for short-term stays in Japan of less than three months. As of the end of 1992, when the number of Nigerians increased sharply in Japan, 90.3% came with short-term stay visas (Figure 10.3).

However, if we check the statistics by legal status, the number of Nigerians with short-term stay visas has decreased since 1992. Instead, the number of Nigerians with the status as "spouse or child of Japanese national" since the mid-1990s began to increase. Moreover, in 1994, the first Nigerian acquired "permanent resident" status, and subsequently, the number of Nigerians with "permanent resident" exceeded the number of those with "spouse or child of Japanese national" status in 2007. By the end of 2018, 14.1% (456) of the 3,245

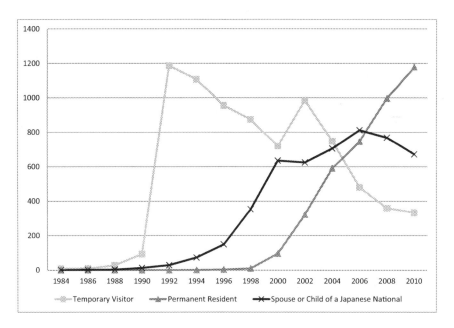

Figure 10.3 Change of legal status among Nigerians in Japan (1984–2010)

Source: Statistics on Foreign Residents in Japan (Immigration Service Agency of Japan, 1985–2019)

Nigerians had the status of "spouse or child of Japanese national" and 49.1% (1592) have obtained "permanent resident" status.

The change in legal status among Nigerians reflects their life course in Japan. After entering Japan with a short-term visa, some chose to overstay the authorized period. Since the Japanese government has not allowed unskilled workers to receive employment visas, many Nigerians stay on as irregular migrants. The most common means to secure a mid- to long-term visa is to marry a Japanese and obtain the status of spouse. As a "spouse or child of Japanese national," they are granted formal resident permission and are free to work. Furthermore, three years after marriage, they can apply for permanent residence under certain conditions, making it possible to staying on, without depending on the Japanese spouse, thereby facilitating more stability.

However, obtaining a spouse visa and resident permits does not necessarily mean that they will settle down in Japan. With a legitimate resident status, Nigerians obtain not only their freedom to work but also the freedom to move, which they lost as irregular migrants. Consequently, it is an opportunity for Nigerians to rethink their relationship with their hometown and transnational movements (Matsumoto, 2014). Therefore, as soon as Nigerians acquire mid- to long-term stay visas, many embark on transnational businesses that link Japan with Nigeria and other countries.

> Alex (pseudonym) was born in Imo State. He came to Japan in 1997. Though he brought four thousand dollars with him, he ran out of money soon. Thereafter, he decided to remain in Japan after the authorized period of stay and began to work at a dry-cleaning plant.
>
> He married a Japanese in 2002 and was able to secure resident permission. He, thus, visited Nigeria temporarily for a period of three months. After returning to Japan, he began working in a printing factory. In the same year, he embarked on cross-border trade between Japan and Nigeria. He buys various kinds of second-hand goods with the money he earns at the factory and ships them to Nigeria.
>
> When these commodities arrive at Nigerian seaports, he quits his job in Japan and returns to Nigeria to receive them. After he arranges for their retail, he returns to Japan and begins work again.
>
> He intends to return home after retirement. He built his own compound in a commercial city near his hometown and bought lands to start businesses.

It has been pointed out that while the unemployment rate among Nigerian living in Japan is high, there are many of those who identify themselves as self-employed. Relying on national census data for 2000, Omagari et al. (2011) analysed the working population of major foreign nationals, except for those from developed countries (i.e. Europe, the United States, and Australia), and found that, Nigerians had the third-highest percentage of self-employed workers in the population, next to that of Koreans and Pakistanis.

This is a matter of self-identification. While Nigerians are engaged in factory work, they identify themselves as a self-employed rather than employees, since they regard their work as their own choice. Moreover, many Nigerians have other businesses in addition to their labour work. Many Nigerians participate in cross-border trade as part-time traders. Like Alex, while they are engaged in manual labour, they buy used automobile parts and other products, pack and ship them in containers to Nigeria and other countries. Some may return to Nigeria to receive these containers as they own stores for distribution in the Ladipo market, the largest used-car parts market in Lagos.

While many work as part-time traders, there are a few Nigerians who are specialized entrepreneurs with licenses, including that of second-hand goods dealer's or used vehicle auctions. In addition, the spread of internet services in Nigeria enables them to find customers while staying in Japan.

To facilitate smooth business, they consider it necessary to know the Japanese language to communicate with Japanese business partners and fulfil the necessary paperwork. Moreover, without a Japanese guarantor, they can rarely rent land and apply for loans from the bank. Thus, Japanese wives and parents-in-law sometimes play significant roles in the setting up of businesses.

New trend of migration: Japanese wives and children heading to Nigeria

Compared to the 1970s, during the oil boom, the Japanese Association, Nigeria, is now remarkably smaller in scale. However, if we look outside the association, there are new developments in the flow of migration from Japan to Nigeria, with a drastic change in the composition of the Japanese population in Nigeria, in recent years.

According to the Embassy of Japan in Nigeria, the number of Japanese nationals residing in Nigeria was 157 in 2019. Contrarily, the official number of members in the Japanese Association was approximately 60. In other words, the majority of Japanese residents no longer belong to the association.

Based on the Annual Report of Statistics on Japanese Nationals Overseas, the number of Japanese staying in Nigeria was 141 as of October 2017. Of these, 18 (12.8%) lived in Nigeria as permanent residents. There were 52 females, accounting for 36.8% of the total population. Dividing the population by age, 45 (31.9%) of 141 Japanese were minors under the age of 20. Since the majority of members of the Japanese Association were male expatriates, this association alone cannot explain the gender and age composition of the current Japanese population in Nigeria.

Women and minors now occupy a certain portion of the Japanese population in Nigeria because they belong to transnational families: Japanese wives and children who followed their Nigerian husband/father home. In the following, we discuss an example of a Japanese woman living in Nigeria, who met her Nigerian husband when he came to Japan for study.

Chiharu (pseudonym) met her Nigerian husband when they were university students in Japan, after which they married. She gave birth to her eldest daughter in 2000 and moved to Nigeria in 2004. In Japan, she worked at a computer company. Owing to the depression, the company called for an early retirement, and she saw this as a good opportunity to move to her husband's home country.

During her first three years in the country, she stayed in a state capital in southeastern Nigeria. Though her children soon acclimatized to living there, she could not enjoy her new life in a regional city, and thought of returning to Japan on several occasions. There were no opportunities to meet Japanese people, nor to speak the Japanese language. If she wanted to have a break, at best, she could have instant coffee at a hotel or surf the Internet using English at a cybercafé.

In 2009, she temporarily returned to Japan for the birth of her second daughter. After her return to Nigeria with her daughter, her family moved to Abuja, the federal capital. This shift to a major city made it easier for her to get accustomed to living in Nigeria. Since the use of Internet and mobile phones have spread rapidly in Nigeria, it now became easier for her to call her parents in Japan, surf the Japanese websites, and get the information on her homeland. It has been approximately ten years since she lived in Abuja, and she now has a third daughter and a son. Her eldest daughter, who was born in Japan, is now in the United States and attends university there.

Of the women living in Nigeria with their Nigerian husbands, only three belong to the Japanese Association. The opportunities for interaction with Japanese people are limited, and communication with local people requires speaking English. Therefore, many Japanese wives have sought divorce and have returned to Japan.

Some Japanese wives also participate in the association called "Nigerwives," a group founded in 1979 with 13 branches across the country. This organization for foreign wives who have Nigerian husbands and live in Nigeria, has approximately 300 women from 40 countries, according to the website. The organization is credited to launching a campaign for the creation of spousal visas that were non-existent in the Nigerian Immigration Policy; as a result, these women are now granted a special residence permit under the name "Niger wife."[4]

Although some Nigerians in Japan return to their homeland, many remain in Japan with their families for economic reasons. Even though their job opportunities are limited in Japan due to language barrier and racial discrimination, they believe they can earn better salaries here. As of today, some of them have stayed in Japan for over 20 years. Those who came to Japan in the early 1990s are now middle aged and have children attending high school or university.

With the growth of second-generation children, the Nigerian community in Japan is increasingly conscious of their cultural identity. Through their voluntary associations, Nigerians began to have events for their children to learn about their father's homeland. For instance, the Igbo Association of Japan, an organization based in Yokohama, introduced an ethnic language class for their children. In addition, every September, this association holds the New Yam Festival, a major cultural event in their homeland. According to the association, this festival gives their children the opportunity to learn about their own culture, where they wear the Igbo traditional dress and give a brief speech in the Igbo language.

Apart from the cases of families moving to Nigeria, and Nigerians trying to create opportunities for their children to learn Nigerian culture in Japan, there are parents who send only their children to Nigeria to have them educated in their father's home country. Paternal relatives take care of these children, while their parents stay in Japan. An example is as follows.

> Hiroshi (pseudonym)'s Nigerian father came to Japan in 1993. He married a Japanese and had three children; Hiroshi was the first son followed by two daughters.
>
> In 2008, when he was in the sixth grade, Hiroshi and the older daughter were sent to Nigeria. Their paternal aunt cared for them. Hiroshi had three second cousins, with Nigerian fathers and Japanese mothers who were living in Nigeria three years prior to his arrival. Therefore, he did not feel lonely, though he was separated from his parents. Hiroshi and his sister learned English from the cousins, and they taught them Japanese.
>
> Hiroshi and his sister enrolled in the sixth grade of a Nigerian primary school and graduated six months later. They then entered a private secondary school that was newly founded near the father's hometown. They lived in the school dormitory for six years until they graduated from senior secondary school. Although Hiroshi sometimes hated living in the dormitory, he had many good memories. He said, "If somebody asks me where my hometown is, my answer is the school dormitory where I spent six years with my friends. I do not know much about my father's hometown."
>
> After graduation, he returned to Japan and got a job. Now, he lives in a shared room with a Japanese friend. His sister, who stayed in Nigeria, now attends a university in Canada.

In addition to learning about their father's culture, some parents consider it better for their children to acquire education in English. Though there are international schools in Japan, the opportunities for admission are limited and their tuitions are expensive.

It is not easy to grasp the actual situation of Nigerian-Japanese children, such as Hiroshi, who were not affiliated with the Japanese Association. The Japanese embassy recognizes them only when they visit to renew their passports with their Nigerian relatives, or when the embassy investigates the location of Japanese nationals for the purpose of a survey. There are several such cases, where parents leave their children with relatives in Nigeria. While child fostering is a common practice among many ethnic groups in Nigeria (e.g. Cohen, 1969), it could be viewed as abandonment and may cause cross-cultural friction between Nigeria and Japan.

Transnational child fostering now becomes easier due to the development of new communication channels. Parents in Japan can use mobile phone and internet video chat-like skype to communicate with their children in Nigeria. It must be noted that mobile handsets are one of the major commodities which Nigerian traders import from East Asia especially China. Thus, the flow of transnational families can be regarded as a by-product of cross-border trade between Nigeria and East Asia.

Conclusion: anisotropic mobility in the migration between Nigeria and Japan

Here, I will discuss the three types of migrations between Nigeria and Japan: the flow of Japanese expatriates to Nigeria, the flow of Nigerians to Japan, and the flow from Japan to Nigeria triggered by cross-national marriages. These flows are not independent phenomena.

The decline in the number of Japanese residents in Nigeria and the increasing number of Nigerians living in Japan are both related to the transition in the Nigerian economy, which is linked to global capitalism. In post-independence African states, the distribution of goods and consumer behaviour have diversified beyond the relationship between former colonial power and ex-protectorates. New trade links are connected to new commodities by new actors (Dobler, 2008). One such change is the flow of made-in-Japan goods and migration between Japan and Nigeria. From the 1970s to the 1980s, during the Nigerian economic boom, this period was marked by the flow of Japanese expatriates who moved to Nigeria for trade of Japanese products. However, since the late 1980s, as the purchasing power of Nigerians declined, a series of Japanese companies withdrew operations, and the number of Japanese residents also declined in Nigeria. Instead, Nigerians who came to Japan became the main players in commercial activities, gathering used commodities that have lost their commercial value in Japan and exporting them to Nigeria.

This migration of Nigerians to Japan leads to another flow of Japanese wives and children moving to Nigeria. At first glance, it appears common to marry and have families in destination countries. However, it is important that there is no similar phenomenon among Japanese expatriates who reside in Nigeria for commercial purposes. The different attitudes towards marriage between Nigerian in Japan and Japanese in Nigeria are influenced by the immigration policy of the host country and the social status of a foreigner.

In her study on Nigerians living in China, Heidi Haugen (2012) uses the concept of "second state of immobility" for the situation which Nigerians encountered in the country of destination. While they left their home country where their social mobility was restricted owing to political instability, they fell into another state of immobility due to China's immigration control. This can be applied to the situations of Nigerians in Japan, where it is difficult for them to obtain work visas. Nigerians must acquire spouse visas and permanent residence to engage in commercial activities.

The flow of Japanese wives and children into Nigeria creates another flow of migration that of Nigerian-Japanese children. While these children have dual nationality, both as Japanese and Nigerians,[5] it is common for them to use their Japanese passport. They cross-borders as "Japanese" because of convenience: firstly, the Nigerian embassy in Japan does not have the function to accept application for new passports for children. And secondly, Japanese passport is said to be the world's most powerful, which enables the holder to cross-borders with visa-free access.

In addition, Nigerian-Japanese children were not bound to these two countries. Like Chihiro's eldest daughter and Hiroshi's younger sister, some Nigerian-Japanese youth enrol in educational institutions in Europe and the United States, not in Japan or Nigeria. Flexible thought about migration gained through their parents' and their own experiences increases their mobility and gives them a broader choice of where to live. At first glance, the practice of the Nigerians living in Japan who want their children to be educated in their home countries appears to be a look back on their own past. However, it is also an act that looks forward to their children's potential relocation in the future.

Notes

1 This chapter is based on a study first reported in a Japanese publication, N. Yoshihara, K. Hashimoto, & H. Konno, eds., *Gurobaruka Jidai no Kaigai Nihonjin Shakai (The Globalized Age and Overseas Japanese Societies)*, Ochanomizu Shobo, 2021. In order to write this chapter, I used data from this publication and added some field data and analyses.
2 *Tokunbo*, a Yoruba word, literally meaning "from across the seas," has been used as an honorary name for children who are born abroad. But later, it came to indicate imported second-hand commodities (Adebayo, 2015: 85).
3 Statistics on the Foreigners Registered in Japan is based on the number of foreigners staying in Japan at the end of the previous year. With the amendment of the Immigration Control and Refugee Recognition Act in 2012, it has been changed to Statistics on the Foreign Residents in Japan. New statistics count foreign nationals based on two categories, "zairyu-gaikokuzin" (registered foreigners) and "souzairyu-gaikokuzin"(total registered foreigners). In the following section, I'll use the latter category, which covers not only foreign residents with mid- to long-term visa but also those with short-term visas.
4 "Nigerwives Nigeria," retrieved on 4 October 2020 from https://nigerwives.wixsite.com/nigeria (2020)
5 According to the Nationality Law in Japan, these children are expected to choose either of the nationalities before they reach 22 years of age.

References

Adebayo, K. (2015). Tokunbo and Chinco Economies in Nigeria: Rethinking Encounters and Continuities in Local Economic Transformations. *African East-Asian Affairs*, 3–4, 80–101.
Ampiah, K. (1997). *The Dynamics of Japan's Relations with Africa: South Africa, Tanzania and Nigeria*. Routledge.

Belanger, P., C. J. Chung, J. Comaroff, M. Cosmas, S. Gandhi, A. D. Hamilton, L.-Y. Ip, J. Kim, G. Shepard, R. Singh, N. Slayton, J. Stone, and S. Wahba. (2001). Lagos: Harvard Design School Project on the City. In C. J. Chung, J. Inaba, R. Koolhaas, and S. Tsung Leong, eds., *MUTATIONS*, Actar/birkhauser, pp. 651–719.

Bodomo, A. (2010). The African Trading Community in Guangzhou: An Emerging Bridge for Africa-China Relations. *The China Quarterly*, 203, 693–707.

Bräutigam, D. (2003). Close Encounters: Chinese Business Networks as Industrial Catalysts in Sub-Saharan Africa. *African Affairs*, 102, 447–467.

Cohen, A. (1969). *Custom and Politics in Urban Africa: A Study of Hausa Migrants in Yoruba Towns*. University of California Press.

Dobler, G. (2008). From Scotch Whisky to Chinese Sneakers: International Commodity Flows and New Trade Networks in Oshikango, Namibia. *Africa*, 78(3), 410–432.

Dobler, G. (2016). The Green, the Grey and the Blue: A Typology of Cross-Border Trade in Africa. *Journal of Modern African Studies*, 54, 145–169.

Gadzala, W. A. (2010). From Formal- to Informal-Sector Employment: Examining the Chinese Presence in Zambia. *Review of African Political Economy*, 37, 41–59.

Gukurume, S. (2019). Chinese Migrants and the Politics of Everyday Life in Zimbabwe. *Asian Ethnicity*, 20(1), 85–102.

Haugen, H. (2011). Chinese Exports to Africa: Competition, Complementarity and Cooperation Between Micro-Level Actors. *Forum for Development Studies*, 38(2), 157–176.

Haugen, H. (2012). Nigerians in China: A Second State of Immobility. *International Migration*, 50, 65–80.

Hsu, E. (2007). Zanzibar and Its Chinese Communities. *Population, Space and Place*, 13, 113–124.

Kawada, K. (2005). Tokyo no Nishiahurika-kei Syussinsya no Seikatsusenryaku: Roppongi niokeru Saabisu-gyou Zyujisya wo Jirei toshite (The Sense of Tactics' of West African Workers in Roppongi). *Studies in Sociology, Psychology, and Education*, 60, 71–92. (in Japanese).

Kernen, A. (2010). Small and Medium-Sized Chinese Businesses in Mali and Senegal. *African and Asian Studies*, 9, 252–268.

Khan Mohammad, G. (2014). The Chinese Presence in Burkina Faso: A Sino-African Cooperation from Below. *Journal of Current Chinese Affairs*, 43(1), 71–101.

Liu, S. (2019). China Town in Lagos: Chinese Migration and the Nigerian State Since the 1990s. *Journal of Asian and African Studies*, 54(6), 783–799.

Lyons, M., B. Alison, and L. Zhigang. (2013). The China-Africa Value Chain: Can Africa's Small-Scale Entrepreneurs Engage Successfully in Global Trade? *African Studies Review*, 56, 77–100.

Matsumoto, H. (2014). Zainichi-ahurikajin no Teizyuuka to Toransunasyonaru na Idou: Naijeriajin no Keizaikatsudo wo Toushite (Settlement and Transnational Movement among African Migrants in Japan: Through the Case Study on Economic Activities among the Igbos from Nigeria). *Journal of African Studies*, 85, 1–12. (in Japanese).

Matsumoto, H. (2017). African Chiefs in the Global Era: Chieftaincy Titles and Igbo Migrants from Nigeria. In Y. Gebre, I. Ohta and M. Matsuda, eds., *African Virtues in the Pursuit of Conviviality: Exploring Local Solutions in Light of Global Prescriptions*. Langaa, pp. 229–247.

Meagher, K. (2012). Weber Meets Godzilla: Social Networks and the Spirit of Capitalism in East Asia and Africa. *Review of African Political Economy*, 39, 261–278.
Okakura, T., and K. Kitagawa. (1993). *Nihon – Ahurika Koyushi: Meiji-ki kara Dainijisekaitaisen-ki made (History of Japan – Africa Relations: From Meiji Period to World War II)*. Dobunkan Shuppan. Co. Ltd. (in Japanese).
Omagari, Y., S. Takahashi, I. Kaji, N. Inaba, and N. Higuchi. (2011). Zainich-Gaikokujin no Shigoto: 2000nen no Kokuseichyosa deta kara (Foreigner's Job in Japan: Analyzing the 2000 Census Data). *Annual report of the Institute of Regional Studies, Ibaraki Universit*, 44, 27–42. (in Japanese).
Röschenthaler, U. (2016). Good Quality or Low Price? Competition between Cameroonian and Chinese Traders. *African East-Asian Affairs*, 1–2, 32–65.
Sumio, A. (1993). *Ahurika ni Watatta Nihonjin (Japanese Who Went Over to Africa)*. Jiji Press, Ltd. (in Japanese).
Sumio, A. (2000). *Nihonjin no Ahurika 'Hakken' ('Discovery' of Africa for Japanese)*. Yamakawa Shuppansha Ltd. (in Japanese).
Wazaki, H. (2009). Chuko jidosyagyou wo Ikiru Tainichi Africajin no Seikatsu Senryaku: Kamerunjin no Seikatsu Senryaku to Bokoku no Seizi-syakai Jyoukyou (Life Strategy among Africans Residing in Japan, Who Work in Second-Hand Motor Business). *JCAS Review*, 9, 260–279. (in Japanese).

Statistics

Immigration Service Agency of Japan. (1985–2019) Immigration Control Statistics. Retrieved from www.moj.go.jp/isa/policies/statistics/toukei_ichiran_nyukan.html
Immigration Service Agency of Japan. (1985–2019) Statistics on Foreign Residents in Japan. Retrieved from www.moj.go.jp/isa/policies/statistics/toukei_ichiran_touroku.html
Ministry of Foreign Affairs of Japan. (1973–2018) Annual Report of Statistics on Japanese Nationals Overseas. Retrieved from www.mofa.go.jp/mofaj/toko/tokei/hojin/index.html

11 Decentralization and conflict prevention in East Africa

Yuichi Sasaoka

In this chapter, focus is placed on decentralization policy, its processes, and its effects on conflict prevention in three East African countries: Uganda, Tanzania, and Kenya. Decentralization policy can also be employed to design and achieve other policy objectives, such as poverty reduction and democratization. Decentralization policy has been promoted in developing countries since the 1990s by northern donor agencies and NGOs. Around the mid-2000s, donors started researching decentralization and its effects on conflict prevention on a significant scale (Braathen & Hellvik, 2006; GTZ, 2006; Siegle & O'Mahony, 2006). However, the application of decentralization policy began slowing around the same time because political regimes in African countries were constructed as hybrid regimes.

Whether decentralization policy can stop intrastate conflict has been debated. Some have argued that decentralization provides a policy environment in which the majority group can allay the frustrations of minorities by constructing local governments, creating public posts (Seely, 2001), and providing public services. Others have complained that promoting decentralization may erode the unity of nation states by enhancing the separatist activities of minorities in certain localities (Posen, 1993). However, both views still regard the concepts and practices of decentralization from the standpoint of the transfer of authority within central and local governments. Much broader perspectives on governance are needed to properly assess these concepts and practices. Therefore, in this chapter and book, the definition of decentralization given by Cheema and Rondinelli (2007) is used: the sharing of power, authority, and responsibilities among broader governance institutions. Decentralization can be considered the coordination mechanisms or partnership principles of three actors: the government, the private sector, and civil society.

African societies were originally fragmented. But when European colonizers arrived on the continent, they combined small villages and established artificial, centralized states. From this point of view, recent decentralization can be seen as a reversion to traditional, precolonial fragmented societies. The centralized political regimes were constructed by colonizers with the character of top-down decision making and no downward mechanism of accountability to people, clients, or taxpayers. The imposed top-down power structure remained in place into modern times, in the centralized political structures following independence, and even after the foundation of democratized states in the 1990s.

Political processes of three East African countries

In the 1960s, three East African countries became independent at almost the same time: Uganda, Kenya, and Tanzania. Within 5 years, Uganda and Kenya became capitalist states, while Tanzania became a socialist state. They had been governed by British indirect rule from 1918 to independence, and after independence the Ugandan and Kenyan governments adopted federalism as stipulated in their constitutions, while Zanzibar in Tanzania applied for quasi-federalism status in 1977. The three countries founded the East African Community (EAC), which lasted from 1967 to the end of the 1970s, the purpose of which was to promote economic integration. This intergovernmental organization was revived in 2001, with a customs union being added in 2005, and Rwanda and Burundi joining in 2007.

In the post–Cold War period, the shift towards multi-party systems, attributable to democratization, has shaken Africa. Pressures from both inside and outside many African nations have compelled their governments to accept a multi-party system (Selbervik, 1999). Consequently, presidential and national parliamentary elections have been introduced in many countries, including three countries. During the political changes, three countries have higher levels of fragility. According to Fragile States Index (Fund for Peace, 2020), Kenya and Uganda are classified as alert countries, and Tanzania is classified as elevated warning country. In 1991, Kenya embraced democratization, authorizing the transition to a multi-party system. However, the government of Daniel Moi retained political power by interfering in otherwise democratic procedures. In 2002, Uhuru Kenyatta, Moi's successor in the ruling party, the Kenyan African National Union (KANU), was defeated by Mwai Kibaki, the unified candidate of the opposition party, the National Alliance for Rainbow Coalition (NARC). Uganda, which had adopted a unique non-party system in 1986 in an effort to mitigate intrastate warfare, introduced multi-party elections in 2006. Since then, the National Resistance Movement (NRM), headed by Yoweri Museveni, has maintained its hold on political power. Tanzania, which at one time had a one-party system, has held multi-party elections since 1995. Chama Cha Mapinduzi (CCM: Revolutionary Party of Tanzania) is the current political regime in Tanzania and the longest ruling party in Africa at present.

Since the 1990s, democratization has been accelerating decentralization in East Africa. Previous decentralization policies were occasionally instituted to reinforce political power in a top-down fashion. The Ugandan and Kenyan federal systems were replaced by authoritarian centralized systems some years after their independence. The Ugandan Obote and Kenyan Kenyatta regimes – and the Nyerere regime in Tanzania – sought to solidify a centralized system by absorbing or outright prohibiting opposition parties. In the 1980s, however, market liberalization policies gained strength and privatization was introduced. Moreover, citizens and donors were increasingly demanding political liberalization, democratization, and public sector reform.

Uganda

Uganda introduced a multi-party system in 2006, four years after Kenya introduced its own. Museveni regarded this system as posing the danger of encouraging sectarianism in the country, believing that it could reignite religious and ethnic confrontations at the central level (Museveni, 1997). Therefore, NRM was eager to promote a decentralization policy in the 1990s to diffuse local frustrations against the government and to encourage grassroots participation in the political process. Before NRM, Uganda was ruled by the dictators Milton Obote and Idi Amin, both of whom were northerners. At first, the Obote regime was a coalition government with leaders of Buganda in the south, but after a confrontation between the two groups, a military dictatorship was installed. Idi Amin, a general at the time, overthrew the Obote regime in a coup and abolished local governments, parties, and parliaments. The earliest incarnation of NRM launched an intrastate war against the second Obote administration based on a claim of election fraud. Museveni and his aides were ethnic Banyankole and had the support of Buganda, which had great antipathy towards Obote.

NRM steadily promoted a decentralization policy. Considering Local Council (LC) as the core, NRM sought to rectify the authoritarian bias by encouraging grassroots participation. NRM needed to promote decentralization as a substitute for democracy. Having experienced harsh domestic conflicts, Uganda was not under immense pressure to democratize its political body by donors. Moreover, the experience of conducting a limited presidential election in 1996 taught NRM a lesson about the importance of service delivery to local people. The origin of the LC was a mutual support system between NRM army and local people. NRM did not exploit people, and it paid for their food. Since the local chief system was not so popular, people generally welcomed the LC to construct a political space in which people could talk freely.

NRM government initially tried to construct a broad-based policy facilitated by power-sharing arrangements. Buganda and even northern groups could be assigned to higher posts in the cabinet and government. This accommodative policy ended around the year 2000, being replaced by patronage politics linked with ethnicity. As NRM fought northerner regimes and military for the sake of the people, northerners had strong antipathy towards NRM, culminating in a conflict instigated by the Lord's Resistance Army (LRA) in the 2000s, exacerbating antipathy. Some Bugandan factions demanded the revival of federalism and the return of the assets sequestered by the Obote I regime. It was said that NRM had promised Buganda these concessions in the midst of the war with the Obote II regime. In the constitution drafting process in 1995, there was a debate about whether Buganda was eligible to receive federal member status. Buganda made a compromise because NRM still promoted the broad-based policy at that time.

However, the debate over a land bill in 1998 irritated Buganda as it adversely affected its king's land.

Museveni announced a deal to abolish the term limit of the president in exchange for a full-fledged democratized election in 2003. Museveni's third term was planned, and bribe money was distributed to NRM parliament members. Dissenting voices were silenced in the preparatory presidential election process. This climate continued until the 2021 presidential election between Museveni and Robert Kyagulanyi. Buganda royalists and a part of young people continued to resent the Banyankole and an emerging elite class, which pretended to forget Buganda's request for autonomy and siphoned money due to their dominant position.

Tanzania

Tanganyika, a continental part of Tanzania, is free from heavy conflict due to a limited level of ethnic tension, the spread of the Swahili language, and inclusive public policy. Based on these favorable factors, CCM could promote both democratization and decentralization simultaneously. However, the Zanzibar islands have retained aspirations of independence from Tanzania, with CCM Zanzibar and the Civic United Front (CUF) having seriously confronted each other in the past. After the 2000 election, for instance, Tanzanian police shot and killed 35 people (and more than 600 people became refugees) during protests by CUF demonstrators, who were claiming that the election was fraudulent.

There was no ethnic faction inside CCM, and the public servants entrance examination was fairly conducted. Although Tanzania had adopted a one-party system, a presidency and prime minister system had also been introduced as a way to balance power. More than two parliament member candidates needed to participate in the election in a constituency, and competition within CCM was strongly encouraged. The electoral law in 1965 prohibited the promotion of racial and regional separation. When the multi-party election system was legalized by an amendment to the constitution in 1992, the prohibition against ethnic, religious, and racial bias was retained to guarantee national unity.

Tanzania followed Uganda's decentralization strategy at the end of the 1990s. In the 1970s, Julius Nyerere, the first president, made the declaration on decentralization, abolishing district governments by absorbing them into regional party units. These measures actually encouraged centralization. In the 1980s, however, the government seriously reviewed this policy framework. Local government was again specified in the revised constitution in 1985, and the government made a wide range of preparations for decentralization and devolution in a policy paper in 1998, as Uganda had done in 1995. While downplaying the role of regions, the government established two layers of local government: district and village. Tanzania's decentralization strategy can also be seen as part of public sector reform. Tanzania recognized the serious failures of centralization, and thus, it sought reforms of local government capacity to implement a more efficient public service delivery. Northern European donors and the World Bank asked for a broad range of public sector reforms beyond the scope of Civil Service Reform (URT, 1996). Development planning shifted from the top-down style in 1972 to the bottom-up style, that is, participation by local people. Rural farmers seemed to be the power base for CCM, and linking central elites and local people was considered an important task.

Confrontations between CCM Zanzibar and CUF became particularly serious concerning Unguja Island and Pemba Island, specifically over racial, ethnic, and historical hallmarks. However, these confrontations seem to be gradually weakening. After independence, Zanzibar was given a quasi-federal autonomous status, and a system was enacted whereby the president of Zanzibar automatically became the vice president of Tanzania. Both CCM and CUF obtained substantial political support in the mainland and in Zanzibar. Since CCM Zanzibar retained power and was reluctant to promote power sharing with CUF, peace negotiations became dead-locked. However, after the end of 2009, both parties made a compromise and held a referendum on the revised constitutional draft on power sharing. In 2010, a two-thirds majority of residents supported the draft, and presidential and parliamentary elections were conducted accordingly.

Kenya

In Kenya, the Moi government delayed the democratic process from 1991 to 2002. Additionally, a centralized governance structure persisted from independence to 2010. The Kikuyu, the largest and wealthiest ethnic group in Kenya, have come into sharp conflict with other groups, especially with the Luo in the west. The centralized system tends to prioritize the interests of the strongest groups, that is, those who hold political power, who are usually located in the center of the country, corresponding to the central distribution of fertile land in the Central and Rift Valley. Moi, originating from the nomadic Kalenjin, was unexpectedly assigned to the presidency but managed to successfully maintain political power; meanwhile, the Kikuyu retained a dominant economic position. In 2002, Kibaki represented the opposition alliance of the NARC and, after serving as president, gradually revealed his group, Kikuyu preference and became confrontational with other groups, especially with the Luo. Since then, the Kikuyu have continued to hold on to political power, and the Uhuru Kenyatta government was formed in 2013 and 2017.

Democratization has progressed since 2002, and meeting and parting of political groups have been repeated. President Mwai Kibaki was deeply involved in the centralized power structure even when he belonged to the opposition party. In that context, the election result in 2007 was dubious (Dagne, 2008). Territorial decentralization was suppressed under the Provincial Administration System (PAS), and the devolution of authority was given to the city and town levels, not to the district level, without transferring the authority to deal with major sectors. Political turmoil inside the centralized structure continued until a power-sharing deal between Kibaki and Prime Minister Odinga was made in 2008, as recommended by former UN Secretary General Kofi Annan. After heated debate, two-thirds of voters in a referendum approved a new constitution draft with the introduction of decentralization in 2010. Three years later, the decentralization process had started and two equal governing bodies, the national and county level governments, were created.

In Kenya, plural channels of local development administration were not well coordinated. The PAS originated in the colonial period. However, local government and the electoral constituency became eligible to receive development funds from the center in the 1990s and 2000s to add service delivery. These mechanisms were introduced to compensate for the insufficient decentralization system, but they were nonetheless signs of progress. After post-election disturbances spawned an ethnic conflict that caused over 1,000 deaths and 300,000 internally displaced persons, Kofi Annan and others met with Kibaki and Odinga and proposed a power-sharing arrangement, a constitutional amendment, and political institutional reform (Dague, 2008). The coalition government was a redemption of the promise made by the two groups five years before, and based on this arrangement, the government made a draft of the constitution that included a prime minister post and local government reform.

Comparative analysis

Centralized East African regimes supported by outside powers in the Cold War were weakened by economic liberalization and intrastate conflicts in the 1980s, ultimately losing their domestic and international support base in the democratization trend of the 1990s. The globalized democratization trend facilitated individual freedom in the political systems in East Africa, and opposition parties started to freely engage in their activities. The ruling parties, however, were reluctant to hold free and fair elections. In Kenya, the political party repeatedly made and broke alliances based on ethnicity. In Uganda, new opposition parties were created such as the FDC (The Forum for Democratic Change) and the NUP (National Unity Party), but Museveni and NRM continued to hold on to power by any possible means. In Tanzania, the opposition party was similarly growing, but CCM continued to maintain its grip on power. The democratization process sensitized people to free elections and citizen rights and urged them to establish financial decentralization through subsidies from the center to local units.

Democratization and decentralization

Decentralization was the means by which to promote and camouflage democratization. Democratization is essentially a system of modern thoughts and practices in relation to state formation, whereas decentralization is the logic linked with any kind of governance at any time. Democratic participation by citizens at the local level is typically used to defend and justify decentralization. The Ugandan NRM stressed citizen participation in the 1990s, stating that a multi-party system could be substituted by decentralization. This position lasted until 2003, when the NRM decided to introduce a multi-party system. The Kenyan Moi administration delayed political reforms for democratization and decentralization, protecting centralized governance systems. The Tanzanian CCM realized the multi-party system in 1995 and shifted towards decentralization at the end of the 1990s. The common dynamic of these three countries is the strong demand for resource allocation to rural areas by citizens.

Another element of decentralization is the elite capture of resources. Fiscal decentralization in Uganda and Tanzania transferred resources to rural areas as a means of realizing their poverty reduction strategy in a de facto one-party system. Likewise, Kenya also diverted financial flows to rural areas in an effort to mitigate conflicts between the center and the periphery. The Kenyan Constituency Development Fund (CDF) and other schemes involving national and local parliament members created a culture of clientelism. Namely, devolution in these three countries was sustained by increasing local demands for central resources. After a system was established in which resources and services were consistently transferred to rural areas, the mindsets and perceptions of citizens changed in a positive way. The Ugandan and Tanzanian decentralization processes, however, were halted when hybrid regimes, including democratic institutions, were virtually constructed (Tripp, 2010). The Ugandan decentralization secretariat was abolished in 2004. Tanzania adopted the CDF in 2009 via parliamentary initiatives. Another indicator of the persistence of the ruling party's patronage was evident in the increase of districts in Uganda. Museveni created new jobs by constructing new districts (Mwenda, 2007), from 39 in 1996 to 111 in 2006 to 135 in 2020.

Effects of conflict prevention

To examine the effects of conflict prevention, we can determine whether the conflict occurred in the centralization or decentralization process of the governance in the three countries. Violence instigated by the dictators Obote and Amin occurred in the centralization process, and NRM's decentralization policy was launched after the end of intrastate war. While constructing a patronage system throughout the nation via decentralization, Uganda has remained peaceful. However, some countries, like Mali and Ethiopia, could not have achieved such a peaceful result through decentralization. This is because Uganda has constructed a fairly well service delivery transfer system via its LC, the nation's major ethnic groups are somewhat disconnected from outside groups in neighbouring countries, and a political power balance exists between the western Banyankole and the central Buganda. Violence tends to occur under a centralized government and political process (Green, 2008). Kenya's ethnic land conflict and disturbance in 2007–2008 occurred under a centralized structure (Kimenyi & Ndung'u, 2005). However, in socialist Tanzania, a centralization policy ordering farmers to resettle in villages was not accompanied by violence. That said, violence and government suppression did occur following a potentially fraudulent election in Zanzibar.

Another effect of conflict prevention was that new governments could gain political legitimacy through the devolution of power, demonstrating to the people the complete change in government structure, policy, and operation. As the former colonies operated according to a centralized and top-down decision-making structure, modern African societies have for the most part maintained a centralized and vertical structure after independence, and small, elite groups have typically dominated the wealth of African nations by exploiting this structure. African intellectuals have considered the centralized structure to be a colonial control device (Mamdani, 1993). Therefore, implementing devolution in African countries can have the effect of altering citizens' perceptions in a constructive way (Kibara, 2005). It has been argued that although Africa is socially decentralized, it is governmentally centralized (Olow, 2003). After independence, many African countries maintained centralized government structures. Tanzania's "decentralization" policy, instantiated in 1972, favored regional government and abolished district parliaments. Kenya began implementing "District Focus" planning in 1966, and yet, this was just a cover for reinforcing top-down control by central ministries despite concerted efforts by policy makers and donors to the contrary. Ordinary citizens did not have any expectations of the government and, as such, made every attempt to evade paying taxes ordered from the center.

In Kenya and Uganda, the power-sharing policy and decentralization policy appeared to be interchangeable. The initial Moi period facilitated the participation of various groups in the cabinet. This de facto power-sharing policy changed in the late Moi Cabinet into a Kalenjin-dominated system. The Kibaki (Kikuyu) – Odinga (Luo) relationship demonstrated that Odinga wished to create a prime minister post to curb Kikuyu's excessive power, a plan realized after mediation by Kofi Annan. Fiscal decentralization measures realized up until the early 2000s had a role in compensating for the lack of inclusiveness among cabinet members. NRM initially encouraged the broad-based cabinet and military and it was gradually replaced by Banyankole dominance, while decentralization policy had been promoted.

Statehood and the federal system

Statehood in the three African countries is closely linked with the history of federalism. The federal system was envisioned to prevent ethnic and religious conflict among various groups by recognizing the political legitimacy of constituent states. Buganda, which had at one time controlled other groups via collaboration with British colonizers, wished to form a federal system that would allow the continued dominance of their identity and culture at the time of independence. Uganda had four kingdoms and one chieftaincy, including Buganda. Tanzania reintegrated Zanzibar, which had once been independent, and thus, a quasi-federal system that permitted a higher level of autonomy in Zanzibar needed to be established. During the socialist period, CCM continued to propagate the centralized development model, but it also recognized its failure in the late 1980s and searched for a new model. Kenya was also given a federal constitution at the time of independence, but the KANU, a coalition of larger groups, immediately abolished it by absorbing the opposition into their party.

At present, Uganda and Tanzania have devolutionary local governments, in operation since the late 1990s. Kenya adopted a similar system 15 years later. These trends are conducive to effective policy coordination in the region. Uganda had a serious motivation for decentralization, whereas Kenyan regime had an instinct for centralization. Buganda had the tendency towards autonomy and division, while Kikuyu tended towards unification and control. Both groups had a relatively higher socio-economic status and could intervene in politics when other groups tried to obtain political power. Similarly, they dominated fertile lands and assumed an intermediary role between British colonizers and other groups. NRM needed to contain Bugandan federalism and thereby promoted district-based devolution, since Bugandan territory is divided into many districts. With this scheme, Banyankole successfully sustained its dominant position in the Ugandan governance.[1] Kikuyu, which had withdrawn from the political center stage under the Moi regime, returned with Kibaki's party in 2003–2004 and has continued to hold onto power since then. Zanzibar, which had experienced turmoil in terms of island politics, stabilized for the most part with further institutional reforms, and antagonistic tensions have at least partly subsided.

These three countries are seeking for a unified federal system of EAC, beyond mere regional economic grouping. At this stage, federalism can imply regional integration. This process, however, is not certain and is in any event quite complicated, but there may be a hypothetical possibility that separatist groups, such as the Buganda, Somali, and Zanzibar CUF, could be accommodated in a larger political unit in the future.

Ethnic group and politics

Looking back on the history of three countries, intrastate conflict has mainly involved conflicts between ethnic groups. An exceptional case in this regard is the LRA, a quasi-religious, cultic group and militia composed of violent non-state actors (VNSAs) that use violence, intimidation, and abductions to terrorize homeland populations in northern Uganda. The ethnic (or identity) composition of Uganda, Kenya, and Zanzibar in Tanzania is somewhat similar and yet diverges significantly from the ethnic composition of mainland Tanzania. What kind of relationship could exist between the conflict process and decentralization or democratization? Here, we can observe some aspects of ethnic group inequality, confrontations between ethnic political parties, and democratization and decentralization trends.

Firstly, group relations are decided by the identities, perceptions, emotions, and memories of people – all subjective images. A typical African group is both ethnic and religious and has been to some extent influenced by European colonizers. Some groups exist beyond state borders but are linked by shared kinship and/or culture. Inside the state, there are many divergent groups, many of which do not share a common language. These groups are all too often mutually suspicious, hostile, and distrustful, with each group viewing the other as a monolithic enemy devoid of nuanced customs, views, and individual differences. African politics have often played out based on such perceptions (Kaufman, 2006) as they offer politicians, group leaders, and conflict entrepreneurs the means with which to manipulate their constituencies for their own ends.

Secondly, each group has differences that can be measured in an objective way – the structural conditions of their conflicts. Stewart (2008) explained that the cause of conflict is group identity based on inequality. Political institutions could be designed to mitigate such group conflicts by establishing an equitable redistribution system for government resources. In the East African context, wealthier groups include the Kikuyu in the central region and the Buganda in the southern region. Poorer groups include the Luo in Nyanza province in Kenya and in northern Uganda. Inter-group hostilities could be alleviated if political and economic inequality is decreased. At present, the Banyankole, a southwestern group, and Museveni's group in Uganda enjoy government privileges and positions and thereby experience frictions with other groups.

Thirdly, the political process may aggravate conflict and reverse the positions of oppressor and oppressed. Obote, the first prime minister of Uganda and a northerner, attained his position by a coup. Kenyan post-election violence in 2007–2008 was instigated by ethnic tensions associated with historical land tenure disputes. Post-election violence in 2000 in Zanzibar was provoked by the killing of CUF demonstrators by the police. These conflicts were ultimately caused by dissatisfaction among poorer groups with resource constraints and election fraud, but they were stoked by violent political groups as well. Buganda's king became the President of Uganda after Buganda gained exceptional autonomy in the constitution. Obote, who was originally the leader of the anti-Buganda party, won the election by forming a coalition of convenience with Buganda (Horowitz, 2000, cited by Elischer, 2008). Thereafter, both groups started criticizing each other. Obote thus launched a coup by mobilizing the northerner-dominated military, abolishing the constitution, the federal system, and the prime minister post in 1966. In Kenya, the Party of National Unity (PNU) and the Orange Democratic Movement (ODM) confronted each other, and post-election violence was attributed to both sides. In Tanzania, Unguja, and Pemba, CCM Zanzibar and the CUF have all engaged in violent confrontations, mainly sponsored by the major oppressor, the CCM-led government.

President Jomo Kenyatta implemented a Kikuyu-biased policy over rich land in central region and Rift Valley, but his rule was persuasive for a time given its historical resistance to the colonial government (Klugman et al., 1999). The next leader, President Moi, gradually revealed his affiliation with the Kalenjin group, but he cautiously adopted a power-sharing policy and later introduced a fiscal decentralization policy after announcing democratization. The politically powerful Kalenjin were balanced against the economically formidable Kikuyu. This relationship is comparable to that between the Banyankole and Buganda. In Zanzibar, Arab descendants, who are concentrated on Pemba Island, were economically active in clove exports and gained political power from this activity.

African descendants revolted against them, and many Arab descendants consequently fled. After independence and the imposition of Tanzanian socialism, the clove trade collapsed. Pemba became poor, while the tourism industry boomed in Unguja. Tanzanian democratization in the 1990s reignited violent confrontations between the islands and groups.

These conflicts took place during the early stages of democratization in the three countries after political leaders began using ethnic symbols to mobilize support for their own party and interests. This is despite the fact that ethnicity can be fluid and boundaryless. The Kalenjin have rapidly grown in number in Kenya since Moi was assigned the presidency, from 3% of the population to over 10% (KNBS, 2020). Political leaders can easily gain solidarity, loyalty, and cooperation from their ethnic electorates by using symbols and concealing internal problems. In Tanzania, ethnic parties were banned due to the sheer number of ethnic groups in the country. In their place, CCM sought to diffuse a socialist identity. Zanzibar is an exception in that it has a strong secessionist movement and group identity is assigned accordingly (ICG, 2019).

In all three of these East African countries, the oppressor often resorts to direct violence against the oppressed. In Uganda, Obote, and Amin, both northerners used military rule to commit ruthless atrocities. In Tanzania, the police killed CUF demonstrators. In such cases, the oppressor carries out mass killings in a systematic, organized way. Other countries, such as Rwanda, Sudan, and Ethiopia, have experienced such violent oppression, in the post–Cold War period. In the recent record, governance in Uganda, Tanzania, and Kenya has been relatively stable and decentralized than in other neighbouring countries.

Fourth, group formation in East Africa is the heritage of indirect rule in colonial times. The Buganda Kingdom was in league with the British colonizers and was designated as an intermediary class between the colonizers and other ethnic groups. This superior position was rather similar to that of the Kikuyu in Kenya and that of the Arab descendants in Zanzibar. Tanganyika, a continental part of Tanzania, was originally colonized by Germany and was unfamiliar with indirect rule. At the time of independence, Buganda, Kikuyu, and Arab descendants were quite dominant, and Buganda and Arab descendants had separationist tendencies for their kingdoms. Indirect rule was designed to run the colonies with fewer personnel and at a lower cost via the separation and antagonization of ethnic groups. Democratization has tended to stimulate such former cleavages when group identity has been combined with political affiliation.

Fifth, democracy can facilitate violence when it is based on group identity politics and political sensitization. The late Moi multi-party system stirred up ethnic hatred among people (Elischer, 2008). However, Uganda had already been facing ethnic divisions and escalating violence in the despotic period when political parties were banned (Okuku, 2002). Therefore, with some conditions, either democratic or authoritarian governance can lead to antagonistic political processes. These processes can be exacerbated by VNSAs, who provide resources to control violence. VNSAs include various groups: warlords, militias, pirates, religious sect, criminal organization, anti-governmental forces, youth group, and private military companies, to name a few. The motivations of these groups can be partly explained by greed theory (Collier & Hoeffler, 2002). This theory suggests that a limited number of people have exclusive interest in capturing natural resources, drugs, and contraband, and that they need to deploy military forces to control certain territories for their activities while simultaneously presenting their intentions as noble and just. In Uganda, the violent activities of LRA can be partly explained by greed theory, but its leader, Joseph Kony, did not appear to have any clear objectives (van Wyk, 2017). For their survival, LRA has engaged in elephant poaching, wildlife trafficking, narcotics smuggling, and illegal trade.

Analysis of conflict prevention

Decentralization can mitigate conflicts between influential groups in control of the government and can address the complaints of various adversarial groups. This is evident in Museveni's strong commitment to decentralization in the 1990s to the 2000s. NRM sought to establish a broad-based government, one that stressed participation by assorted ethnic groups and females, in the 1980–1990s. This power-sharing process was sustained for over 10 years – and in the second half of 1990s, NRM started a genuine decentralization policy. The motivation of NRM in this regard was that the Banyankole group wanted to stop Buganda federalism by dividing their kingdom into pieces. NRM also considered implementing poverty reduction programs through decentralization so that the party could become more popular among people in rural areas. While Museveni and NRM bowed to the pressure for democratization from donors, they nonetheless pursued decentralization as a substitutive policy for democratization. In the LC system, any adult can run for election as an individual candidate, not a party candidate. With these refined strategies, Uganda has attained world-wide popularity and support.

What about the effects of conflict prevention? Banyankole's support base has expanded, while confrontations have decreased in intensity because local service delivery is working. And even though Buganda and northern people may still have been discontented and antipathic towards Banyankole, they nevertheless had to admit that the economic performance of the country was optimal, at least in the 2000s. That said, political tensions between NRM and the opposition party have been growing since the 2010s and have continued into the 2020s, and there is suspicion that the recent elections were rigged. Western donors have expressed disappointment with Museveni for his unlimited extension of presidential terms, becoming essentially a presidential monarchy. Human rights issues have arisen, especially the suppression of freedom of speech and political activities. In Uganda, decentralization preceded democratization under NRM rule. In the initial stage of decentralization, people could speak more freely in LCs and had high hopes for the future. Meanwhile, serious conflicts could have been avoided.

Tanzania has learned from the failure of socialism and initiated a liberalist policy and related institutional reforms as a consequence. In 1995, the nation held a multi-party election and implemented a variety of institutional reforms of public services, the financial and auditing system, and legal systems. Local government changes were considered one of these reforms, and Regional Administration Act in 1998 stipulated that the district government was the core level of service delivery, with the regional government being reduced to a subordinate role. Since Tanganyika is rather free from ethnic conflicts, and as democratization preceded decentralization, CCM did not have an internal motivation to utilize decentralization as a tool. The common motivations between CCM and NRM were twofold: one was the improvement of service delivery in the whole restructuring of the government in order to reduce poverty; the other was that the ruling party wanted to foster close relations between central elites and local elites in order to diffuse the power base into local grassroots organizations. Zanzibar was given a special status in the quasi-federal system but internally faced harsh party confrontations. The 2010 power-sharing agreement added accommodative elements between the two groups.

Among the three countries, Kenya was the slowest to implement decentralization. Kikuyu, the KANU, and central ministries wanted to preserve centralization, whereas the opposition party and civil society wanted to promote decentralization. In this political climate, bargaining among political leaders and parties was linked with ethnic groups, which is a problematic issue. The most important factor in this respect was what kind of coalition would be forged among influential groups, especially the Kikuyu, the Luo, and the Kalenjin. The government, established in 2013 and 2017, was based on the Kikuyu–Kalenjin coalition. Decentralization was agreed to by a power-sharing arrangement in 2010, and it was made the cornerstone of the governance system. Kenya experienced democratization prior to decentralization, and the disturbances following the 2007 election were caused by ethnic confrontations and political sensitization under centralization.

Decentralization seemed to work for conflict prevention in general, but it should be noted that some conditions must be attached: ethnic group allocation, historical governance structure, party structure and its mode of behaviour, and bottom-up political support. The state borders among these three countries cannot be easily controlled, but there is no need to strengthen them because only a limited number of trans-border conflicts have occurred, and there is a common vision for economic integration. The good level of decentralization among these three countries can serve as a model for other African countries.

Firstly, if multi-party democracy is linked with political sensitization, ethnic group inequality, and historical conditions, then it can lead to political instability and the risk of conflict. Decentralization could mitigate such conflicts by providing posts and resources in the local government. If budget resources are transferred to local areas, power struggles at the center would be at least partially ameliorated. A decentralization policy can provide relatively fair resource allocation under democratization or under the pressure or necessity for democratization. Political decentralization can facilitate participatory democracy at the grassroots level while also contributing to the establishment of a strong support base for service delivery. Promoting decentralization after a de facto power-sharing arrangement among political groups can be found in NRM policy in the 1990s and Kenyan power sharing in the 2010s.

Secondly, whether decentralization can be successful, including a federal system, depends on the historical state formation process. While Kenya and Tanzania became colonized as a unified bloc owing to the rivalry of suzerain countries, the Ugandan territory was organized by British colonizers arbitrarily as a bloc of Buganda and other groups. Moreover, Buganda royalists and Arab descendants sought authority for their kingdoms after independence, but the other groups strongly opposed such a vision. Thereafter, a special autonomous position was obtained in Zanzibar, but not in Buganda. If historical sociopolitical structures can be built into the present decentralized structure as a subtext, it could work as a method for conflict prevention. Buganda and other kingdoms must be treated fairly in this respect with non-territorial and sociocultural decentralization.

Thirdly, the political legitimacy needed to break the colonial legacy requires devolution to negate the vertical and centralized governance structure. This is the antithesis of colonialism and could work to stabilize the society. As a theory, citizens expect devolution to actively mobilize the government. On the one hand, Ugandan and Tanzanian devolution can be supported in the search for a decision-making process from the bottom up instead of traditional local chief system. On the other hand, the Kenyan chief system became the base for a local governance system until the year 2010, and it maintained a vertical and centralized structure, not at all accommodative to the voices from below. However, Kenya finally abandoned the administrative system of colonial legacy.

Effects of decentralization on state borders

What kinds of effects does decentralization have on state borders from a conflict prevention perspective? The most fragile border is the Kenya–Somalia border. Some politicians and merchants from both countries have close relationships, including smuggling. The north-eastern part of Kenya is a part of the Somali cultural area. Although LRA operations were conducted in northern Uganda, LRA has also established a geo-political zone in Sudan, the Democratic Republic of Congo (DRC), and the Central African Republic (CAR). In 1991, LRA finally gained the support of the Sudanese government and obtained arms and bases. Sudan was engaged in a civil war against the Sudan People's Liberation Army (SPLA) and was thus critical of the Ugandan government's support of SPLA. LRA could escape northern Uganda when they were pushed into a corner by the Ugandan government army, and they could return when they recovered their strength. In October 2020, Kitaya village in southern Tanzania was attacked by a militia called Islamic States – Central African Province (IS-CAP), which came from the province of Cabo Delgado, Mozambique.[2] IS-CAP was considered partly a splinter group of the Allied Democratic Forces (ADF), a militia carrying out violent attacks in Uganda and DRC and once supported by Sudan. But there is no concrete evidence for the existence of IS networks in DRC, Tanzania, and Mozambique.

Loose border control cannot prevent the flow of smuggled goods and VNSAs, and VNSAs tend to utilize borders as a tool for expanding their activities. For local people, militia is harmful and dangerous – but in some cases, they are considered beneficial to local people. If the state border is firmly controlled, benefits accrue to the government, central powers, and central groups living in the capital city. The reason why African state borders are so loose is that intrastate conflict was more harmful than interstate conflict until the 2000s. In the three countries examined here, interstate conflict once occurred as well: between Uganda and Tanzania, when General Amin provoked President Nyerere in 1978. Intrastate conflicts occurred more often: for example, between Obote and Buganda, Obote II and NRM (Museveni), LRA and NRM, PDU (Kibaki) and ODM (Odinga), African descendants and Arab descendants, and CCM Zanzibar and the CUF. However, intrastate conflicts are decreasing, while trans-state conflicts provoked by VNSAs are rather rapidly increasing.

The impact of democratization after the Cold War has persisted for about 20 years. Ethnic group captured the central area of a country, the capital, can be a dominant group, while a weaker group tends to stay in the periphery. The Kikuyu live in the central region of Kenya and have thus retained both political and economic power. Likewise, Buganda in central Uganda has maintained economic and cultural power as well, but political power has shifted to the Banyankole, that is, the westerners. In Zanzibar, the power center has shifted from Pemba to Unguja Island. These contrasting groups have experienced ethnic conflicts in many parts of Africa. After the rulers had constructed a hybrid regime combining democratic institutions and informal authority, intrastate conflict has decreased but has remained in very weak states such as Somalia and South Sudan. VNSAs have become active in resource exploitation and transnational networks. Trans-state conflicts have been driven by VNSAs, combined with rural communities. The change of conflict type has been evident in East Africa, while all the types remain as open options.

The role of decentralization beyond conflict types

Decentralization works well in the three countries discussed here, although they have experienced problems and challenging tasks. A good element can soothe confrontation among ethnic political parties under the democratization process. The conflict over a zero-sum game at the center would be reduced. Another element is that decentralization allows local people to participate, and in doing so they can realize their power as voters and clients in service delivery. However, the decentralization policy crucially depends on a real sense of resource allocation to rural areas and peripheral groups. The three East African countries described here are rather satisfactory concerning these conditions compared with other African countries. Decentralization can be risky when peripheral groups have connections with other groups in an adjacent country. The northeast region of Kenya is a case in point because Somalis are a trans-border ethnic group. However, there is little chance that all Somalis will unite to promote a secessionist movement. Somalis continue to fight against each other, at the clan and sub-clan level.

The roots of intrastate conflict are derived from politicians' exploitation of identity divisions to mobilize people. However, as shown here, ethnic conflict has tended to decrease in Uganda, Kenya, and Tanzania. The new type of conflict is trans-border conflict, which was once sparked by anti-NRM forces, LRA, and ADF, and more recently by Al-Shabaab, Somali warlords, and IS-CAP. The frequency of VNSA activities in the three countries is less than the average for East Africa as a whole. Protecting the border is considered an easier way to stop the inflow of militias, but it is very difficult and costly to do so, and doing so can eliminate future opportunities. There is another way to solve the problem of VNSAs: making local people and VNSAs non-violent via a decentralization policy. If the state border becomes fully open, an extended cooperation framework beyond the nation state could occur. Therefore, decentralization is a useful measure for circumventing or preventing violence and struggles over resources.

Notes

1 Abbey K. Semuwemba, Comment, Museveni, Buganda can make peace, 4 February 2021. The Independent.
2 George Obulutsa, "Militants from Mozambique staged deadly attack in Tanzania, police say," Reuters 23 October 2020.

References

Braathen, E. & Hellvik, S. (2006). Role of Decentralization on Peace Making and Conflict, *NIBR Working Paper 125*, Norwegian Institute for Urban and Regional Research.
Cheema, G. & Rondinelli, D. (eds) (2007). *Decentralizing Governance-Emerging Concepts and Practices*, Brookings Institution Press.
Collier, P. & Hoeffler, A. (2002). Greed and Grievance in Civil War, *Policy Research Working Paper, 2355*, The World Bank.
Dagne, T. (2008). *Kenya: The December 2007 Elections and the Challenges Ahead*, No. 34378, CRS Report for Congress, Washington, DC: Congressional Research Service.
Elischer, S. (2008). Ethnic Coalitions of Convenience and Commitment: Political Parties and Party System in Kenya, *GIGA Working Papers 68*, German Institute of Global and Area Studies.
Fund for Peace. (2020). Fragile States Index, Washington, DC. https://fragilestates index.org
Green, E. (2008). Decentralisation and Conflict in Uganda, *Conflict, Security and Development* 884, pp. 427–450.
GTZ. (2006). *Decentralization and Conflicts: A Guideline*, Eschborn, Division Governance and Democracy, Federal Ministry for Economic Cooperation and Development.
Horowitz, D. (2000). *Ethnic Groups in Conflict*, Berkeley, CA: University of California Press.

International Crisis Group. (2019). Averting Violence in Zanzibar's Knife-edge Election, *Briefing No. 144*, Washington, DC.
Kaufman, S. (2006). Symbolic Politics or Rational Choice? – Testing Theories or Extreme Ethnic Violence, *International Security* 30(4), pp. 45–86.
Kenya National Bureau of Statistics. (2000). 2019 Kenya Population and Housing Census, Nairobi. https://www.knbs.or.ke
Kibara, G. (2005). Prerequisites for Democratic Consolidation in Kenya. In *Democratic Transition in East Africa*, Research for Democracy in Tanzania (REDET), University of Dar es Salaam.
Kimenyi, M. & Ndung'u, N. (2005). Sporadic Ethnic Violence – Why Has Kenya Not Experienced a Full-Blown Civil War? In: Collier, P., Sambanis, N. (eds) *Understanding Civil-War Evidence and Analysis, Vol. I Africa*, Chapter 5, World Bank.
Klugman, J., Neyapti, B. & Stewart, F. (1999). *Conflict and Growth in Africa, Vol.2: Kenya, Tanzania and Uganda*, Development Centre Studies, OECD.
Mamdani, M. (1993). *Imperialism and Facism in Uganda*, Nairobi: Heinemann.
Museveni, Y. (1997). *Sowing the Mustard Seeds: The Struggle for Freedom and Democracy in Uganda*, Oxford: Macmillan.
Mwenda, A. (2007). Personalizing Power in Uganda, *Journal of Democracy* 18 (3), pp. 23–37.
Okuku, J. (2002). Ethnicity, State Power and the Democratization Process in Uganda, *Discussion Paper 17*, Uppsala: Nordiska Afrikainstitutet.
Olow, D. (2003). Local Institutional and Political Structures and Processes: Recent Experience in Africa, *Public Administration and Development* 23, pp. 41–52.
Posen, B. (1993). The Security Dilemma and Ethnic Conflict, *Survival* 35 (1), pp. 27–47.
Seely, J. C. (2001). A Political Analysis of Decentralization: A Coping the Tuareg Threat in Mali, *Journal of Modern African Studies* 39 (3), pp. 499–524.
Selbervik, H. (1999). *Aid and Conditionality*, OECD.
Siegle, J. & O'Mahony, P. (2006). "Assessing the Merits of Decentralization as a Conflict Mitigation Strategy," Paper Submitted to Office of Democracy and Governance, Washington, DC: UEAID.
Stewart, F. (ed.) (2008). *Holizontal Inequalities and Conflict – Understanding Group Violence in Multiethnic Sciences*, New York: Palgrave Macmillan.
Tripp, A. (2010). *Museveni's Uganda – Paradoxes of Power in a Hybrid Regime*, Boulder and London: Lynne Rienner Publishers.
United Republic of Tanzania. (1996). *The Local Government Reform Agenda 1996–2000*, Dar es Salaam.
van Wyk J. A. (2017). Joseph Kony and the Lord's Resistance Army. In: Varin C., Abubakar D. (eds) *Violent Non-State Actors in Africa*, Palgrave Macmillan.

Conclusion

Yuichi Sasaoka, Aimé Raoul Sumo Tayo, and Sayoko Uesu

Following different and complementary perspectives, the various chapters in this volume have described the current state of African borders. From their key findings, some proposals can be made in light of this book's three initial research questions. Our case studies try to capture the current status of "porous and fragile" borders or "marginalized" borderland; those cases can be categorized into two types of thinking: (i) where the hardening of borders is needed and justified, with the expansion of Violent Non-State Actors (VNSAs) or a migration crisis, and the recent outburst of global pandemic (Chapter 9). While there are accumulations of literature on this former aspect, this volume tries to shed light on another trend, (ii) where the opening of borders is encouraged, by adopting the suitable institutional framework (i.e. free movement of people or decentralization) and supporting the borderland's actors in this process. As presented by Sasaoka in Introduction (Chapter 1), analysing the borderlands with Dobler's (2016) "blue, grey and green" borders offers another, less grim perspective; as most of the cases deal with the specific borderlands and their institutional settings or actors, they fall under the "green" and "grey" borders or its mixture, as shown by Yamazaki (Chapter 3), Kamei (Chapter 4), Sekiya (Chapter 5), Uesu (Chapter 7), and Sumo Tayo (Chapter 9). The "blue" borders are described by Sasaoka (Chapter 6) and Matsumoto (Chapter 10). Sumo Tayo (Chapter 2) and Takezawa (Chapter 8) discuss the new trend of regional organization and cooperation to cope with interstate conflicts. Another categorization is, regarding actor's type, Sumo Tayo (Chapter 2), Uesu (Chapter 7), and Takezawa (Chapter 8) pick up the issue of VNSA that instigate the new type of conflict demonstrated in Chapter 1. Sasaoka (Chapter 11) also addresses the experiences of three East African countries and examines how the broad meaning of decentralization had helped to ease the conflicts, and this part is discussed in the following section (second question).

Firstly, what kind of state borders exist in Africa? Yamazaki's case study, a mixture of "green" and "grey" borders, focuses on the evolution of cross-border trade in marginalized borderland in West Nile in northern Uganda and assesses how the provision of road infrastructure and the resulting expansion of logistics have positively affected people's lives. West Nile region had been unstable from the 1970s to the early 2000s, and after the signing of the peace agreement in

2002, the development did not take off despite the improvement of the security situation. At the same time, with the support of the Local Government (LG) of Uganda, new markets were created by the trans-border movement of people (including the refugee) affected by the outbreak of conflict and its end. In this process, the implementation of National Development Plans since 2011 was crucial in connecting the borderlands to the larger cities and regional markets as far as Mombasa and Dar es Salaam; the establishment of One-Stop Border Posts (OSBP) in East Africa have also helped the intensification of cross-border trade. It is worth noting that residents in the DRC side also benefit from Uganda's development plans and scenes.

Kamei presents another good (somewhat struggling) aspect of managing refugees in West Nile, again a mixture of "green" and "grey" borders. Uganda has long been subjected to trans-regional movements and intrastate displacements of people. These unique conditions have made Uganda among the world's top refugee-hosting nations and have profoundly shaped Uganda's acknowledged refugee protection policy. Uganda is also known as one of the successful cases in decentralization in Africa (Chapter 11 and summarized later to argue the *state-building approach*). The unique feature of refugee-hosting in West Nile lies in the mindset of people in borderland: historically, peripheral West Nile had been demoted and deprived of backing from the center. It seems likely that long years of marginalization and hardships inflicted upon the population have profoundly influenced the formation of their frontier mindsets. Cross-border migration is also enabled because, while a large part of the state boundary exits, there is no clear fencing or physical demarcation. Hence, the residents come and go between the borderlands for practical reasons. For them, state borders are artificial and impractical: they are historical remnants from colonial supremacy and today's administrative divisions rather than political, as discussed by Dobler. Based on those observations, Kamei's chapter assesses the impact of recent refugee influxes in the LGs and draws some policy implications. This aspect will later be summarized in the second question, on the validity of the *state-building approach*.

Sekiya's case opens up a different perspective of economic migration from rural Africa, especially how mobility as a culture is entrenched in African societies. Inspired by Urry's (2007) mobility theory, Sekiya argues that the mobility paradigm is taking a turn in various fields including anthropology; while the livelihood of people in rural Africa has traditionally been treated as static, he attempts to reconsider the topic from a more dynamic perspective in which sedentariness and mobility coexist. He retraces the trajectories of young rural immigrants in Niger to find that their connection with their place of origin and the family is maintained by sending money and communication, and this communal connection continues unbroken. As rural Africa is facing structural transformation with mobility as culture, this transformation is becoming increasingly complex and diverse. Sekiya stresses that there is an essential task for researchers who wish to deepen their understanding of the structural transformation of rural Africa today; they must depict the livelihoods and lifestyles practiced by rural communities and people in terms of sedentariness and mobility and consider how the two coexist.

In this regard, Dobler's typology and his way of analysing borderland dynamics provide a helpful hint for understanding the dynamic transformation in rural Africa. While Dobler classifies actors into three groups according to his typology, Sekiya instead proposes to see the same society or people face the three types of borders in different situations of their life.

In another case of "green," "grey," and a bit of "blue" borders with a grim perspective, Uesu analyses the expansion of VNSAs in the Sahel to illustrate Sumo Tayo's argument for hardening the border. She described how the violent, malicious, or victimized narratives and perceptions had been created by VNSAs and security actors who persecute it. Consequently, the politically and economically marginalized communities tend to find their accounts and construct their narratives in the peripheries/borderlands; we have seen many other cases with the rise and fall of the Islamic State (third question). Uesu then assesses the management of borderlands and their actors by local governments and the international community, including Japan. While African governments put little resources on borderlands and let smugglers or other grey actors in the periphery to control the zone, the international community has concentrated on border controls and counterterrorism operations. At the same time, a new trend has emerged to assist the borderland and its actors in re-engaging their normal economic activities or rebuilding the trust among neighbouring communities and local authorities through different levels of mediation. Overall, Sahelian countries are still in the middle of political and security instability and the future perspective looks grim, but there are lessons learned that could also apply to other borderlands under crisis.

Sumo Tayo has described the forms, characteristics, and functions of the symbolic, legal, and material border hardening mechanisms in Africa. From the analysis of border securitization processes and daily functioning, it emerges that borders must be reaffirmed as a framework of sovereignty and responsibility in some contexts. However, states should make use of them in an intelligent, moderated manner. Border hardening is adequate for shorter terms, but it would isolate the root cause of problems instead of solving them in the long run. Therefore, it is imperative to strengthen the capacity for border management stakeholders in Africa while paying attention to the harmful effects of hardening borders on human rights and the environment.

Sasaoka reviews the experience of Development Corridors (DCs) in Mozambique, a "blue" border case, planned and implemented as a means to promote the regional integration (or "micro-regionalism" in the case of DCs). Many DCs occur across state borders and link-up ports, mineral resource areas, industrial estates, and forests. As they are often linked to the national interests and political elites, it relies on a *top-down development* approach since its inception. Against such a backdrop, he assesses whether the Non-State Actors (NSAs), notably African Civil Society (CSO), have been involved in the process, who are expected to counterbalance the top-down development approach. Mozambique has various DCs plans; the major one is the Maputo DC (MDC) located in the south, others are the Beira DC (BDC), and the Nacara DC (NDC). Here, we take up the case of NDC to examine how the local civil society and small-scale farmers had gradually organized and raised concerns over the NDC agricultural project (ProSavana), which was planned as triangular cooperation among Mozambique, Brazil, and Japan. However, NGOs in Mozambique, Brazil, and Japan, and a group of researchers, expressed concern about the expulsion of small-scale farmers from their homes. Criticized as a land grab, and coupled with the corruption of President Guebuza, Prosavana was perceived as a revival of Portugal's colonialism. After numerous consultations among stakeholders, its termination was announced by Mozambique and Japanese governments in July 2020. Among many lessons learned, Sasaoka highlights that while DCs provide macroeconomic impacts on the Southern African region, the promoters of DCs reside in the capital city and are deeply entrenched in African neopatrimonialism, and the grassroots and borderland people get the lesser benefits from the existence of "blue" border.

As another case of a "blue" border, Matsumoto examines the migration between Nigeria and Japan, triggered by cross-border trade. Instead of focusing on a single direction flow, the bilateral migration of Japanese and Nigerians and the multiple actors' interrelationships are examined. He points out that current African markets are connected to various countries and cities through road networks and transport corridors to ports and airports, and it symbolizes contemporary African borders. Concerning imagined borders, he argues, African states share their boundaries with countries in other continents, including those in East Asia. We observe today the increase of cross-border trade between East Asia and Africa and the flow of migration. Matsumoto points out that while Africa's porous borders indicate the vulnerability of its states, the borderland and trans-region approaches reconsider its contribution to sociocultural networking. He agrees with Dobler (2016) that cross-border activities can enable the participants to construct new links among themselves. For this, Matsumoto discusses the three types of migrations between Nigeria and Japan: the flow of Japanese expatriates to Nigeria, the flow of Nigerians to Japan, and the flow from Japan to Nigeria triggered by cross-national marriages. These flows are not independent phenomena; the decline in the number of Japanese residents in Nigeria and the increasing number of Nigerians living in Japan are both related to the transition in the Nigerian economy, which is linked to global capitalism. Inter-continental immigration is nothing new, but imagined borders are now activated through globalized human contacts and the progress of information technology.

Secondly, this volume tries to assess the validity of the *state-building approach* in light of African borderlands. Each chapter has directly or indirectly addressed this issue; the role of regional cooperation and decentralization is highlighted in this concluding part.

The following cases discuss the regional aspects in coping with the countries that share unstable borders. Takezawa highlights that the role of IGAD is unique in focusing on regional security, where other regional organizations are more economically oriented. It is due to the characteristics of the security situation in the Horn of Africa. The Horn is distinct from other sub-regions of the continent in having severe internal conflicts caused not only by clan, sub-clan, ethnic or religious factors but often intensified by weak borders, state rivalries, and cross-border elite alliances. Although peace processes are the most visible activities of IGAD, it carries out various conventional operations and launched mechanisms to address the mid-term and long-term security challenges. As one example, Takezawa illustrates the Conflict Early Warning and Response Mechanism (CEWARN) established in 2003, one of the key IGAD projects to date. The concept of conflict early warning emerged globally in the 1990s as an instrument of preventive diplomacy. CEWARN enhances security and develops peace infrastructure at the regional level as pastoralist conflict was treated as a low priority subject to the control of individual governments before its launch. The objective is to "receive and share information concerning potentially violent conflicts as well as their outbreak and escalation in the IGAD region." Since its launch, CEWARN has developed step by step in monitoring pastoral conflicts. The CEWARN secretariat works with lower-level institutions down to the district level, and in each country, a national research institute is also involved in monitoring. While the clusters still cover only a limited part of the Horn of Africa, there has been a steady growth in the program's scope and the inclusion of further member states.

Sasaoka's chapter on DCs in Southern Africa presents another policy implication to assess the validity of the *state-building approach*, so we shortly discuss it here. As we have seen, the top-down development approach differentiates the beneficiary and the victim clearly, and external resources tend to be linked to concessions for power elites through unclear channels. The disbursement of the development budgets to the northern regions has been quite limited, and land appropriation in the NDC area has been facilitated by buyers linking with the local chiefs, thus suppressing resistance from small-scale farmers and CSOs to land acquisition. His case study shows that the development of DCs can be considered as the growth source of macro-economy and the construction of neo-patrimonial interest systems that link the center with the local, from which the periphery tends to be excluded without the proactive intervention from national and global CSOs.

The successful experience of decentralization in Uganda also offers important lessons learned in the area of conflict prevention. Sasaoka, in Chapter 11, compares the processes of decentralization policies in Uganda, Tanzania, and Kenya, and concludes that it can mitigate conflicts between the dominant groups in control of the government and the adversarial groups if the policy was adequately designed and implemented, and promoted by higher level, which was shown by Uganda. The National Resistance Movement (NRM), led by President Museveni, steadily promoted a decentralization policy since the late 1990s and put the LGs as a focus of governance, although the present overall governance situation has been deteriorated by long-term Museveni's rule. It strengthened the service delivery to local people and constructing a broad-based policy facilitated by the power-sharing arrangement in the 1980–90s. The devolution can have a positive impact on the perception of the local population. On the other hand, Sasaoka points out that the effect of decentralization on conflict-prone state borders will need careful attention, as the policy crucially depends on a real sense of resource allocation to rural areas and peripheral groups. In addition, decentralization can be risky when peripheral groups have connections with other groups in the adjacent country. Making local people and VNSAs autonomous via a decentralization policy helps prevent violence. To complement Sasaoka's view, Kamei's case also provides important policy implications; Uganda's decentralized governance structure places LGs to be essentially responsible for providing shelters and essential social services to the refugees who have settled within the LG's jurisdiction. While LGs crucially need fiscal budgets to support the influx of refugees from neighbours, strengthening the refugee-hosting policy is also crucial in preventing the instability in borderlands.

Thirdly, while we see the expansion of VNSAs across the continent, the root causes of African Jihadism may be found in the social structures and governance of the state and region rather than their radical and alleged ideologies and the lack of border controls. At the same time, we shall ask, what kind of policy and strategies to adopt when the borderland and actors face multiple and entangled difficulties? Sumo Tayo, Chapter 2, described that the Lake Chad basin has long been the scene of political, ecological, economic, and security issues. A sense of distrust among four countries (Nigeria, Cameroon, Chad, and Niger) is strong, and notably, Nigeria has difficult relations with francophone countries. Such mutual distrust has allowed Boko Haram to use the Chad Basin as space for recruitment and safe heaven. Because of its strategic location, historical border disputes, and a lack of coordination, and more recently, the effect of climate change that triggers the land conflicts between populations, all these factors have given Boko Haram an opportunity and space to develop and extend its area of activities. Sumo Tayo has argued that demarcating borders are the prerequisite for genuine cross-border cooperation and mindset change among stakeholders. The Sahelian countries face the same structural problem as the Lake Chad Basin, and as Uesu has described, the local population has a strong sense of distrust against the local authorities. The legacy, ideological structure of past Jihads was so attractive that some residents perceive VNSAs as a more reliable service provider (Miles, 2018; Kaufman, 2006). While there are no quick solutions to fix the entangled social problems, Uesu keeps in mind the importance to hear from the marginalized population and support them so that they can construct their place voluntarily.

Regional integration

The examination of New Perspectives on Africa's Borders also considers the dynamics of regional integration, both formal and informal, and the logic of decentralized cooperation. In effect, borders are social and political objects that respond to the universal need for limits. These political artifacts can be seen more as opportunities rather than as obstacles to sub-regional integration. To this extent, the researcher should emancipate himself from militant and victim-oriented approaches that emphasize the separatist function of African borders and present them as the main obstacle to realizing the Pan-Africanist dream. This victim-based and militant approach to African borders does not make it possible to grasp the dynamics that cross them. The limits of these approaches to African border studies have been pointed out by former Malian President, Alpha Omar Konaré (2005): "for a long time, we thought with exhilaration that history was a fight fought on the simple model of morality, colonialists, neo-colonialisms, imperialists, and capitalists on the one hand, and enslaved, despoiled and exploited peoples on the other." This "infantile" disease of African borders studies has long prevented researchers from "bringing theory into Africa and Africa into theory" (Aborne, 2009).

The diversity and richness of the various contributions to this volume show the interest of an ontological, epistemological, and methodological *aggiornamento* on African border studies to grasp the dynamic that affects them. On the ontological level, it is necessary to decolonize many commonplaces. It involves the definition of new epistemic frameworks through which Africa will think its borders because, until now, many clichés, clichés, and pseudo-certitudes (Sarr, 2020) obscure the logics that cross them. The persistent discourse on the artificiality of African borders, for example, calls into question the need for critical reflection on this colonial intellectual legacy that later became the banner of anti-colonialism (Lefebvre, 2011).

On the methodological level, the main challenge for perceiving the dynamics that cross African borders is field surveys that can better explain the reality. It is not a question of fetishizing the terrain but of making it one of the main criteria for validating arguments on African borders. It soon became apparent, for example, that while the political and intellectual elites hold forth over the artificiality of African borders and the weakness of regional integration, on the ground, local populations are weakly affected by the borders. For example, for one borderland resident on the Ghana–Togo border, "the international border is an 'imaginary line', one that exists only in the imagination of the cartographers, colonial officials and postcolonial security apparatus" (Adotey, 2021).

In the field, there is a consensus on the disappointing performance of regional integration in Africa (Asiwaju, 2012). Regionalization projects have focused on trade integration, capital and monetary integration, and sectorial cooperation (Söderbaum, 2000). However, beyond the institutional, occidental-centric, and economic perspective, a vernacular approach to African borders that analyzes integration through the prism of people's daily practices shows a weak formal regionalism on the continent on the one side and informal integration or regionalization on another side. Informal integration exploits dysfunction and disparity that derive from existing boundaries (Bach, 1999). That is the case with border markets such as the Mai Duwa market at the Niger–Nigeria border (Oculi, 2005). In the Sahel, for example, formal borders are ignored by the local population and local traders. Even state representatives use borders as a source of resources and rent. Scholars have noticed formal and informal micro-regionalism in the West African Sahel (Söderbaum & Taylor, 2007). Informal regional exchanges are based on the complementarity of ecosystems. Nationalized spaces and deterritorialized practices create a "floating population." Indeed, "by losing its ability to control men, the state sees diminish its ability to control its territory" (Egg & Herrera, 1998). Today, the buoyancy of populations is manifested by the possession of multiple national identity cards and international participation in votes following a logic of subversion of elections, among others (Roitman, 2003).

Cross-border communities have long been seen as a stigma of colonization. However, the reality is that their presence can be a factor of regional integration, as shown by Feyissa and Hoehne in their study on the Horn of Africa. They realized that it could favor the creation of informal economies, trans-border networks, and alliances (Onah, 2015). Considering the individualized dimension of relations to borders shows the process of regional integration "from below." This dynamic goes along with an informal dynamic of decentralized cooperation between cross-border communities and authorities in certain parts of the continent.

Moreover, local authorities' external action dates from the colonial period when it had inter-and intra-imperial dimension. The authorities of the national states have taken up this practice, and half a century later, this sub-state diplomacy remains in the informal realm. At the same time, however, cross-border para-diplomacy has been institutionalized as far as North–South relations are being played. However, gradually, the proximity of the challenges and the support of joint partners have encouraged some cooperation initiatives of local communities and authorities. The Dank Project, led by the metropolis of Nantes, has enabled a South–South territorial rapprochement between the cities of Dschang (Cameroon) and Kindia (Guinea) (Stravens, 2019).

At the regional level, African Union has adopted a Convention on cross-border cooperation on 14 June 2014, to promote cross-border cooperation at local, sub-regional, and regional levels. The convention has not yet entered into force, but some councils as Adjara or Ifangui in Benin have cross-border agreements with Ogun State's local governments in Nigeria (Aning & Pokoo, 2017). The European Union also sponsors a program through the Emergency Trust Fund for Africa in the borderland between Ethiopia and its neighbours, Sudan, Kenya, and Somalia. However, overall, the dynamics of cross-border cooperation between cross-border communities and authorities remain informal. Therefore, they must be institutionalized by speeding up, for example, the process of ratifying the Niamey Convention and, above all, by financing cross-border projects.

This process of collaborating across borders to achieve a common goal (Pavlakovich-Kochi, 2011) is also linked with an increasing sub-regional interdependence and interstate interaction. In the Sahel and the Lake Chad Basin, for example, the various countries are part of a security complex as defined by Barry Buzan (2000): "a set of states whose major security perceptions and concerns are so interlinked that their national security problems cannot reasonably be analyzed or resolved apart from one another." The regionalization of insecurity leads to the multiplication of ad hoc and integrated military responses as G5 Sahel or the MJTF. Besides informal regional integration due to common security problems, there are forms of bioregionalism in Africa with cross-border cooperation to manage watersheds and conservation efforts (Smart & Smart, 2012). There is also a process of sanitary integration in Africa to fight against pandemics and epizootics. Gradually, linear borders are giving way to networked borders in Africa. Beyond their instrumental aspect, past experiences of bordering on infectious diseases do not work because they induce logics of circumvention when they do not consider the geographical, social, anthropological, and political configurations of borderlands.

On the other hand, the logics of co-building reticular borders and especially cross-border cooperation in biosecurity are of formidable effectiveness. In fact, due to common problems, African states are gradually devaluating some of their border functions to achieve regional integration. There is a changing paradigm, from barrier to bridge (Asiwaju, 2012). This dynamic is facilitated by realities such as transnational regional religious dynamics as Pentecostalism in the West African coast, for example (Adogame & Spickard, 2010).

In the end, a bottom-up approach to African borders can hold some pleasant surprises. It makes it possible to reconsider or, at least, relativize the pessimistic reading of the dynamics of regional integration in Africa. It also makes it possible to propose models of regional integration that are co-constructed and consider border areas' characteristics. Examining positive experiences in this direction on the continent shows that clearly defined, accepted, and demarcated boundaries are the precondition for cross-border cooperation and socio-economic growth.

Governance in the borderland

Borderland governance is affected by multiple actors. Not only the central and local government but also the relationships between central groups and peripheral groups in a country and even the existence of militia and external donors influence the governance in border areas. There are complementary actors such as traditional authority, ethnic and religious groups, CSOs, foreign donors, IOs, ROs, and transnational informal networks. If local militia provides security to border people, it is involved in shaping the governance. The same composition of actors can be assumed in a neighbouring country. Network governance theory became quite suitable to capture the new phenomena occurring in border areas to understand the indiscernible area consisted of the government, market, and civil society (Rhodes, 1997). Governance theory is said to be born from the tradition of International Relations (Rosenau & Czempiel, 1992) and the New Public Management (Osborne & Gaebler, 1992), but now it is considered the best theory to deal with borderland politics.

The active interaction of various actors may be more important than strengthening a single actor – a central government. At the state level, hardening the border and strengthening border control may be necessary as an urgent measure, but it could lead to future undesirable development. Hardening the border has bad effects on the border community and little support seems to be provided from border society. The pre-modern cultural connection with adjacent societies and the borderless principle of globalization rarely requires strong borders. Only modern state tends to require strong borders due to centrifugal forces and nationalistic slogan. Many shabby state border signboards have been transformed into robust facilities recently. That is the interest of the political elite because many countries have a fear of disintegrated into some units and they have a distrust with neighbouring countries. An effective and democratic state needs to achieve various minimum conditions: security, political order, and basic service provisions (Evans, 1995). Since the state not fulfilling these conditions cannot assume social contract with people, power elites need to promote interest-induced politics with narrow-based supporters or control people by using threat, coercion, and physical forces. In either case, border politics can suffer instability.

The minimum conditions tend to be lacking at the border area. Therefore, people do not rely on the government and seek the help of other actors. If people are not protected and even persecuted, people turn to the CSOs, traditional authority, and local militia (Herbst, 2014). If people cannot solve land property rights with the government, they need to claim to other bodies. Zambian chief arbitrages land issues among people, but it was abolished by Tanganyika African National Union (TANU). Without land arbitration system, efforts to delineate state border is almost impossible. A foreign militia is aiming at the opportunities to sneak into such a chaotic situation in the borderland. Inversely, the border area can be affluent by facilitating trade and people's mobility. Uganda's West Nile can enjoy the trade expansion between Uganda and DRC as soon as West Nile has been gaining modern state infrastructure after LRA sneaked out. Refugees from South Sudan are not classified as dangerous foreigners due to the free flow of people between Uganda and South Sudan, while Kakuma and Dadaab camp in Kenya was ordered to close by the government.[1] Uganda's decentralized structure assumes the major role of LGs in the implementation of refugee programs. Local commitments must be reinforced with additional funding by donors. In this way, the state border areas show different patterns.

In Africa, the sub-national conflict became fervent when politically powerful majority continued to dominate the wealth over politically weak minority. This type of division can be seen in Cameroon, Mali, Nigeria, Mozambique, and many other states. Sometimes minority area happens to be resource-rich and secessionist movement could occur. Often weak minorities share group identity with outsiders beyond state boundaries. Makonde and Makua between Tanzania and Mozambique are such a place. Some groups such as Hausa, Fulani, and Kongo are settled in many countries. Southern Libya, a stateless society at present, accommodates a lot of VNSAs such as Mali Al-Qaida, Chad anti-government militia, and Sudanese anti-government groups. From this place, a militia tried to collapse the Chad government in 2021. Any group can easily enter and start a dirty business. The other type is that a weak state is utilized by a strong neighbour as observed in eastern DRC exploited by Rwanda. Also, the support for anti-government force by a neighbour is quite common, but these interstate interventions were rather a past thing. At central Africa, President Déby in Chad sent troops to

Sudan while Sudan made an act of revenge and tried to confuse CAF by weakening the border area intentionally.

Decentralization can be an inclusiveness indicator of the whole society. While political decentralization is promoted under democracy or democratic pressure, fiscal decentralization can be facilitated even under authoritarian regimes. Since many African states are largely aid dependent, it is not so difficult to set the subsidy scheme to local government utilizing donor funds. It crucially depends on the will of political elites. The decentralized local governments can promote initiative and discretionary power to implement social and agricultural programs with resident's support and establish local infrastructure with the help of development agencies to gain revenues from local markets. Also, a new element is the potential need to consider sedentariness and mobility of rural people. Local development projects under decentralization need to cope with people's bifurcated lifestyle. Decentralized cross-border development (CBD) can be new trial. They require the coordination mechanism of adjacent communities, states, and concerned groups to promote a joint project, including border cities by transferring authority and resources to local actors (Trémolières & Walther, 2019). With the appropriate measure of CBD, decentralization, and regional integration, there seems little pressing need to divide the country and increase the state border.

Relating to CBD, various border programs have recently started after AU's Convention on cross-border cooperation in 2014: UNDP set up Africa Borderlands Centre in Nairobi and started the program of CBT as drivers of peace in the Liptako-Gourma region in west Africa with the collaboration of Japanese government[2]; AU started AUBP; World Bank published a report on "Horn of Africa Borderland Communities can achieve Economic prosperity" in 2020.[3] World Bank report considers that cross-border initiatives should address livelihoods, institutions, and stability/security. "Central to this response is a call for regional integration through additional support to existing development initiatives including those formulated by IGAD and AU on borderlands, to strengthen platforms for dialogue as well as technical capacities." Therefore, the significance of CBD is deeply recognized by the governments, civil society, ROs, and donor communities.

CBD can have a preventive effect on violence. The main tendency of violent conflict today is increasing trans-state conflicts by VNSA, which tries to utilize stateless or weak state territory to get haven and is often supported by neighbouring countries, expatriates, and Jihadist networks. CBD can block the inflow of such bad visitors. As seen in West Nile and Maputo, successful CBD areas are peaceful and stable, even though not everything is going well. Or, we can estimate that based on a certain level of cross-border security (CBS), CBD can be facilitated. From this standpoint, many areas of Sahel and West Africa lack in the positive loop between CBD and CBS, inviting a lot of annoying guests. In Mozambique, southern part regions including MDC have been stable due to the home base of the Frelimo ruling party, but northern part regions connected with the opposition party Renamo have been marginalized. IS-CAP took advantage of the weak border area between Cabo Delgado, Mozambique, and Mtwara, Tanzania. Therefore, CBD should be targeted as the main plan. Relatedly, SADC joint-military intervention in Cabo Delgado announced in June 2021 can be justified as just an urgent measure of CBS.[4] ROs should have the adaptability to respond to trans-state conflicts by VNSA and trans-border crimes in the region, but much more focus should be given to CBD. One of the problems in the Sahel is that western African RO did not encompass northern African states.

We need to develop a regional governance network while checking the trend of trans-state conflicts. The transnational threat often tends to improve the borderland governance. Since the French type decentralization process pays much attention to the city capacity enhancement, the city collaboration scheme becomes undoubtedly important in western Africa. The collaboration of RO, AfDB, WB, NGOs, and bilateral donors is essentially important to fill the administrative and financial gap to make an appropriate level of investment in infrastructure and social sectors in border cities. African people need to establish a sort of neutral zone in the borderland to facilitate the works of joint programs, trade, and mobility of people, while jointly monitoring CBS.

Eastern and southern Africa have the common tasks of the economic corridor, OSBP, cable network linking more modern and super-modern infrastructures. Southern Africa can enjoy a more stable economic environment and try to establish a common prosperous area through advanced infrastructure, except for Cabo Delgado. South Africa is the center of regional economic development, the hub of airports and ports, gathering spot of foreign immigrants. Eastern Africa can be located between southern Africa and western Africa from the standpoint of stability and transportation facility, while OSBP and cold chain are nicely advanced. The southern part of East Africa is stable and is equipped with advanced infrastructure, whereas the northern part of East Africa is left behind in many aspects, where climate and environmental conditions are generally worsening. Western Africa faces the most challenging tasks: CBS should be constructed, the great challenge of road and IT networks, and heavy environmental degradation.

"The field of international relations (IR) is witnessing growing efforts to challenge Western centrism and give more space and voice to the Global South. These efforts are happening under a variety of labels, such as, but not limited to, non-Western IR, post-Western IR, Global IR, etc (Acharya & Buzan, 2017)." In this line of thought, we can recommend *the borderland and trans-region approach*, rather than *state-building approach* to construct a stable and prosperous border area. Africa went through different state formation processes as confirmed by Herbst (2014). His view on the difference of African state-making process is based on the recognition of low population density. This point of view is debatable when compared with other regions' low population density track record (Robinson, 2002), but alarms the potential risk that the African state system is becoming closer to the European state system, as the population grows rapidly. Africans need to avoid such a self-fulfilling prophecy by promoting the non-European state formation process consciously.

African second-level governance, the state, is weak, and its historical formation process has been shorter and blocked by colonialism gravely, compared with other regions. Therefore, state level governance should be combined with other levels of governance, culture, and globalization. However, the present situation is rather opposite: the interaction of culture and globalization has formed the risk of instability such as the penetration of Salafism and Pentecostal movement in the borderland. We need to find a reversal way of stabilizing society, loosening antagonism between groups, and providing basic services and infrastructure in the borderland. Non-military interventions such as *L'Alliance Sahel*, decentralization policy, regional integration, refugee policy, immigration policy, FTA, all are vital. The wrong direction is concentrating on a statist, militaristic, hardliner approach to invite a harsh intrastate confrontation as a reaction and the risk of future interstate conflicts.

The important clue is *the borderland and trans-region approach*, which combines the importance of modern transportation route (grey border) community level route (green border), and globalized transportation route (blue border). Here what kind of perception, identities, and determination should residents have, while referring to social construction. Through our observations and analyses, the coexistence of three levels' governance and transportation route is quite important and the state formation process needs to go through such a delicate and well-balanced multilayer approach. This "alternative" understanding is different from the ordinary *fragile states'* perspective which is derived from Western centrism. Therefore, researchers, practitioners, and citizens need to promote trans-border cooperation by encouraging all the relevant actors to join and relate to each other. Multiple actor's participation and joint work are vital when designing and implementing trans-border cooperation of any kind.

Notes

1 Giulia Paravicini, Kenya orders closure of two refugee camps, gives ultimatum to UN agency, Reuters 24 March 2021.
2 UNDP, Cross-border trade as driver of peace in the Liptako-Gourma region, May 4, 2021.
www.africa.undp.org/content/rba/en/home/presscenter/pressreleases/2021/
3 The World Bank, Report: Horn of Africa Borderland Communities can Achieve Economic Prosperity, 19 May 2020.
www.worldbank.org/en/news/press-release/2020/05/19/
4 Emma Ramney, African nations send troops to tackle Mozambique insurgency, Reuters June 24, 2021. www.reuters.com/world/africa/

References

ABORNE. (2009). Call for papers: ABORNE Conference on 'How Is Africa Transforming Border Studies?', Hosted by the School of Social Sciences, University of the Witwatersrand, Johannesburg, South Africa, 10–14 September 2009, www.africa.upenn.edu/Current_Events/bordersaf-cfp0909.html retrieved on July 2, 2021.

Acharya, A. & Buzan, B. (2017). Why Is There No Non-Western International Relations Theory, Ten Years on. *International Relations of the Asia-Pacific* Vol. 17 (pp. 341–370). Japan Association of International Relations, Oxford: Oxford University Press.

Adogame, A. U. & Spickard, J. V. (Éds.). (2010). *Religion Crossing Boundaries: Transnational Religious and Social Dynamics in Africa and the New African Diaspora*, Brill.

Adotey, E. (2021). An Imaginary Line? Decolonization, Bordering and Borderscapes on the Ghana – Togo Border. *Third World Quarterly*, 42(5), 1069–1086.

Aning, K. & Pokoo, J. (2017). Between Conflict and Integration: Border Governance in Africa in Times of Migration. *International Reports*, 1, 54–65.

Asiwaju, A. I. (2012). The African Union Border Programme in European Comparative Perspective. In T. M. Wilson & H. Donnan (Éds.), *The African Union Border Programme in European Comparative Perspective* (pp. 66–82), John Wiley & Sons, Ltd. https://doi.org/10.1002/9781118255223.ch4

Bach, D. C. (1999). Regionalism Versus Regional Integration: The Emergence of a New Paradigm in Africa. In J. Grugel, & W. Hout (Eds.), *Regionalism across the North/South Divide: State Strategies and Globalization*, London: Routledge.

Buzan, B. (2000). The Logic of Regional Security in the Post-Cold War World. In B. Hettne, A. Inotai, & O. Sunkel (Eds.)., *The New Regionalism and the Future of Security and Development* (pp. 1–25), London: Palgrave Macmillan. https://doi.org/10.1007/978-1-137-11498-3_1

Dobler, G. (2016). The Green, the Grey and the Blue: A Typology of Cross-Border Trade in Africa. *Modern African Studies*, 54(1), 145–169.

Egg, J. & Herrera, J. (1998). Echanges transfrontaliers et integration regionale en Afrique subsaharienne : Introduction. *Autrepart-revue de sciences sociales au Sud*, 6, 5–25.

Evans, P. B. (1995). *Embedded Autonomy: States and Industrial Transformation*, Princeton: Princeton University Press.

Herbst, J. (2014, 2010) *States and Power in Africa – Comparative Lessons in Authority and Control, New Edition*, Princeton and Oxford: Princeton University Press.

Kaufman, S. (2006). Symbolic Politics or Rational Choice? – Testing Theories or Extreme Ethnic Violence. *International Security*, 31(4), 180–191.

Lefebvre, C. (2011). La décolonisation d'un lieu commun. *Revue d'histoire des sciences humaines*, 1, 77–104.

Miles, W. (2018). Jihads and Borders – Social Networks and Spatial Patterns in Africa, Present, Past and Future. In O. J. Walther & W. Miles (Eds.), *African Border Disorders – Addressing Transnational Extremist Organizations*, London: Routledge.

Oculi, O. (2005). Cooperation and Integration in African : The Case of Informal Cross Border Trade. *Africa Vision*, 525, 3.

Omar Konaré, A. (2005). Opening address of the symposium "Histoire et perception des frontières en Afrique du XIIe au XXe siècle dans la cadre d'une culture de la paix", Bamako, 15–19 March 1999, in *Des frontières en Afrique du XIIe au XXe siècle*, Paris: UNESCO/CISH.

Onah, E. I. (2015). Trans-Border Ethnic Solidarity and Citizenship Conflicts in Some West and Central African States. *African Security Review*, 24(1), 63–74. https://doi.org/10.1080/10246029.2014.995192

Osborne, D. & Gaebler, T. (1992). *Reinventing Government: How the Entrepreneurial Spirit Is Transforming the Public Sector*, New York: Penguin Books.

Pavlakovich-Kochi, V. (2011). Cross-border Cooperation and Regional Responses to NAFTA and Globalization. In D. Wastl-Walter (Ed.), *The Routledge Research Companion to Border Studies*. Farnham: Ashgate. https://doi.org/10.4324/9781315612782.ch23

Rhodes, R. A. W. (1997). *Understanding Governance: Policy Networks, Governance, Reflexivity and Accountability*, Buckingham: Open University Press.

Robinson, J. (2002). States and Power in Africa by Jeffrey I. Herbst: A Review Essay. *Journal of Economic Literature, XL*, 510–519, Pittsburgh: American Economic Association.

Roitman, J. (2003). La garnison-entrepôt : Une manière de gouverner dans le bassin du lac Tchad. *Critique internationale, 2*, 93–115.

Rosenau, J. & Czempiel, E.-O. (Eds.). (1992). *Governance Without Government: System of Rule in World Politics*, Cambridge: Cambridge University Press.

Sarr, F. (2020). *Afrotopia* (D. S. Burk & S. Jones-Boardman, Trad. & 1st ed.), Minneapolis: University of Minnesota Press.

Smart, A. & Smart, J. (2012). Biosecurity, Quarantine and Life across the Border. In T. M. Wilson & H. Donnan (Eds.), *A Companion to Border Studies*, Blackwell Companions to Anthropology 19 (pp. 354–370), Chichester: Wiley-Blackwell. https://doi.org/10.1002/9781118255223.ch20

Söderbaum, F. (2000). The Role of the Regional Factor in West Africa. In Hettne, B., Inotai A., Sunkel O. (Eds.). *The New Regionalism and the Future of Security and Development* (pp. 121–143), London: Palgrave Macmillan.

Söderbaum, F. & Taylor, I. (2007). *Micro-regionalism in West Africa: Evidence from Two Case Studies*, Uppsala: Nordiska Afrikainstitutet.

Stravens, L. (2019). Les coopérations décentralisées de la ville de Nantes, levier d'une diplomatie territoriale Sud-Sud pour le développement. *Relations internationales, 3*, 41–52.

Trémolières, M. & Walther, O. J. (2019). *Regional Integration in Border Cities*, West African Papers. No. 20, OECD.

Urry, Y. J. (2007). *Mobilities*, Cambridge/Malden: Polity Press.

Index

Africa Borderlands Centre (ABC) 110, 124, 197
African National Congress (ANC) 90
African Union (AU) 3, 9, 19, 28, 58, 128–129, 194; African Union Border Governance Strategy (AUBGS) 3
AIDS 12, 80, 145
airport xiii, 9, 11, 49, 83, 140–141, 150, 155, 190, 198
Al-Qa'ida in the Islamic Maghreb (AQIM) 103–104, 106–108, 116–117
al-Shabab 122, 125–126, 147
anisotropic mobility/nature xxi, 155–156
Ansar Dine 103, 105–106
Ansaroul Islam 104, 108–109
anthropology xviii, 72, 75, 188
Arua District 36, 38, 44, 46, 56–57, 59, 60, 62–65
Atlantic slave trade 71
Azande 75

Beira 88, 93, 189
Benin 77, 103–104, 112, 115–116, 141, 194
biometrics 77
Boko Haram xiv, 19, 20, 25–28, 103–104, 106, 115–117, 119, 143–144, 147, 149, 192
border community(ies) 21–22, 118, 148, 194–195
border control(s) xii, xv–xvi, 1, 2, 6, 11, 110, 112, 131, 139, 140–141, 150, 156, 184, 189, 192, 195
border crossing xxi, 12, 23
border governance xix, 17, 22, 29
borderland(s) 1–2, 6–7, 9, 12–13, 22, 25, 34–35, 47–50, 56–57, 60–61, 63, 67–69, 84, 102–105, 107–112, 115, 123–124, 130, 135n2, 138, 155, 187–190, 192–199; governance 195, 198; and trans-region approach i, xii, xiii, xix, 1, 2, 13, 155, 190, 198–199
border security 11, 68, 139, 140, 140, 149, 150, 197; border security management 143
border society 195
bottom-up xxi, 96, 99, 174, 182; approach 89, 97, 195
Braudel, F. xvii
Bremmer, I. xvi, xvii, 8
budgetary support 68
build-operate-transfer (BOT) 88
Burkina Faso 3, 5, 103–105, 107–110, 112, 115–118
Buzan, B. xiii, 8, 18, 24, 102, 139, 147, 194, 198; Acharya and 8; and Lawson xiii

Cameroon xv, xix, xxi, 3, 17, 19, 20–29, 74, 86, 106, 118, 140–141, 143–145, 147, 149, 150, 156, 192, 194, 196
cash income 42–43, 50–51
centralization xviii, 173, 176, 178, 182
centralized political regimes 170
Chad xv, xviii, xix, xxi, 3, 17, 19–24, 26–29, 112, 118n43, 192, 196
Chama Cha Mapinduzi (CCM) 171, 173–177, 179, 180, 182, 184
China/Chinese xvi, 10–11, 45, 81, 91, 93, 129, 155–156, 166
Civic United Front (CUF) 173–174, 178–179, 180, 184
Civil Society Organizations (CSOs) 61, 91–92, 98, 191, 195–196
Collier, P. 11; and Dercon 91; and Hoeffler 181
colonial control device 177

Index

colonial times 1, 180
Common Market for Eastern and Southern Africa (COMESA) 48
community(ies) xx, 1, 6, 17, 20, 24, 54, 58, 60, 62, 66, 68, 71, 76, 79, 80, 83, 91, 104, 108–109, 111, 115, 199; African community xix; expatriate community 159; Nigerian community 28, 164; Peul/Fulani community 76, 103, 106–107, 116; Toloobe community 108
community-based organizations (CBOs) 80–84
conflict early warning and response mechanism (CEWARN) 130, 191
conflict prevention 127, 130, 133, 170, 176–177, 181–183, 191
coronavirus/COVID-19 xvii, 11, 59, 60, 82, 125, 141–142
Cote d'Ivoire/Ivory Coast 74, 77–78, 96, 103–105, 110, 115–116, 118
Counter-Insurgency (COIN) 110–111, 117, 147
Counter-Terrorism Operations (CTOs) 103, 106, 108, 117
cross-border xii, xix, 12, 17, 21–24, 27–29, 59, 63–64, 67, 69, 78, 84, 97, 122, 125–127, 140, 167, 194, 197; cross-border communities 21–22, 194; cross-border cooperation xx, 17, 21–22, 25–26, 28, 148, 192, 194–195; cross-border development (CBD) 197; cross-border elite alliances 122, 126–127, 191; cross-border migration 54, 57, 188; cross-border movements 26, 60, 67, 125; cross-border refugees xix, 54, 64; cross-border security (CBS) xv, 22, 197; cross-border trade xx, 5, 34, 48–49, 56, 83, 155–156, 159, 162, 166, 187–188, 190
cross-national marriages 166, 190
culture xiii, xv, xvii–xviii, xix, xx, 2, 4, 6–9, 60, 71–85, 126, 165, 177–178, 188, 199; mobility as xx, 71–85

Debray, R. xvi, 110, 138, 144
decentralization xiv, xviii, xxi, 5, 7, 12, 26, 35, 57–58, 170–179, 181–185, 187–188, 190–192, 197–199; decentralized governance and structure 54, 64, 68, 192
Democratic Republic of Congo (DRC), the xix, 34–38, 41, 45, 48–50, 54, 56–57, 59–61, 74, 183, 188, 196

democratization 2–4, 8–9, 170–176, 178–179, 180–182, 184
deterritorialization xvi, 138
development assistance/aid 60, 81, 91, 133–134
development corridors (DCs) 86–87, 91, 96, 98–99, 189–191
devolution 58, 173–174, 176–178, 183, 191
Djelgodi/Djelgodji 115, 116–118
Djibouti 127–128, 131, 135
Dobler, G. xiii, xxii, 7, 35–36, 49, 60, 83–84, 156, 159, 166, 187–189, 190

East African Community (EAC) 11, 48, 54, 171, 178
East Asia 155–156, 159, 166, 190
Economic Community of West African States (ECOWAS) 24, 26, 116, 118, 141–142
elite capture of resources 176
Eritrea 51, 123, 126–128, 131–132, 135, 146
ethnicity 24, 105–106, 117–118, 135, 156, 172, 175, 180
Ethiopia xiv, xvii, xx, 3, 74, 81, 122–124, 127–132, 145, 146, 176, 180, 194
ethnic and religious conflict 177–178
ethnography 75–76, 82
expatriates 156, 158–159, 161, 163, 166, 197; Japanese expatriates 112, 156, 159, 166, 190

federalism 171–172, 197–198, 181
fragile state(s) xii, xxii, 6, 57, 59, 171, 199
France/French xiv, 3, 19, 27, 88, 103, 106–108, 110, 112, 115, 117–118, 146, 198; French National Centre for Scientific Research (CNRS) 72
Frelimo (Frente de Libertacao de Mozambique) 87, 92–93, 95–98, 197
Fulani/Fulbe (Peul) 5, 76, 103–109, 115–119, 196
Funada, S. 87, 91, 95

Gambia 73, 75, 79, 82–83
Ghana 77–78, 103–105, 107, 109, 115, 140, 142, 150, 193
global governance xiii, xvi, 7–9, 12
globalization i, xiii, xvi–xviii, xix, xx, 2, 4–12, 75, 109, 138, 196, 199

Index

globalized i, xii–xiii, xvi–xvii, xx, 1, 12, 60–61, 68–69, 74–75, 80–85, 166–167, 175, 190, 199
governance xii–xvii, xix, 1–4, 7–9, 12, 17, 21–22, 28–29, 54–55, 57–58, 60, 64–66, 68, 103–104, 127, 134, 139, 170, 174–176, 178, 180, 182–183, 191–192, 195, 198–199
group identity 179–180, 196

Haouka 77
hardening of border(s) xvi, 103, 112, 139–140, 144, 187
Herbst, J. xii, xv, 196, 198
herdsmen/herder 20, 26, 106–107, 109, 111–112, 116–118
Horn of Africa xx, 58, 122–127, 129–130, 132, 134–135, 190–191, 194, 197
host communities 62, 65–66, 69
Huntington, S. xvii, 7
hybrid regime(s) 2, 4, 170, 176, 184

identity(ies) xii, xvi–xvii, 2, 8, 9, 12, 23, 82, 102, 105, 107, 138, 142, 147–148, 156, 159, 164, 177–185, 194, 196, 199
immigrant(s) i, xii, 10, 188, 198
immigration 6, 20, 36, 64, 82, 138, 140, 145, 147, 160, 166–167, 190; policies xviii, 139, 161, 164, 166, 199
imported commodities 159
industrial development zones (IDZs) 90
inequality 10, 156, 178–179, 182
informal cross border trade (ICBT) 5, 48
informal economy 26
informal micro-regionalism 89, 193
informal regionalism 12
information technology (IT) xvii, 74, 190
insurgency xiv, 23, 27, 29, 57, 122, 124–125
Intergovernmental Authority on Development (IGAD) xx, 122, 124, 128–135, 190–191, 197; IGAD Capacity Building Program Against Terrorism (ICPAT) 131
internally displaced person (IDP) xiv, 57, 175
international community/global community 29, 54, 62, 68, 104, 108, 110, 129, 132, 189

International Crisis Group (ICG) xiv, 3, 27, 29, 103, 112, 115–117, 129, 147, 180
international donor community xx, 58, 60, 62, 68
international organization (IOs) xiv, 115, 131, 159, 195
International Organization for Migration (IOM) 74, 110–112, 141
interstate/inter-state xiv, 18–19, 86, 96, 99, 128, 190, 194–196
inter-state conflict(s) xxi, 1, 3, 4, 6, 128, 184, 187, 199
interstate system xiii, xvi–xviii, 7–11
Islamic State (IS) 109, 115, 183, 189; Islamic State in Central Africa Province (ISCAP) 183; Islamic State in Greater Sahara (ISGS) 103–105, 107–109, 116–117, 119; Islamic State in West Africa Province (ISWAP) 115, 119

Jama'at Nusrat al-Islam wa-I-Muslimin (JNIM) 103–107, 116
Japan/Japanese xx, 7, 10, 27, 80–81, 88, 90–94, 102, 104, 111–112, 114–115, 118, 122, 132–135, 155–169, 189, 190; Japanese Government 90–81, 94, 111, 133, 162, 190, 197; Japan International Cooperation Agency (JICA) 78, 91, 118, 133–134; Japan Self Defense Force (JSDF) 133; Japan Volunteer Center (JVC) 92; JOCA 78; JOCV 76–77
jihad/jihadism, jihadi, jihadist xiv, xv, xviii, 5, 12, 19, 24–26, 103–107, 109, 116–118, 125, 139, 140, 143–144, 146–148, 192, 197

Kanuri(s) xv, 22, 116
Kaufman, S. 179, 192
Kenya xx, xxi, 1, 3, 36, 48–49, 54, 59, 54, 59, 71, 73–74, 80–85, 122–131, 135, 144, 170–172, 174–180, 182–185, 191, 194, 196, 199; Kenyan African National Union (KANU) 171, 178, 182
Kumasi 77

Lake Chad Basin, the xiv–xv, xix, 17–28, 146–147, 192, 194; Lake Chad Basin Commission (LCBC) 17, 19–21, 25
land deprivation 91

Index

Liptako-Gourma 103, 111, 115, 118, 197
livelihood(s) xiv, xviii, 35, 44, 47, 60, 63, 67, 72–73, 75, 77–78, 81, 83, 94–95, 97, 118, 124, 188, 197
local chief 172, 183
Local Council (LC) 37, 51, 58, 66, 172, 176, 181
local governments (LGs) xx, 5, 37, 46–48, 52, 54, 56–59, 63–66, 68–69, 108, 111, 115, 170, 172–173, 175, 178, 182, 188–189, 191–192, 194–197; peripheral LGs 59, 61, 64–66
local market(s) xix, 10, 34, 37, 48, 98, 197
long-distance trade 72; long-distance traders 43, 48
Lord's Resistance Army (LRA) xiv, xv, 44, 51, 57, 172, 178, 181, 183–185, 196
Lugbara 36, 38, 41, 56, 60

Macina Liberation Front (FLM) 103–104, 106
Malawi xx, 71, 73, 78–79, 81–83, 88–89, 93, 95–97
Mali 3, 103–112, 115–118, 140, 150, 176, 193, 196
Mamdani, M. 177
Maputo Development Corridor (MDC) 86–90, 92–98, 189, 197
mediation 111, 115, 128–129, 132–133, 177, 189
micro-regionalism xx, xxi, 12, 69, 86–89, 94, 96–97, 99, 189, 193
migrants 73–74, 77, 79, 81–82, 102, 143, 148, 161; illegal migrants 143–145; irregular migrants 162
migration xx, xxi, 2, 54, 57, 60–61, 68, 71, 74–75, 77, 79, 81–83, 103, 105, 139, 141, 143, 147–148, 150, 155–169, 187–188, 190
minority area 196
mobile phone xiii, 5, 7, 10, 48–49, 74–79, 164, 166
mobility xii, xvi–xvii, xx–xxi, 1, 5–6, 24, 34, 67, 71–85, 96, 142, 166–167, 188, 196–198
Morocco 142, 144, 146, 148
Movement for Oneness and Jihad in West Africa (MUJAO) 106, 117
Mozambique xiv, 7, 80, 86–98, 118, 143, 148, 183, 189–190, 196–198;

Northern Mozambique 111, 115–116, 119
Multinational Joint Task Force (MNJTF) xiv, 26–27
multi-party system 171–172, 175–176, 180
Museveni, Yoweri 44, 57–59, 129, 171–173, 175–176, 179, 181, 184–185, 191

Nacala Development Corridor (NDC) 22, 88, 91–92, 94–99, 189–191
national boundary(ies) 34, 80, 124, 156, 175–178, 181–185; state boundary 58, 60
nationalities 18
National Resistance Movement (NRM) 57, 171–173, 191
network governance 195
neutral zone 198
New Approach for Peace and Stability in Africa (NAPSA) 104, 112, 115–116
Niger xv, xix, xx, 3, 17, 19, 21, 24–27, 71, 73, 76–79, 82–84, 103–104, 106–108, 110, 112, 116–118, 148
Nigeria/Nigerian xv, xix, xx–xxi, 3, 9, 17, 19–22, 24–29, 74, 77, 105–106, 110, 115, 118n43, 119n49, 141, 143–145, 147, 149, 155–167, 190, 192–194, 196
nomad(s) xviii, 102, 105, 109, 116
non-party system 171
nonprofit organizations (NPO) 80
non-state actors (NSAs) 12, 62, 63, 66, 68, 86, 110, 125, 189
Nuer 75, 84

Office of the Prime Minister (OPM) 62
Office of the United Nations High Commissioner for Refugees (UNHCR), the 51, 54, 59, 61–62, 64, 112
one-party system 97, 171, 173, 176
One Stop Border Posts (OSBPs) xvii, 9, 48, 188, 198

passports xviii, xx, 36, 142, 165, 167
pastoral/pastoralist xvi, xviii, 22, 25, 103, 108, 116, 118, 123, 130, 191; agro-pastoral 20, 24
peacebuilding xxii, 118, 132–135
peace process 128–130, 132–134, 191
periphery/peripheral xvii, xx, xxi, 56, 59, 61, 64, 67, 69, 102, 123, 184,

188, 192, 195; West Nile xx, 56, 67, 69, 188
porosity xviii, 5–6, 12, 59, 150, 156
porous border i, xii, xix, 1, 6, 13, 34, 59, 103, 155, 190
Portuguese 88, 92
power-sharing 77, 79, 172, 174–175, 181–183
private financial investments (PFI) 87
ProSavana 91–94, 96, 98, 190
Provincial Administrative System (PAS), the 174–175
public-private partnerships (PPPs) 89, 91, 93, 96–98
public sector reform(s) 172–174

rebel(s) xviii, 21, 59, 62, 102, 115, 124, 126
refugee(s) i, xii, xix, xx, 10, 37, 44, 54, 57, 59, 61–69, 81, 95, 126, 140, 167, 173, 188, 188, 192, 196, 199
refugee crisis xx, 54, 61, 63–65, 67–68
refugee hosting LGs xx, 61–63, 65–66, 68; refugee hosting districts 64–65; refugee hosting government 68; refugee hosting nations 68, 188
refugee protection policy 54, 61–62, 65, 67–68, 188
refugee responses xx, 62, 65, 68
refugee settlement 37, 57, 61–65
Regional Economic Communities (RECs) xvii, 3, 9
regional governance network 198
regionalism xvii, 5, 8, 11–12, 86, 110, 122, 127, 134, 189
regional organizations (ROs) xx, 5, 11, 122, 127–128, 133–134, 187, 190, 195, 197–198
religion(s) xvii, 12, 144
Renamo (Resistencia Nacional Mozambicana) 87, 95–97, 198
road infrastructure xix, 34, 43, 48–50, 187
Rosenau, J. 8, 18; and Czempiel xiii, xvi, 7
Rwanda 48, 51, 54, 59, 171, 180, 196

safe haven/sanctuary(ies) 103–104, 116, 124, 125, 146, 147
Sahel xiv–xvi, xviii, 102–104, 106–107, 108, 110–113, 115–118.189, 193–194, 197–198; L'Alliance Sahel xiv, 199; Sahel G5 xiv, 3, 103, 107, 112, 116, 118, 194

secessionist movement 123, 180, 185, 196
second-hand: clothing 47; commodities 167; goods 162–163; products 155
security xiv–xvi, xviii–xx, xxiin3, 3–5, 11, 17–22, 24–27, 29, 36, 44, 49, 59–60, 62–63, 68, 74, 96, 102–105, 107–112, 115, 117n16, 117n21, 118nn40–41, 118n46, 122–134, 138–141, 143–150, 159, 188–197; food security 62–63
sedentariness xx, 71–72, 74–76, 79, 81–84, 188, 197
separationist tendencies 180
Shaw, T. 90; Soderbaum and 12
Soderbaum, F. 86, 89, 97, 193
Sokoto 105, 109, 115; Sokoto Caliphate 105, 116
Somalia/Somali xiv, xxi, 3, 6, 51n20, 58–59, 122–131, 134, 135n1, 144, 147, 178, 183–185, 194
Songhay-Zarma 76–77, 83
Soninke 73, 75, 83
Southern African Customs Union (SACU) 89–90
Southern African Development Community (SADC) 48, 87, 90, 98, 198
South Sudan 54, 57, 59–63, 122, 123, 129, 130, 131, 133, 134
Spatial Development Initiative (SDI) 87, 89–90, 93, 97–98
stakeholder consultations 90
state border(s) i, xii–xiv, xviii, xix, xx, xxi, 1, 3–5, 9, 11–12, 57, 59–61, 63, 67, 83, 86, 148, 178, 182–184, 187–189, 191
state-building (approach) i, xii–xiii, xv, xviii, xix, xxi–xxii, 1, 2, 4, 6, 54, 68, 124, 126, 188, 190–191, 198
state formation process xv, 1, 4, 183, 198–199
Stewart, F. xvii, 179
sub-regional/regionalism xxii, xxi, 2, 5–6, 12, 24, 28, 56, 135, 192, 194
Sudan 55–57, 60, 74, 122, 123, 127, 128, 129, 130, 131, 133, 134
Sustainable Development Goals (SDGs) 75

Taylor, I. 86, 89, 97, 193
terrorism i, xii, xvi, 3, 5, 59, 68, 102, 111–112, 116–117, 123, 127, 131, 141, 146–147

Tokyo International Conference for African Development (TICAD), the: TICAD V 91, 111; TICAD VI 112, 135; TICAD VII 112; TICAD 8 116
Tilly, C. xiv, 4
Toloobe 103, 108, 115, 117
top-down development xx, 86, 89, 90, 92, 96, 99, 189, 191
trans-border/transborder xvi, xviii, xix, xxi, 5, 22, 37, 90, 110, 124, 140, 182, 184–185, 188, 194, 198–199; transborder communities 22; transborder conflicts 182, 185; transborder cooperation 5, 140, 199; transborder crimes 198; transborder ethnic group 184; transborder movement 37, 188; transborder networks 194; transborder trade; xix, xxi
transnational/transnationalism xii–xiv, xviii, xx, xxi, 1, 2, 4, 6, 11–12, 18, 86, 98, 103, 109, 139, 141, 162–163, 166, 184, 195, 198; transnational civil society 86, 98; transnational families 163, 166; transnational movements 139, 162; transnational networks 6, 184; transnational society xii, xix, 1; transnational threat/transnationality of threat xix, 17, 27, 198
trans-region/regional 34, 59, 68, 105; trans-region/regional approach i, xii–xiii, xviii, xix, 1, 2, 13, 155, 190–199; trans-regional movements 34, 54, 67, 188
trans-state conflict(s) xv, 2, 4, 68, 184, 197–198
Tuareg 76, 103, 105–106, 108, 117–118
Tumbuka 78, 83

Uganda xiv–xv, xix, xxi, 1, 34–38, 44–45, 47–50, 51n3, 51n20, 52n29, 52n31, 54–62, 64–68, 74, 123, 125, 127, 129–132, 135n1, 170–173, 175–181, 183–185, 187–188, 191, 196; Uganda National Rescue Front (UNRF) 44; Uganda Revenue Authority (URA) 36
Uniao Nacional de Camponeses (UNAC) 91–92
United Nations Development Programme (UNDP) 25, 27, 110–112, 124, 135, 197
United Nations Mission in the Republic of South Sudan (UNMISS) 134
unskilled workers 162

Violent Extremist Organization (VEO) 102–107, 109–111, 115–118
Violent Non-State Actors (VNSA) xvi, xxi, 2, 122, 125–126, 187
visas 36, 48, 51, 141, 145, 160–162, 164, 166–167
vulnerability 6, 59, 68, 127, 142, 146, 155, 190

wall(s) xvi, 51, 138–140, 142–150
war on terror 102, 107, 116, 138, 146
West Africa xiv, xv, 72–73, 77, 103, 105–106, 109–111, 116–118, 122–124, 138, 142, 155, 159
Western Centrism 198–199
Western Sahara 142, 144, 146, 149
West Nile xix, xx, 34–38, 43–45, 47–52, 54–57, 59–69, 187–188, 196–197

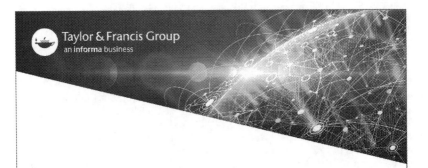